LAW AND ORDER IN HISTORICAL PERSPECTIVE

STUDIES IN SOCIAL DISCONTINUITY

Under The Consulting Editorship of:

CHARLES TILLY *University of Michigan*	EDWARD SHORTER *University of Toronto*

William A. Christian, Jr. Person and God in a Spanish Valley

Joel Samaha. Law and Order in Historical Perspective: The Case of Elizabethan Essex

John W. Cole and Eric R. Wolf. The Hidden Frontier: Ecology and Ethnicity in an Alpine Valley

In preparation

Immanuel Wallerstein. The Modern World System: Capitalist Agriculture and the Origins of the European World-Economy in the Sixteenth Century

D. E. H. Russell. Rebellion, Revolution, and Armed Force

John R. Gillis. Youth and History

Kristian Hvidt. Flight to America

Law and Order in Historical Perspective

THE CASE OF ELIZABETHAN ESSEX

JOEL SAMAHA
University of Minnesota

ACADEMIC PRESS New York and London
A Subsidiary of Harcourt Brace Jovanovich, Publishers

ACADEMIC PRESS, INC.
111 Fifth Avenue, New York, New York 10003

United Kingdom Edition published by
ACADEMIC PRESS, INC. (LONDON) LTD.
24/28 Oval Road, London NW1

Library of Congress Cataloging in Publication Data

Samaha, Joel.
Law & order in historical perspective.

(Studies in social discontinuity)
Bibliography: p.
1. Criminal justice, Administration of–Essex, Eng.–History. 2. Crime and criminals–Essex, Eng.–History. I. Title. II. Series.
HV8197.E75S3 364'.9426'7 73-812
ISBN 0–12–785756–7

PRINTED IN THE UNITED STATES OF AMERICA

To Jennifer

CONTENTS

PREFACE

The life of a virgin queen, the execution of Mary Queen of Scots, the defeat of the Spanish Armada, and the rise and fall of the Earl of Essex have all lent an air of spectacle to the last half of the sixteenth century in England, a spectacle which has appealed both to politicians looking back to what they thought to be a Golden Age and to romantics who, in every generation from the death of Queen Elizabeth onward have dramatized, fictionalized, cinematized, and televised those outstanding personalities and events in a light that has not separated history from artistic license. On the more factual historic side, religious revolution, embryonic empire building, the unfolding genius of Tudor statecraft, and the growth of political institutions have engaged the energies of historians for at least a century.[1] Some contemporary scholars who have studied the economics of the period think, and not without reason, that the birth of industrial society took place in England in the 1500s. These scholars claim that these fundamental changes in society gave rise to both the spectacular events that romantics have always extolled, and to the political, economic, and social

[1] See for example James A. Froude, *The History of England From the Fall of Wolsey to the Defeat of the Spanish Armada* (revised edition 1862–1870), 12 volumes. Naturally, the work of Albert F. Pollard falls into place here as well, especially his famous *Factors in Modern History* (1907), which became the standard interpretation of the period until later scholars came along to challenge his preeminence. It remained largely in the hands of one man, Geoffrey R. Elton, to add a newer view of the Tudor century; his works are too numerous to mention here but it goes without saying that no student of the period can overlook his brilliant *Tudor Revolution* and his sparkling narrative of the period, *England Under the Tudors*. There are many other historians and works that span this century and cover political, social, and religious history as well. See Mortimer, Levine, *Tudor England 1485–1603*.

developments that serious scholars have more recently begun to study.[2]

In the past decade, a growing band of students who are critical of the vague and untidy difference between the terms and facts of traditional and modern society has entered the field. Their demand for more precision has come at a time when statistical measurement and machines to speed it up have become more popular and more accessible.[3] Moreover, it has coincided with a rapidly growing curiosity about the way ordinary people actually lived during the past. Armed with the weapons of statistics, they have set out to bring early modern "ordinary man" back to life. Disenchanted with the traditional approaches, they have not dwelt upon the sources about kings, ministers, and central institutions of government. Rather, they have left the capitols and gone into the provinces, where they have found and studied an increasingly accessible collection of local archives concerning ordinary people. Through analysis of these old sources, the lives of peasants, farmers, craftsmen, tradesmen, farm and manufacturing workers are being reconstructed.[4] Questions never before asked about the most fundamental dimensions of life during these times are now being answered: How many of these people were there, and how were they distributed between city and countryside? What was the size of their families? When did they marry and when did they die? What were their religious beliefs and their sexual behavior, their habits of work and their modes of play? What did they eat and how much food was there? How was it produced and how was it distributed? To answer these questions, students have borrowed both the methods and findings of economics, political science, sociology, and anthropology and have put them to use sharpening the

[2] Most prominent in this field have been Professors Fisher and Nef. See, for example, F. J. Fisher, "Commercial Trends and Policies in Sixteenth-Century England" *Economic History Review*, Volume 10, pp. 95–117; John U. Nef, "A Comparison of Industrial Growth in France and England, 1540–1640," *Journal of Political Economy*, Volume 44, pp. 289–317, 505–533, 643–666. And we have two recent surveys of economic history that are extremely useful in understanding the Elizabethan economy in its proper historical perspective: Sidney Pollard and David W. Crossley, *The Wealth of Britain* (London, 1968) and L. A. Clarkson, *The Pre-Industrial Economy in England* (London, 1971).

[3] Most of the individuals working in this field are just now coming into prominence and it is not possible to cite published works, but Professor Charles Tilly has shown in an unpublished paper that the whole question of the transition from preindustrial to industrial society is still wide open. He cites there the work being done by men such as Franklin Mendels in demographic history who has given us the happy working term "proto-industrial" in order to come closer to grips with realities of the span of time encompassed in early modern history.

[4] See, in particular, the work of the Cambridge Group on Population Studies and the provocative book written by one of its members, Peter Laslett, *The World We Have Lost*. This group is engaged in a full-fledged demographic reconstruction of Britain from the earliest possible time for which records exist. They have enlisted the aid of numerous local private persons to help them compile data which will make it more than likely that we can find the world Peter Laslett thinks we have lost.

historical perspective.[5] Historians have finally accepted the value of the methodology and results of other disciplines to their work; hopefully, scholars in other disciplines will realize the contribution that the historical perspective can make to their research.

These new studies in history nearly always concentrate on small geographical areas.[6] Instead of the country of England, we learn about the counties (and even they loom as universes under the historian's microscopic eye); rather than British industry, we speak of Colchester woolens. In place of English agriculture, we have Essex butter; in lieu of kings, queens, ministers and bishops, we read of judges of Assize,[7] justices of the peace,[8] overseers of the poor and parish priests. Although perhaps something has been lost by replacing the grand style of Victorian writing with the historical monograph, the results of work by these new generation historians has been anything but parochial, despite the restricted geographical boundaries of their studies. They have proved that a West European population explosion took place during the sixteenth century, and have forced scholars of all persuasions to ask why this should have happened when it did. Furthermore, they have brought into the forefront a fundamental problem that the growing population created. How did society shift its methods of production and its utilization of resources in order to house and—more important—to clothe and feed increasing numbers of people.[9]

New questions, new methods, and more disciplines have been enlisted, therefore, to stretch the contours of life in the past. One discipline and the body of knowledge contained within it has been largely overlooked, if not specifically ignored, in this impressive growth of historical scholarship—the law.[10] And yet, there is no institution so rooted in society, and few

[5] See, for example, Alan MacFarlane, *Witchcraft in Tudor-Stuart England*, in which Dr. MacFarlane has used the methods of anthropology to reconstruct and interpret the witchcraft prosecutions of early modern England. Also see Kai T. Erikson's *Wayward Puritans* for an attempt to relate sociological findings and methodology to historical data.

[6] Professor MacFarlane's book, for instance, deals almost exclusively with Essex county in England and Erikson's with Essex county, Massachusetts. And in perhaps the finest studies we have to date, *The Agrarian History of England and Wales 1500–1640*, edited by Joan Thirsk, nearly all the conclusions are based on careful local case studies.

[7] See, for example, J. S. Cockburn, *A History of the English Assizes* (Cambridge, 1972) for a careful look at the doings of these judges on circuit.

[8] James Gleason, *The Justices of the Peace in England* (Cambridge 1969) relies heavily on data drawn from records that deal with history at least at the county level.

[9] Pollard and Crossly, *Wealth of Britain*, Ch. 3.

[10] Professor Cockburn's recent book on Assize judges, *History of English Assizes*, is an exception to this general rule of no studies of the law. That is not to say that no one has written of law in the traditional sense; naturally they have. But what is needed is more studies that place law in a broad social context—in a setting that will help to explain the nature of early modern society.

local repositories, at least in England, house longer and more complete archives than those connected with the law. When viewed as a reflection of social reality and not as a series of tricky procedural gimmicks and flowery oratory expended only to win the most attractive game known to Anglo-American society—the criminal trial, the study of law in sixteenth-century England affords a rare opportunity to fill a major gap in our knowledge of early modern society. The laws that Parliament wrote in the form of legislation, the rules and decisions set down by the great courts in Westminster—The Queen's Bench, the Exchequer, and the Common Pleas—on momentous legal questions of the day, the commentaries on law written by the great scholars of the time are all the stuff of intellectual history and important individuals' aspirations toward what they wanted the social order to be. But the criminal law as it actually operated in a community—who was prosecuted for what crimes; who was punished, who went free and for what reasons; how the system of criminal justice was administered—how, in short, it dealt with the residents and workers of the community can shed a bright light on the day-to-day circumstances of ordinary people's lives.

Viewed as it worked in fact on a local level, and not the way educated lawyers and jurists in London thought it should work in an ideal world, law points to crime as an outgrowth of the changes that recent scholars have been pointing out with such force. And the statistics of law are a way, however imperfect, to measure some of those changes. Furthermore, the administration of justice, taken here to mean society's response to those who violate its laws, is a fair guide to how the community dealt with its lawbreakers.

Since many of the references made to criminal law, procedures, personnel, and institutions will be thoroughly familiar only to those readers connected professionally to the law, what follows is a brief general description of what happened in the sixteenth-century criminal justice system from the time a felony was committed until the final disposition of the case occurred.

The start of any case was, of course, the commission of a crime—for purposes of this study, it will be mainly felony. What usually happened following the crime was that the victim—if he intended to do anything about it—went to the nearest justice of the peace, a country gentleman who lived in the vicinity and whom the Queen had appointed to perform many legal duties, one of which was enforcing the law of felony. When the victim arrived he told his story and the justice, if he believed him, issued a hue and cry—an order to the constable, the local policeman who had either been elected by his parish or appointed by the justices of the peace, whose job it was to go out and find the suspect. He pursued the accused to his parish boundary, where his authority ended, the constable of the neighboring parish took it from there, and so on until the suspect was apprehended—if indeed he ever was.

If the constable found the suspect, he had the authority to arrest him and bring him before the justice of the peace. If suspects refused to comply, as sometimes they did, they were subject to criminal prosecution for resisting arrest, or worse, the constable could kill them if they warded him off with force. What of the suspect? Did he have any rights? Surprisingly, he had a considerable array of very familiar ones at this point. He could go along with the officer and if he was not convicted of the crime, he could sue for false imprisonment or false arrest or both. As we shall show, the record shows that defendants were well aware of their "civil rights." Once the suspect was brought before the justice of the peace he was carefully examined, along with the victim and any other witnesses who were present, as to the facts of the case. Though the justices were bound by certain proprieties, it is clear that this examination in the country gentleman's house could be both inquisitional in its form and very intimidating in its manner. Most felony suspects were poor men, and to face their "betters" right in their "worship's" own home must have been an unduly oppressive experience in many cases.

Once the justice determined the probability of guilt, he either set the suspect free if he did not think there was "reasonable cause" to believe the accused had committed the crime, put him to bail if he was a "substantial" person, that is, a gentleman or yeoman, or send him to jail if he was too poor to await further action in his case. At the same time, he bound all witnesses and suspects put to bail to appear at the next Quarter Sessions—courts held four times each year in all English counties and over which the justices of the peace presided.

At the Quarter Sessions, the suspect was brought before the grand jury—24 good men and true from the county—to determine whether or not sufficient evidence existed to send him on to trial. Before these men, the justices again questioned victims, witnesses, and the accused. If the body of men from the county thought there was enough evidence, they found a "true bill" against the suspect, and he was returned to jail to await the Assizes—the courts held twice a year in the county and over which the great Westminster judges presided—where he would be tried. If the grand jury decided there was not enough evidence against the accused—or, what was equally likely, if victim or bailed defendant did not show up for the proceedings—the bill was "ignoramus" or dismissed and the accused went free.

At the Assizes, defendants who had been indicted were tried before the Westminster judges and by juries of their peers, while the justices acted as prosecuting attorneys. Since the defendant could not defend himself the trial was a quick affair: The witnesses (usually the victim) accused the defendant, and he pleaded guilty or "put himself on the country," that is, pleaded not guilty. The jury retired without food or drink until they reached a verdict. Since they often gave verdicts in more than 100 cases a day, it is not likely that they got very hungry or thirsty—their deliberations were notable, if for nothing else, at least for their speed. If the jury found the defendant not guilty, that was the end of it: He went free immediately. If he was found guilty, several things might happen. The penalty for felony was hanging, but no one could be hanged before judgment was rendered. Before the judge did this, he was required to ask if there was any reason why the convict should not have judgment passed on him. There were several reasons why not. He might have bought a pardon, in which case he displayed it and went free; he might have been a lunatic or a minor and then, too, the guilty man or child went free. If the accused was a woman, she might be pregnant, and if a jury of matrons found upon physical examination that this was true, then she was formally "respited" until the child was delivered but in fact often went free for good. If a man could recite a verse from the Bible, he too went free on the grounds that he was literate and literacy was a legitimate defense against final judgment, at least in some cases. Should there be no reason to avoid judgment, it was formally passed and the convicted felon then had only to await the sheriff to take him a few blocks away to the public hanging place, where the hangman did his job in front of anyone who wanted to come—and by most accounts it was a popular event, even if it was a neighbor on the gallows.

This was, in short, the road from crime to execution or freedom. Much in the text modifies or takes exception to this general outline. But this is the way most criminal cases were handled, and in all the discussions that follow this description should keep clear the usual, the typical, the ordinary felony proceedings.

Surely the crimes that were committed, the persons chosen for prosecution, the punishment meted out to convicts and the machinery used to process illegality formed an integral part of ordinary people's lives in early modern society, a part which legitimately demands reconstruction. Furthermore, an intensive study of law enforcement in one early modern community, Elizabethan Essex, demonstrates some timeless if also some unique elements in the problem of crime and the administration of justice. To view law and order in historical perspective ought then to comfort some who see our own society as verging on the brink of a precipice of chaos and disorder—all societies in all ages have their law-and-order fanatics. By contrast, intellectuals and reformers will find little satisfaction in the discovery that the criminal justice system and the law it administers has changed so little in the past four centuries. The greater value, however, lies in emphasizing that law and order has had a considerable history in Anglo-American society.

ACKNOWLEDGMENTS

Community values, not those of the individual, ranked high in the ideology of the Elizabethans, and in a somewhat smaller sense, community produced this book. Had it not been for Lacey Baldwin Smith, who is the most inspiring teacher I ever had, I would have remained a lawyer and not turned historian. How fortuitous that boredom in 1966 took me to one of his classes which laziness had driven me from in 1957, a chance encounter that set off my excursion into legal history. Or that one late autumn afternoon in 1967 I happened in on a seminar of Peter Laslett's. An aside in his prepared text had a profound impact on me. He told of how scholars had accumulated stacks of detail concerning kings and queens and still we did not know how much our forefathers had to eat. That remark made me want to go out and help his group fill up their forms that very day. (Of course, I learned later how unbearably tedious that task can be.) And had I not attended another seminar—this one by F. G. Emmison—I would never have known that Essex county had tons of records that might tell us something more about ordinary people and their lives in preindustrial English society.

Thus was the groundwork laid. But there is more. Without Geoffrey Elton to guide, criticize, and discuss the research and writing of the manuscript, I could not have completed this book in its present form. Only those who know him and have had his help and support can fully appreciate how significant was his contribution. What is more, he taught me what a "community of scholars" truly is.

The Essex Record Office staff were also indispensable to the final product. Mr. K. C. Newton, Miss Nancy Briggs, Mr. Arthur Searle, and Mr. A. C. Edwards gave me not only the technical advice that I so desperately needed but they also taught me more about Essex than I could ever have learned from books. To those students at UCLA and Minnesota who have had to listen to my theories about law and order in historical perspective and who had the fortitude to go out and test some of them, I owe more than gratitude—I had to meet the challenge of satisfying their inquiring minds.

Charles Tilly and Ned Shorter, the editors of this series, encouraged me to forge ahead when times were rough. More than that, they also made invaluable suggestions that definitely made the manuscript much more than it was when their critical minds were put to work on it. Stanford Lehmberg saved me from many embarrassments by his careful scrutiny of the manuscript in its early stages. He also gave me sage advice in its later stages, which only a senior colleague can do. The people at Academic Press have made this business of publishing a very pleasant experience—and I had heard it could be otherwise.

To four friends, I want to put in print what I never said to them. Dan taught me how to think critically about quantitative material. Fontaine proved that it was possible to show in a picture what it takes a thousand words to say. And Liz, though I admit it was not easy, pointed out that it *is* possible to communicate in writing by means of the English language. Finally, Steve kept telling me that I could put all of this massive material into meaningful form.

Jennifer's contribution, however, was greatest of all. She lived with me and with this from its inception and despite overwhelming odds, kept on being her own woman.

PROLOGUE

AN ENGLISH "GOSHEN"

Elizabethan Essex county, lying immediately adjacent to London on the east, was a community which should have had few problems. Contemporaries called it the "English Goshen" and thought that it was "most fat, fruitful and full of profitable things, exceeding any other shire for general commodities and . . . plenty."[1] Such a conclusion was, in some respects, clearly warranted. Mutton and beef, milk and butter, and especially the famous Essex cheeses, "those cheeses of an extraordinary bigness which are used in foreign places as well as in England, to satisfy the coarse stomachs of husbandmen and laborers,"[2] were produced in large quantities in the south and east. A combination of large farms (the result of pasture requirements), damp climate, and poor drainage (which made it dangerously unhealthy) all contributed to a population thinly scattered across the whole southeastern region of Essex—that area stretching inward from the banks of the Thames and the southern coast of the North Sea. Thus did the abundance of food and lack of people create a rich surplus for other areas.

Corn, wheat, saffron, and the profitable "new" hops were all grown in the northwest, the only part of the county with predominantly open field farming in the sixteenth century. True to the old method, village farmers tilled intermingled strips of land, heavily dependent upon their neighbors' habits and communal practice to bring their crops to harvest. This portion of the county was not enclosed until the nineteenth century, a development all the more striking because the rest of the shire was far advanced over

[1] John Norden, *Speculi Britanniae Pars* (Camden Society, London, 1840) p. 7. See also Fig. 3 on p. 30.

[2] *Ibid.*

much of England in being enclosed.[3] Long before Elizabeth's time, small independent farms surrounded by hedges were the dominant feature on the Essex agricultural landscape.[4] Indeed, some evidence suggests that most of the shire was always enclosed.[5] Open fields did not prevent large quantities of food from being grown there, just as they were in the south and east.

The core of the county and county life was the mixed farming area in the center. It was here that oats, wheat, barley, and other grains were produced in abundance, here that the county's reputation for prosperous independent yeoman farmers was made,[6] and here that the county's powerful new London magnates Petre, Mildmay, and Riche made their homes and built their magnificent mansions. And square in the middle was the county town of Chelmsford.

> This town is called the shire town . . . by the keeping of all the assizes and Sessions of the Peace, and many other certifications and inquisitions there. It is also a great thoroughfare and market town, weekly upon the Friday. In which market are to be sold abundance both of victuals and wares in respect of time and place.[7]

Here it was that some 300 households of townsmen lived, plied their trades and crafts, worked as apprentices or journeymen or for wages by day and, of course, farmed their own small plots of ground to supplement either their income or diets or, if fortunate, both. They had a crude form of rotation, planting in turn first one side in corn and the other in garden crops, alternating from year to year to keep the ground healthy.[8]

Dotting the landscape all over the county were market towns of modest size. Several, like Halstead, had only 700 inhabitants, and hardly any except Chelmsford and Colchester had more than 1000.[9] These small provincial towns were the prime distributors of food, clothing, and other needs for local people, as well as weekly meeting places for pleasure, rowdiness, violence, and crime. From Harwich in the extreme northeast to Epping on the western edge of the county and from Thaxted and Saffron Walden in the northern tip to Barking in the extreme south, and of course Chelmsford in the center, these market towns are a dramatic reminder that this was still a time when most people relied on their neighborhood to satisfy basic needs—food for the stomach and pleasure for the heart—though the way they went about it was not always calm or legal.

[3] Felix Hull, *Agriculture and Rural Society in Essex 1540–1640* (Ph. D. Thesis, London University, 1950).

[4] *Ibid.*

[5] *Ibid.*

[6] *Ibid.*

[7] E.R.O. DD/Ge M50, Survey of Manor of Chelmsford, 1591.

[8] *Ibid.*

[9] Essex Record Office Publications, *The Towns of Essex*.

Essex was overwhelmingly rural, but it would be misleading to think of the county exclusively in agrarian terms. In the first place, the borough of Colchester was a city second in size in eastern England only to Norwich. A wool industry flourished in the city, due, it should by stressed, in no small part to the heavy concentration of people there.[10] During the second half of the sixteenth century, the borough and a number of towns nearby—Halstead, Dedham, and Ardleigh to mention a few—moved well ahead of older cloth-producing centers that were suffering a decline in the second half of the sixteenth century.[11] With the aid of Dutch immigrants who at first were made very unwelcome in Colchester, Essex clothiers developed a finer fabric (the so-called bays and says) and gained a preeminent position in the industry, their Coggeshall whites winning even an international reputation for superior quality.[12] Though dense population enhanced the "industrial sector's" growth, it was a benefit not without its cost. Workers in the woolen industry as well as other inhabitants in the vicinity were crowded onto the smallest plots of ground in the county, patches so paltry that their occupants could not eke enough out of them to feed even the poorest man and his family.[13] The northeast, therefore, had to rely almost entirely upon the rural sector to supply it with food, a specialization in production that perhaps marked an advance in the county's economic history but spelled economic disaster for many local workers of the time. The declining real wages of laborers aggravated—and indeed were at least in part the result of—the relatively dwindling food supply. The situation was especially acute for those who had to buy their bread, mainly the poor wage earners. But, naturally, not everyone suffered. The overall wealth of the region was expanding, and to no one's surprise, the clothiers did not feel the bite of higher food prices. What with the profits in wool soaring, how could a rise in the price of bread, especially that which was made from the grain that the workers ate—rye and barley—affect them adversely? No, it was the workers who were at the mercy of the cloth market's precarious health (it would suffer a severe depression and final death in the following two centuries) for their livelihood and the fickle East Anglian weather (which led to many a famine in preindustrial England) to produce sufficient harvests to feed them.

In the opposite corner of the county—in the southwest—was an urban sector spawned almost entirely from London's overspill of population. It was similarly dependent on local agricultural production for its food. Situated right next door to London as it were, Essex was naturally affected

[10] See population density map, p. 6.

[11] Victoria County History of Essex Vol. II (London 1907), pp. 329–333.

[12] *Ibid.*

[13] *Ibid.*

by the city. London was the urban heart of the kingdom. It housed more people, handled more trade, and attracted more wealth than any other part of Elizabethan England. Experiencing a mushroom-like growth during the late sixteenth century that doubled its population during the reign of Elizabeth, its demands for space were nearly insatiable, and a cluster of parishes in southwestern Essex was flooded with the burgeoning metropolis' excess population. The crowded nature of these parishes and the petition of one of them, West Ham, that there were more than 60 suspected felons apprehended there in one year and that most men who owned land there resided in London, strongly suggests that they were urban slums exploited by absentee landlords and wanton criminals alike. The problem of ghetto crime and the scourge of the urban slumlords is not simply a twentieth-century phenomenon.

It would be impossible to measure but equally impossible to discount the significance that location had on county development during the period. London's impact was profound. Not only did the capital make significant demands on the shire's land for living space, but far more important, the waxing populace quickly devoured any food it could get from the county. The burden of supplying the hungrier and hungrier metropolis was a heavy one and not always welcomed by the county. Due to London's reliance on Essex for its food—"their chaundlers haunt all of the market towns . . . and sweep the market of all the corn that comes"—any shortage in the shire was quickly felt in the city. The Privy Council's orders that Essex send corn to the capital during every food supply crisis (and there were many) and the county's polite but firm replies excusing itself from doing so because the shire's own people were in need of food demonstrate the precarious state of both London's and the county's subsistence.[14] In any event, the catastrophic effects of dearth are strong reminders that in Tudor London, as in Elizabethan Essex, weather and the harvest primarily ordered life and determined the community's well-being.

The relationship of city and county that proximity and the need for food and space fostered is symbolized by the ancient Colchester–London Road. Initially built by the Romans, it became easily the most heavily traveled highway in Essex, beginning on the coast at Harwich, going into Colchester and straight through the middle of the shire, cutting through the center of Chelmsford, the county town, and continuing on into the heart of London. Despite modern railway lines and new highway bypasses around these provincial centers, today's travelers and farmers' produce still follow the same path to and from London as did their Elizabethan forebears. And even though it is hidden under new buildings, concrete highways, and

[14] There are several of these orders in the *Acts of the Privy Council* for the reign of Elizabeth. There are further references to them in P.R.O. *State Papers Domestic*, 12.

changing land boundaries, scraps of the old road still remain, reminders of the close and tough ties between London and her rural neighbor to the east. Troublesome as the contacts with London were at times, the expansion of London and the contacts it fostered contributed far more to the county's welfare than the city's slums to its detriment. Not only criminals and poor people, but also many of the city's wealthiest merchants and the Tudor government's most successful servants came to live in Essex, where the latter built large estates and used their wealth and expertise not only to advance the shire's general well-being but also to overhaul and to run efficiently the machinery of local government.

London was not the only, though it surely was the most important, external influence on Essex life during the sixteenth century. Cambridge University was just to the north. A hotbed of puritan radicalism and general intellectual ferment, its seething discontent was bound to spread to its neighbor in the south. And it did. Essex JPs and parish rectors were educated there and the puritan headquarters, Emmanuel College, was founded by the scion of an Essex family, Sir Walter Mildmay.[15] It is easy, however, to exaggerate the degree to which religious feeling determined social behavior. In the end, it is much sounder to think in terms of weather, wages, farming methods, demand for wool, and above all, food supply when uncovering the moving forces behind the actions of ordinary sixteenth-century people. And it is more accurate to write of profit, good husbandry, and the price of wool when characterizing the upper ranks of society. Indeed, most Elizabethan gentlemen for the greater part of their lives had far more interest in their pocketbooks than they did in life after death.[16] Time enough for the afterlife when the day approached; in the meantime, it was the world here and the rewards in it that mattered.

It is well to remember that all of Essex, including the "urban" southwest and the "industrial" northeast, were clearly preindustrial. But to associate with that term a static, traditional, hierarchical, organic community would not tell the whole truth, because along with these attributes of an older society were telling new departures. So, although much remained the same, powerful new influences were making themselves felt in this bustling sixteenth-century community. In the first place, the population grew rapidly during Elizabeth's reign, and even if it is impossible to be very accurate about specific figures, it would not be far off the mark to think of at least a $33\frac{1}{3}\%$ increase from roughly 60,000 inhabitants in 1558 to 80,000 in 1603.[17] These people were spread unevenly over about 400

[15] For a good public life of Walter Mildmay, see Stanford E. Lehmberg, *Sir Walter Mildmay and Tudor Government* (Austin, Texas, 1964).

[16] See Chapter I.

[17] See p. 32–33.

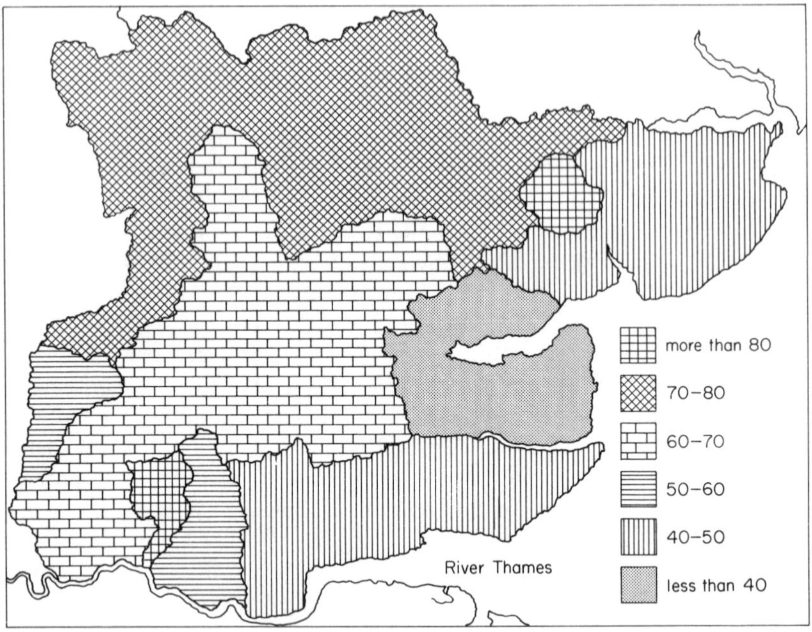

Fig. 1. Population density based on subsidy list of 1638.

parishes, hamlets, and towns. In 1638, for example, the density ranged from less than 40 persons per square mile in the south and southeast to more than 70 in Colchester and around London.[18] In the latter, the effects were aggravated because of the even more spectacular rise in neighboring London's populace during the same period.[19] Moreover, inflation joined hands with the intensified demand for food, encouraging landowners to raise grain, cattle, and dairy products for the market rather than rely on rents, fixed or even racked, for income. Thus was Essex agriculture shoved well on its way toward commercialization in the second half of the Tudor century.

Behind these changes were forces that may well have been impersonal, but the shifts were engineered by individuals, a collection of men who had backgrounds that were significant in determining how successfully the county made the transformation from traditional to commercial farming. The most famous of them stemmed from London marketplaces and the royal bureaucracy—not from Essex soil—and were close enough to their

[18] See population density map, above.

[19] F. J. Fisher, "The development of the London Food Market, 1540–1640," *Economic History Review* (V., 1935).

administrative and commercial origins to use their managerial talents to good advantage in shifting the county's resources, a shift which significantly affected, indeed disrupted, social and economic life in the county.

Impressive as the new landowner's efforts to produce more food and other products were, the brutal and pervasive effects of famine on the lives of ordinary people and the terrific rise in food prices compared to other products, especially nonessentials, should act as warnings against jumping to any simplistic conclusions about the success that commercialized agriculture in its early stages had in meeting the subsistence crisis that Essex and indeed all Western Europe faced in the sixteenth century.[20] Surplus farming, good husbandry clauses, and efficient, consolidated land management did not produce bounty sufficient to prevent a steady and steep upward turn in food prices or to keep many poor people in the county from starvation even during short-term economic crises. As in modern underdeveloped countries, the impact of dearth was immediate and catastrophic.

What has crime to do with the varied dimensions of Elizabethan Essex life? How did population increase and the commercialization of agriculture, dearth in harvest and inflation on the market, proletariazation of labor and religious strife, limited facilities and the subsistence crisis affect crime and the administration of justice? All of them to greater or lesser degree undoubtedly had their impact on the nature and amount of lawlessness in the county as well as on society's response to that misconduct, that is, on law and order in Elizabethan Essex.

A word of warning is in order about reading too much into conclusions about one county. The varied economic life of the county makes it look, at first glance, as if it might be a laboratory in which to study crime and criminal justice in general in early modern society. Traditional open fields in the north, long-standing enclosure in the middle, commercial dairy farming in the south, embryonic urbanization in the southwest, and the expanding cloth industry in the northeast all point to a diversity that might well embrace all of sixteenth-century life. Furthermore, the invasion of the county by "new" families, the so-called "rising gentry" of Professor Tawney, accentuates standard notions of Tudor–Stuart society. The dangers, however, in trying to generalize from one county to make conclusions about a whole kingdom are so striking that to do so would call into question their soundness. Political and administrative boundaries, in the first place, are largely artificial and make poorly defined limits for intensive study. So, to speak of all preindustrial society or even all England is not the intent of this study, for only when analyzing a restricted and compact area is it possible to speak at all precisely and with even a measure of accuracy and to escape the glib and often trivial generalizations that are attached to

[20] Pollard and Crossley, *Wealth of Britain*, Ch. 3.

England as a whole in the early modern period. Hence the decision to reconstruct the experience of a single community that felt the impact of intellectual, political, and religious turmoil, that faced the general problems of discontinuity produced by the commercialization of agriculture, and that suffered the basic pain of having insufficient food at impossibly high prices. To measure the effect such forces had on the lives of people who turned or were driven to crime and to trace society's response to this criminal behavior, both through the institutions that sought to root out or control antisocial behavior (the law and its courts) and through the men who controlled these institutions (the JPs, clerks, constables, and jurors) are reason enough for undertaking a study of law and order in Elizabethan Essex.

PART I

THE STATISTICS OF CRIME

CHAPTER I

CRIME AND CRIMINALS

"There is no country in the world where there are more robbers and thieves than in England."[1] Thus did one Italian visitor sum up his gloomy view of crime and criminals in sixteenth-century England, an opinion shared by many Elizabethans themselves. The Queen took numerous opportunities to chastise her subjects for their unruliness[2]; Lord Burghley on one occasion took singular pains to probe into picayune improprieties of some Essex parish residents[3]; Sir Francis Walsingham on another manifested hearty displeasure over a trifling rucus in the borough of Colchester.[4] Not only Burghley and Walsingham but also other counselors and the Queen herself took major and direct responsibility for personal surveillance over even the most minor disorders in society, a care born not simply of a fetish over order but from what seemed to them at least, the clear and present danger of massive lawlessness. The House of Commons, a quite accurate barometer of English upper-class opinion in the sixteenth century, shared the worry of the Queen and her council, lacing preambles to multitudinous statutes with harangues against evil-doing.[5]

Fear of disorder was not confined to higher circles of government, that is, the Crown, Privy Council, and Parliament. Shakespeare's "take but degree away" poetically expressed a basic fear among propertied men that permeated the whole realm, percolating down into the counties where it

[1] *Italian Relation of England* (Camden Society, 1847), p. 34.

[2] P. Hughes and J. Larkin, *Tudor Royal Proclamations*, Vol. II and III (London, 1969).

[3] B.M. *Egerton MS 2644/61.*

[4] E.R.O. *Morant MS 47/331.*

[5] Fernando Pulton, *An Abstract of All Penal Statutes* (London, 1577).

generated a demand by country gentlemen all over England that crime must be curbed. William Lambarde, Kentish JP and commentator on local law and order, summed up the feelings of most of his contemporaries when he said, "with grief, that sin [lawlessness] of all sorts swarmeth and that evildoers go on with all license and impunity,"[6] and he warned that:

> It is an ancient truth . . . that even as no man can live comfortably without the fellowship of men, so no fellowship can stand without law and discipline; . . . laws be ordained . . . to the end that men may direct the steps of their conversation according to the right rule and prescript, knowing that as obedience is the end of the law, so the safety of the people is the end of that obedience.[7]

Modern historians, like Tudor critics, tend to highlight fear of disorder in men of the sixteenth century and to stress the high incidence of lawbreaking. A. L. Rowse cautions against "underestimating" the "latent violence" and "endemic strife" in Elizabethan England[8]; A. V. Judges claims that "thieves abounded everywhere,"[9] and the social science-oriented Lawrence Stone, while judiciously stipulating that the aristocracy's bent toward lawlessness was waning under the Tudors, still insists that the "lower classes did not lose their habits of violence until the twentieth century."[10]

Complaints against the administration of justice and crime in the streets are as old as recorded history.[11] The Anglo-Saxon laws repeatedly harp on justice and how it should be done to rich and poor alike. The medieval kings complained that their peace was not being sufficiently kept. The Mirror of Justices lists 150 abuses in legal administration. In the fourteenth century, Wycliff moaned that "lawyers make process . . . by heathen men's laws" while Starkey, during Henry VIII's reign, bitterly wrote that "everyone that can color reason maketh a stop to the best law that is . . . devised." And complaints continued after the sixteenth century. Law reform was a persistent plea in the revolutionary fervor of the seventeenth century, whereas in the eighteenth century it was argued that judges ignored human nature and the affairs of men. Even the momentous achievements in the nineteenth-century reform movement both in England and in America did not stem the tide nor alter the nature of the blanket complaints against the administration of justice in Anglo-American Law.

[6] Conyers Read, ed., *William Lambarde and Local Government* (Ithaca, 1962) p. 68.
[7] *Ibid.*, p. 128.
[8] A.L.Rowse, *The England of Elizabeth* (New York, 1966) p. 344.
[9] A.V.Judges, *The Elizabethan Underworld* (London, 1930) p. xv.
[10] Lawrence Stone, *The Crisis of the Aristocracy* (abridged edition, 1967) p. 97.
[11] The following is based almost entirely on Roscoe Pound's famous address "The causes of popular dissatisfaction with the administration of justice," *American Bar Association Report* (1906, Vol. 29) pp. 395–417.

> In other words as long as there have been law and laywers, conscientious and well meaning men have believed that laws were mere arbitrary technicalities, and that the attempt to regulate the relations of mankind in accordance with them resulted largely in injustice.[12]

More than contemporary, if timeless, individual or upper-class complaints point to at least an apparent crime wave in late Tudor Essex. A plethora of legal records which began in the reign of Philip and Mary verifies the general impressions that contemporary critics and modern historians have portrayed—a society of growing lawlessness measured by swelling felony statistics.[13]

But crime indices are forever rising, whether the time and place is twentieth-century "violent" America, modern "law-abiding" England or sixteenth-century Essex county, and these increasing numbers always cause law-abiding citizens to become alarmed. Simply counting criminal cases recorded in the extant court files without careful refinements does not accurately portray the nature or level of lawlessness in preindustrial society. In order to get at the meaning of crime in early modern Essex it is necessary to attack two vexing problems: How to extract conclusions about actual crime from the recorded evidence on felony, and how to reconstruct the system of criminal justice that brought the system into being. Chapter I sorts out the elements that went into making up the criminal statistics, and the remaining three chapters reconstruct the system which processed those crimes, that is, the chapter looks at the criminal law in operation. Obviously the two are related, and therefore an overlapping will occur because the efficiency of the system that administered justice and the practices of criminal procedure vitally affected the statistics of crime, whereas the amount of crime in turn had its impact on how and to what extent the law of crimes was enforced. At times, this circularity will pose delicate problems of accurate analysis and always will act as a red flag of caution waving in front of all conclusions reached. But it is a central problem that faces anyone who would unravel the workings of the criminal justice system.

The evidence used here requires careful attention. In the first place, the general problem of records retention is a critical one for historians, and it has become especially prominent with the onset of quantitative analysis in history. Gaps in records, sloppy record keeping and "weeding" done since the time the records were created all throw unknown quantities into the court records and thereby affect the conclusions that can be extracted from them. For too long, historians have accepted the custodial integrity of archivists on faith. Most of this faith is not misplaced; nonetheless it does no harm to point out that the records are no better than the care and

[12] *Ibid.*
[13] E.R.O. Q/SR 1–160 and P.R.Q., Asz. 35, 1–45.

concern that their keepers have given them. One notorius case should suffice to make the point of the harm that an irresponsible Essex custodian could have done. In the eighteenth century, a prominent Colchester clergyman, William Morant, raided the documents of the borough and made a scrap-book of all the "juicy tidbits" and scandalous goings on in the town. A large assortment from the Elizabethan period includes everything from preparations for the Queen's progress through Essex to information surrounding felonies and treasons. Fortunately, the manuscripts were retrieved and are now in the Essex Record Office.[14] One would not want to suggest that archivists are all of this ilk. But dishonesty is not the only reason for the failure to keep records in their proper form and place, especially since as the pressures of space and quantity increase, the problem facing archivists becomes an enormous one. We know of extensive weeding as early as the eighteenth century.[15]

This is aggravated in the case of legal records, because lawyers have different things in mind when they talk of retention of records than do historians and other scholars. Like their sixteenth-century counterparts who created them, they are pondering the "legal" importance of the records, considerations that are at variance with historians' interests.[16] The Essex criminal court records have obviously suffered from all of these problems. The most critical deficiency for this study is that the Assize Files are not complete, especially for the early years in the period.[17] Most of the missing files fall in the 1560s, a factor that exaggerates the overall rise in crime.[18] One should be careful, however, not to conclude that a file is lost merely on the assumption that there must have been two files for every year because Assizes were supposed to meet twice a year. It is entirely possible that due to plague or other crises courts were either postponed or absorbed into the following session, or that cases were even heard and determined at the Quarter Sessions.[19] Quarter Sessions suffer least from deficiencies. Due to the efforts of Sir William Petre, who became *Custos Rotulorum* (keeper of the records) during Mary's reign, and his faithful Clerk of the Peace, John Carrowe, a tradition of complete record keeping began. Everything seems to have been saved, at times with a vengeance—scraps and bits with no legal significance were kept, perhaps for their sheer value as paper and parchment but also due to a new attitude toward written records in general. As the period progressed, record keeping

[14] E.R.O. *Morant MS.*

[15] Cockburn, *A History of the Assizes*, p. xii.

[16] See below, p. 15.

[17] This is based on the remaining files for several years in the early period, for which only one survives. This does not necessarily mean they are missing.

[18] See p. 19ff.

[19] See p. 96–97, Chapter IV.

continued to improve and its orderliness was enhanced, both of which significantly affected the felony statistics and the evidence for an analysis of the criminal justice system.[20]

Another problem is that early modern English court rolls are, unfortunately, meagre repositories of the intimate details surrounding the commission of particular crimes. The reason for this is a matter of law—records were kept because they were *legally* important, and the record keepers often discarded what the historian would most desperately liked to have had.

Second, much information acquired prior to indictment, that is, before a grand jury formally charged a suspect with a felony, has been lost. Examinations taken by JPs at preliminary investigations of felony (see Chapter III) were often thrown away, probably because they were not "matters of record."[21] The valuable historical evidence that disappeared with these "legally useless" storehouses of information is a staggering loss, but then Tudor clerks were not writing for modern scholars but for sixteenth-century lawyers. What is left for the historian of crime are almost exclusively indictments and coroner's inquisitions. These are laconic statements written in very bad Latin mixed, fortunately, with some useful English; their brevity is matched only by the drudgery of their uniformity—a fact of their legal nature. A typical one reads like this in translation: "The jurors for the queen (meaning the grand jury)[22] present that Richard Harrison of Baumont, laborer, on 18 November 1588 broke into the close of Thomas Ward at Moze and stole one ewe sheep worth 5s."[23] Notice that the indictment refers not at all to crucial matters (crucial for the historian that is, not for legal record keepers) such as whether Richard sheared the sheep and sold the wool or killed and ate it, and it obscures the reason why he committed the crime. Was he simply greedy, was he an enemy of Thomas, or was he cold and hungry without money to buy food and clothes? The answers to these and other questions are forever lost.

Third, not even all the available indictments were used in this study. Witchcraft, having been explored in Alan MacFarlane's full-length study of that crime in Essex, has not been treated here, though it is a necessary adjunct to this one. It not only adds another dimension to a rather limited topic, but also the abundance of extralegal evidence about that felony enabled him to get behind many witchcraft cases, an enviable

[20] See p. 100–103, Ch. IV.

[21] Not all examinations have been lost. Fortunately, a nearly complete series is extant for the borough of Colchester for the sixteenth and seventeenth centuries and are being transcribed and edited by the author for publication.

[22] See Chapter II.

[23] E.R.O. *Q/SR 95/17*.

position impossible to emulate more in other felony cases.[24] Sedition, though obviously a significant offense, especially in a time of crisis such as the late sixteenth century, was also omitted from discussion, though the total number of cases is listed in the tables in Appendix I. The reasons for leaving it out of the general analysis were that in the first place, relatively few cases of it appeared in Essex during Elizabeth's reign; but even more important, it covered such a broad range of vaguely defined behavior—embracing everything from unpleasant gossip about royalty (one woman, for example, spread a rumor that the Queen was pregnant by Dudley and that she stuffed the bastard up a chimney flu to be burned alive) all the way to political agitation which becomes blurred with treason.

Perhaps most serious for this study was the elimination of indictments for misdemeanor. They are rich in detail about such misbehavior in sixteenth-century life as disturbing the peace, scolding wives, incontinency, stirring up lawsuits, assaults, affrays, and riots. But they are extremely difficult to categorize and study systematically. It is especially tricky to sort out the meaning of the violent ones, in particular assault and riot. Sixteenth-century law formally blurred the distinction between private suits (our term is tort) and public wrongs (what we would call crimes) when it came to these offenses. Because of this, it is never clear whether or not what the indictment calls an assault or a riot really is one, because both in real riots and assaults and private suits between individuals in which one hoped to recover damages for trespass and damage to property, the plaintiff could use the indictment form, which required that the defendant use force and arms against the Queen *(vi et armis contra pacem domina regina)*.

The historian will never know which of the indictments really involved violence, naturally of special concern in this study, or whether the words "force and arms" was only a legal fiction to get a private lawsuit involving no violence whatsoever into court. Probably very few riot indictments were indicative of violent crime. The number of them which were clearly written to fulfill the statutory requirements is large, and the ones that point to major public disturbance are invariably mentioned elsewhere. There was only one major riot in Essex during Elizabeth's reign. Wistan Browne, sheriff of Essex, had recently inherited some land upon which stood a church. This house of God was not being used by the townsmen of Brentwood for a place of worship but as a meeting hall. When Browne attempted to tear it down, some 30 townsmen appeared and barricaded the place, holding the local schoolmaster inside for ransom. When the authorities tried to enter they were attacked with everything from boiling water to pickaxes, many of the weapons being wielded by women. The

[24] MacFarlane, *Witchcraft 1560–1680.*

sheriff and JPs were able to take over finally and with little if any harm to anyone.[25]

In the case of assaults it is more difficult to speak with assurance. The standard form of the indictment gives no hint about the true nature of the offense. Nor did serious ones, except those resulting in death and counted elsewhere, reach public notice in other forms. But, that nearly all of them state that the defendant not only assaulted the plaintiff but also dissiesed him (the legal term for putting him out of possession of his land) strongly suggests that these plaintiffs were using the criminal law to try property cases. This view is reinforced by the clerk's note on many of them, giving the plaintiff restitution, that is, putting him back in possession of his land. One should, however, not lose sight of the distortion in the figures that omitting assault produces. Violent crime figures would have undoubtedly been higher in this study had assault indictments been included. Less inaccuracy, however, seemed to arise from omitting them all than either including them all or putting them in piecemeal after judging them individually, since the latter would have been guesses.

Despite loss, destruction, omission, paucity of detail, and problems in definition, much valuable data is included in the remaining indictments. They include murder, manslaughter, suicide, rape, buggery, robbery, burglary, and theft, and the records of them tell a large part of the story of lawlessness in Elizabethan society. Society's definition of what constituted murder or manslaughter, robbery or burglary or mere theft rested upon distinctions in the quantity of violence each embodied, and because of this the law provides a ready measure of the dispersion of force among felonious acts. Homicide, suicide, and rape all violated the body; robbery and burglary harmed an individual and his possessions (the robber took valuables directly from a person by threat or force); and the burglar put his victim in fear in his own home. Theft damaged only property, as the English verb "to steal" clearly indicates: to sneak away a man's property without his knowledge. Thus the law with meticulous care and great precision set up a hierarchy of illicit conduct, a practice which historians can use to good advantage in penetrating to the essence of late Tudor lawlessness.

Moreover, an indictment had to include the defendant's name, residence, and social status, making it possible to map out the sociology and geography of crime as well as its typology. The inconsistency of residence and social status which is sometimes encountered in the indictments (a man may be labeled, for example, a Chelmsford glazier in one indictment and the same person might be called a Brentwood laborer in another indictment) might suggest that information regarding these two important facts is unreliable.

[25] *Acts of the Privy Council*, 1577.

To some extent that may well be true. However, given our knowledge about the high geographical mobility of sixteenth-century persons[26] and the growing fluidity of certain occupational lines,[27] it is not apparent that the conclusion to be drawn from these inconsistencies in the indictments is due to inaccuracy rather than to actual changes in residence and social status. To be sure, however, one must recognize the possibility that those who drew up the indictments were most interested in filling up the required spaces and not terribly dedicated to making certain the information was correct. On the other hand, it seems unlikely that clerks would have any motivation to be wrong on purpose. In the end, then, it seems most plausible, in view both of the facts we know of the demography of the period and of the notable lack of motivation of clerks-to-be, to assume that the indictments reflect the truth about location and status of criminal defendants.

Finally, clerks' notes provide valuable information about the consequences of violence, because these faithful bureaucrats recorded the court's decision, when there was one, on every indictment. The clerks recorded the plea of the defendant, guilty or not guilty, the jury's verdict, guilty or not guilty, the value of the defendant's goods, if he had any and was found guilty, and the punishment to be meted out or the circumstances such as pardons and benefit of clergy which would forestall or eliminate punishment altogether. Even the absence of clerks' notes are important because they mean the party charged and indicted was never tried. The growing care with which clerks did their job and the mentality that made recording almost a mania during the period argues against the conclusion that no clerks' notes on the indictments means that the bureaucracy did not record a sentence, though to be sure one must again allow for the possibility that blank spaces here mean poor record keeping and not purposeful omission due to lack of action of the part of the court.[28]

What does this legal evidence with all of its pitfalls add to our knowledge of early modern history? The sensational features of the Elizabethan age, as we have seen, have oft been told (probably overtold), and they add nothing to that dimension of sixteenth-century life. Moreover, the institutions as well as the workings of central government have been fully explored in literally thousands of volumes, and the Essex criminal files have little to say about them. Change the perspective, however, from the drama of history and the world of high politics, foreign adventure and religious debate to crime in the shires perpetrated by ordinary people, and it creates

[26] E. E. Rich, "The Population of Elizabethan England," *Economic History Review*, 2nd series, 1950 Vol. 2.

[27] Joan Thirsk, ed., *Agrarian History of England and Wales 1500–1640* (1967), Ch. 7.

[28] See pp. 53–55.

a new picture of the era. As we have noted already, the evidence paints a clear picture of rising registered local crime during the reign of Elizabeth—in every decade the amount of felonies recorded in Essex surged relentlessly upward, and not until the last 5 years of her reign did it begin to taper off.[29] Overall, the increase was more than 400% (from 319 felonies recorded in the opening decades to 1,389 in the closing 10 years). The rate of growth was even more dramatic. In the first 30 years, from 1558 to 1589, the number just about doubled, but in the last 15 years it doubled again, so that more than half the felonies registered during the reign were put on the books between the years 1589 and 1603 or in the last third of the period (see Tables 1 and 2).

TABLE 1 *Felonies in Five-Year Totals*[a]

	Violent crimes (Murder; manslaughter, rape)		Body and goods (Robbery and burglary)		Theft		
Year	Number	%	Number	%	Number	%	Total number
1559–1563	22	14	54	35	76	51	152
1564–1568	27	16	63	31	77	53	167
1569–1573	24	10	38	16	176	74	238
1574–1578	40	12	52	16	241	72	333
1579–1583	66	13	76	17	289	70	431
1584–1588	50	10	104	21	337	69	491
1589–1593	40	7	63	10	436	83	539
1594–1598	37	4	130	15	699	81	866
1599–1603	53	12	101	20	366	68	520

[a] The figures are based on the Assize Files and Quarter Sessions Rolls as well as coroners' inquests.

Totals of recorded felonies, that is, numbers by themselves, only vaguely tell about offenses registered by the authorities, hence the necessity to describe their contents in detail. In the first place, totals obscure geographical distribution. For instance, in surveying the rise in the number of felonies, it is at once apparent, and necessary to caution, that very few felonies were recorded for any particular neighborhood in the county. Many parishes went for years without a single registered crime, and even where the rate was relatively high, as for example in Chelmsford, only about three felonies annually were put on the books—an insignificant number when one considers that Chelmsford had nearly 300 households, or 1200 people.[30]

[29] See Appendix I.
[30] E.R.O. *D/DGe M 50.*

TABLE 2 *Annual Crime Totals*[a]

	Violent crime						Body and goods				
	Murder	Man-slaughter	In-fanticide	Suicide	Rape	Total	Robbery	Burglary	Total	Grand larceny	Total crimes
1559	0	2	0	0	0	2	6	23	29	17	48
1560	0	4	0	1	3	8	3	1	4	22	34
1561	3	1	1	0	0	5	0	10	11	21	36
1562	0	0	0	3	0	3	0	0	0	0	3
1563	0	0	2	2	0	4	3	8	11	16	31
1564	1	0	1	2	0	4	8	1	9	2	15
1564	0	0	1	2	0	3	2	5	7	10	20
1566	1	1	2	0	1	5	2	13	15	30	50
1567	3	1	0	7	1	12	0	19	19	19	50
1568	0	2	0	1	1	4	8	5	13	16	33
1569	0	0	0	2	0	2	2	3	5	27	34
1570	0	2	0	5	0	7	3	6	9	46	62
1571	3	1	1	4	0	9	3	8	11	34	54
1572	0	0	0	3	0	3	0	5	5	29	37
1573	0	1	0	1	1	3	3	5	8	40	51
1574	1	2	2	10	0	15	13	0	13	69	97
1575	0	2	0	5	1	8	5	2	7	40	55
1576	0	0	1	0	3	4	4	10	14	52	70
1577	0	7	0	2	0	9	8	6	14	33	56
1578	0	2	0	1	0	3	3	2	5	44	52
1579	1	4	1	0	2	8	14	13	27	35	70
1580	2	4	3	3	4	16	0	18	18	64	98
1581	0	10	1	2	7	20	14	2	16	70	116
1582	1	2	1	0	3	7	5	6	11	84	102
1583	1	5	2	3	4	15	2	2	4	36	55
1584	0	4	1	4	1	10	4	6	10	53	73
1585	0	4	0	3	0	7	12	9	21	68	101
1586	2	3	4	4	1	14	14	7	21	65	100
1587	1	0	0	3	0	4	15	14	29	62	95
1588	3	6	1	3	2	15	8	15	23	83	121
1589	0	3	1	0	0	4	6	16	22	82	108
1590	1	5	0	0	1	7	9	8	17	101	125
1591	0	7	1	1	3	12	4	6	10	160	182
1592	2	2	1	1	0	6	0	8	8	29	43
1593	0	10	1	2	1	14	0	5	5	74	93
1594	0	5	1	3	1	10	4	10	14	71	95
1595	0	3	2	0	1	6	0	16	16	89	111
1596	0	0	0	0	0	0	3	2	5	111	119
1597	0	4	1	4	0	9	12	23	35	258	305
1598	0	5	1	5	0	11	18	39	57	165	233
1599	3	0	0	5	0	8	1	8	9	27	44
1600	3	2	0	3	2	10	12	8	20	120	150
1601	4	0	3	2	0	9	14	22	36	104	149
1602	2	17	2	1	0	22	5	10	15	91	128
1603	0	4	1	1	0	6	22	0	22	27	71

[a] Figures based again on Assize Files, Quarter Sessions Rolls, and coroners' inquests.

The greatest number of felonies were committed in market towns or in other populated areas along roads and riverbanks, the two important modes of transportation during the early modern period in Essex. Perhaps this is why a common preoccupation of justices of the peace at their quarter sessions and of stewards in manor courts was hearing parish's presentments that bridges were falling down, and a constant effort was made in manor courts to keep roads cleared of trees and bushes by the statutory 20 feet on either side. Furthermore, complaints about refuse and other roadblocks were frequently made by residents, suggesting that overgrowth near the road's edge was a happy hiding place and that broken bridges and impediments in the roadways caused passersby enough delay to allow prospective criminals to jump from this convenient lair and steal away with tradesmen's, farmers', or other travelers' goods.

Nor do general totals reveal the specific types of crimes that were committed. For example, they obscure the savagery in some criminal acts: One Pagelsham amazon gripped a neighboring tailor's throat and twisted it until it broke; a day laborer smashed in a neighbor's head with an axe and stabbed him in the throat, turning afterward to dash out the brains of the victim's sister; and a local tailor, after he got his girl pregnant, kicked her in the belly and "did spurn and crush her to make the child untimely born."

Shocking as these atrocities were, they certainly were not, as one recent historian has called them, "typical . . . of what was happening all over the county in every decade of Elizabeth's reign."[31] Quite the contrary. Murder was the most infrequent of felonies. Never more than four were recorded in any single year, and in many years none occurred (see Tables 1 and 2 and Appendix I.) These official records probably reflect actual murders better than other felonies because of the difficulty in hiding a dead body. Furthermore, even when the other crimes of violence against the person—manslaughter, infanticide, suicide, and sex offenses—are added to murder, violent crimes constitute an average of only 10% of the total number of recorded felonies. The proportion, of course, varied. For instance, it rose in one 5-year period to 16%, while dropping at one point as low as 4%. Between the first and last five years of Elizabeth's reign, the number of violent felonies recorded rose from 50 to 99, or nearly 100%. At first this seems extraordinarily high, but compared to total felonies, which multiplied 400%, the rate of growth in violent felony was only one-quarter as great as that of other kinds. According to these figures, then, violent crime was rising, but at a much slower rate than other felonies.

Theft was the real culprit in swelling crime figures in late Tudor Essex (see Fig. 2). Larceny accounted for more than 70% of all felonies recorded

[31] Fredrick G. Emmison, *Elizabethan Life: Disorder*. Chelmsford, England (1970) p. 148.

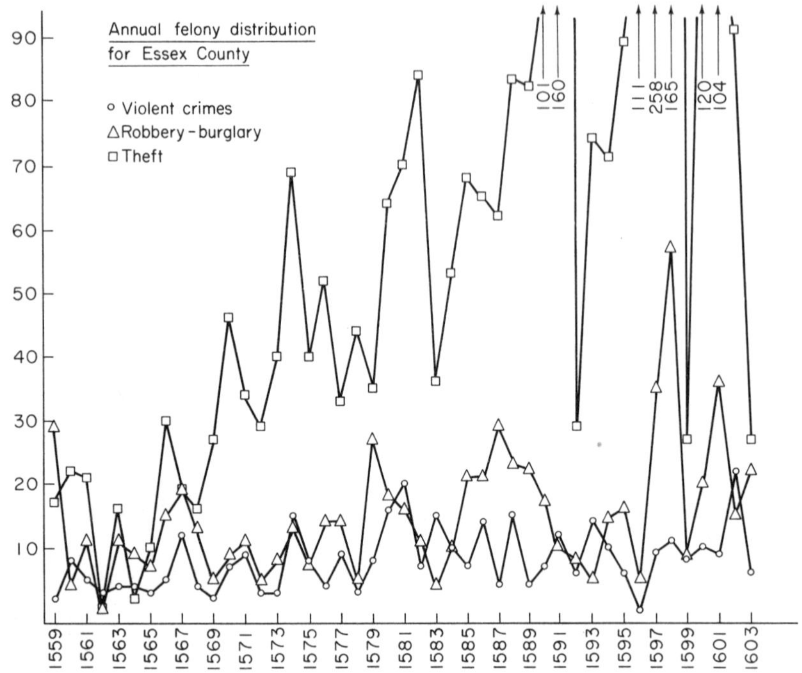

Fig. 2. The graph included here is based on three sources: the felony indictments in the Assize files, the indictments in the Quarter Sessions rolls and the coroners' inquests extant for the county of Essex during the reign of Elizabeth. They are records of offenses, not offenders. The distinction is important because the numbers here are thus larger than the total number of individuals involved in felony cases.

from 1559–1603 (a portion comparable to that of modern-day Britain). Furthermore, it rose dramatically during the 45 years of Elizabeth's reign. A striking tenfold increase in theft can be seen between 1559 and 1563, when 153 were recorded, and in the last five years when 1,100 larcenies were registered. If robbery and burglary are added to larceny, the result shows that crimes against property accounted for 90% of the total felonies reported. Though annual figures fluctuated, in general the trend was definitely up, especially toward the end of the century (see Fig. 2). For example, in 1596, 111 thefts were recorded; a year later the number rose to 258. In 1598, however, the number dropped back to 165.[32]

Turning from crime to criminals, certain features stand out. In the first place, most Elizabethan felons were one-time offenders (see Table 3)

[32] The explanation for the erratic pattern of these numbers, unlike anything seen in modern-day graphs of crime, is difficult to pin down, but it seems to lie in wildly fluctuating grain prices and periodic famine.

TABLE 3 *Total Number of Offenders by Number of Offenses*

Number of offenses	Absolute frequency	Relative frequency (%)	Adjusted frequency (%)	Cumulative adjusted frequency (%)
One offense	2,044	84.0	84.8	84.8
Two offenses	265	10.9	11.0	95.8
Three offenses	62	2.5	2.6	98.4
Three or more offenses	38	1.6	1.6	100.0
Blank	22	.9	missing	100.0
Total	2,432[a]	100.0	100.0	100.0

[a] Total includes valid observations (2,395) and missing observations (37).

and not for the reason that one might expect—the extensive use of hanging in felony cases.[33] Eighty-five percent of all defendants in the period were charged with but a single crime. When combined with those who committed two felonies, the percentage jumps all the way to 95.8. Furthermore, almost all the multiple offenders were individuals who went on a crime spree, killing, robbing, burgling, and stealing on several occasions in the space of only a few days. Such careless men and women rarely went unapprehended. The real significance of the figures, however, lies in the paucity of professional criminals who were recorded in operation in Essex. Whether this meant that there were not many professional criminals or whether it signifies that the professional thief went unapprehended, either because he was clever or because the law was enforced selectively in favor of him cannot be ascertained with certainty, but possible explanations will be explored further on.[34]

Furthermore, Elizabethan felons tended to follow the rhythm of the seasons and the agricultural year in their criminal behavior. Beginning in November and lasting until April, that is, the coldest months and slackest period in the farming year, lawbreaking climbed steadily upward and then tapered off until it reached a low in July and August, the warmest and busiest months in the agrarian calendar. Only May is an exception, and an important one which might provide a clue that there was more to the explanation of crime than the economics of farming in the community reveals. Since May was a month of merriment and games, celebrations tied to agricultural and seasonal rhythms, it is likely that crime was a

[33] See Chapter II.
[34] *Ibid.*

concomitant to these activities. Modern crime patterns tend to bear out that offenses fluctuate with sports events and holidays.[35]

Finally, most Elizabethan felons tended to be very respectful of status lines in their criminal acts with two exceptions. Gentlemen and yeomen were indiscriminate in choosing whom to injure. Laborers and small tradesmen and craftsmen as well as women, on the other hand, rarely did a wrong to anyone above them in social status. Nearly all felonies committed by laborers were against other workers. The time had not yet come (if indeed it ever would, since it is exaggerated in all societies) when gentlemen needed to fear the lower orders attacking them in the streets, murdering them in their beds, or taking their property from their houses. Ironically, it was not those who got the lion's share of the expanding wealth of Elizabethan England that the suffering poor turned against—it was their poverty-stricken fellow workers.

The problem of the relationship of social status and crime is perplexing because the meaning of the figures is hidden in some critical ambiguities in the legal definitions of social status. The reason for this is an obvious one—the law, as usual, lagged behind social reality and was still using in the sixteenth century a terminology that fit the legal technicalities of the day but described a community that had greatly changed since the twelfth to the fourteenth centuries, during which the definitions became fixed. The law recognized six classes of persons. In the first were included the nobility, esquires, and gentlemen. Since the nobility was legally exempt from trial at the courts analyzed here, they never appear as defendants in felony trials at manor courts, Assizes, or Quarter Sessions. Though esquires and gentlemen were subject to the tribune's jurisdiction (an esquire by the sixteenth century was merely a man who had bought a coat of arms, and a gentleman's status, too, was purchased),[36] they were nonetheless the rulers of county society. Second were the yeomen, or 40s. freeholders—men who "owned" land from which an annual income of £2 rent or fees could be realized. In the late medieval period, these were the sturdy, prosperous farmers of the countryside, but inflation had long since erased the importance of 40s. as a measure of wealth, and large leaseholdings wiped out the value of freehold land tenure as a mark of status.

Third were the peasants, or husbandmen as they were called in England. They were the men who held their land by something less than freehold, usually by either copyhold or increasingly, as the sixteenth century progressed, by lease.[37] Since many of the new "capitalist" farmers and even

[35] Certain crimes rise during December, and an interesting drop in crime figures has been registered for the District of Columbia when the Washington Redskins are in a winning streak.

[36] See Chapter III.

[37] Hull, *Agricultural and Rural Society* pp. 313–326.

the enterprising old tenant farmers were lessees of vast tracts of land, they were by Elizabethan times often much richer and higher in the social scale than many yeomen. Still, the law clung to the feudal formula, by which social status was defined almost exclusively in terms of land tenure and the personal relationship between lord and tenant that tied the two together, the essence of both medieval landholding and social structure.

Furthermore, by Elizabethan times large segments of society had grown up on the periphery of the feudal legal and social system, particularly trades and crafts. To be sure, the feudal system did recognize this, and the law followed it in attaching to the names of criminal defendants some trades and crafts, but the ones that were legally noticed were not at all coextensive with the social realities of the sixteenth century, especially of rural society. Many agricultural "crafts," as we shall see, were excluded from the formal category, artisan, whereas medieval guilds were represented despite the waning influence they played in Tudor society.

The law was most indiscriminate about laborers and women. Women were known only as widow, wife, or spinster, not always very helpful descriptions for the historian. It should also be stressed that the label attached to an individual could change from season to season, a fact particularly applicable to laborers. A man might work for wages in winter and farm a plot of ground in summer—and his status in an indictment depend on the season in which he committed his crime. Third, the term laborer is inadequate because it neither reflects social reality nor economic worth. The law did not always recognize many of the rural occupations that were considered by the community to be virtual crafts. One might find a man in an informal—but very real—reference called ploughman because that is what he was, that is what his father had been and what his sons would probably be, and nevertheless, because he was paid by the day, or the rood, or the acre he plowed, he was indicted as a laborer. Distinctions recognized and held proudly by local men therefore were treated lightly or ignored entirely by the law. Nor did the law notice that the range of wealth was wide amongst those called laborer. Some laborers—the majority, one suspects—were landless or held only enough land for a very small garden and a clay hut with a roof of straw. A considerable portion, however. were like Christopher Tomlinson, who put together a fortune of £40 held farms, and had enough interest in one of them to bequeath it to his wife. Some "bondmen in blood" are known to have left fortunes worth up to £30 or £40.[38] Thus it is never certain which type or how well off laborers in the criminal records were, though other evidence indicates strongly they were very poor and landless.

Most important, if toughest to do, is sorting out the process of selection

[38] Thirsk, *Agrarian History*, pp. 424–425.

used in prosecuting certain groups in society.[39] That gentlemen and yeomen were less frequently prosecuted was, as we shall see, absolutely certain, but how much the proportion of laborers in the records was due to selective enforcement, how much to their economic position, and how much to their numbers in the population as a whole is susceptible, to be perfectly honest, only to hunch supported by circumstantial evidence, not to certainty based on direct proof. Laborers are the largest group in the records, and we would like to know a great deal about them. Unfortunately the law paid them little heed, a fact of especial significance since it points up immediately a bias, a prejudice against, indeed a clear disregard on the part of the educated elite of the law, especially by its higher echelons, for the realities of life in the world of ordinary people. One should, therefore, be warned against total reliance upon legal definitions of social status to reflect social realities accurately.

Recognizing these caveats, it is nonetheless revealing to look at the "criminal classes" according to their occupation or position in society, even if it is through the eyes of sixteenth-century law and its preoccupation with outmoded medieval definitions and the prejudiced view of Tudor gentlemen against wage laborers. The picture that emerges from an analysis of these figures is not a surprising one. Gentlemen felons made up only 1.1% of the offenders, or about half their noncriminal counterpart in society. Yeoman wrongdoers also made up less of the criminal population than their "class" counterpart; about one-third of the population of Essex during the sixteenth century can be described as belonging to yeomanry, whereas only 10% of the criminals were yeoman. Peasants or husbandmen made up only 7.5% of the deviant subculture, even though somewhat over 20% of Essex people came from that class. Laborers, those who worked for wages either on farms or in the woolen industry, on the other hand, made up about half the criminal population—a proportion that corresponded to their numbers in society at large.[40] The number of tradesmen and craftsmen who were criminals is far more difficult to assess. No statistics for their numbers in Essex society are available, yet because

TABLE 4 *Tradesmen and Craftsmen Indicted for Felony*

Butchers	91	Millers	23
Tailors	56	Sailors	16
Blacksmiths	32	Baker	1
Shoemakers	31	Grocer	1
Carpenters	30	Poulterer	1
Glovers	29		

[39] See Chapter II.
[40] *Ibid.*

they made up one-quarter of all the criminals on record, they were either a significant segment in criminal society, or one which the law was particularly eager to prosecute; a fact of great importance but difficult to ascertain. The variety of trades and crafts represented in the category is broad, and unfortunately its rich textures are blurred by throwing together so many distinct occupations (See Table 4).[41] It ranged from sailors and fishermen to locksmiths and collarmakers, but the predominance of peculiarly rural artisans is only to be expected. Butchers, blacksmiths, and millers were the greatest in numbers while tailors, weavers, and carpenters fell close behind them, not at all surprising in a community in which the clothing industry was prominent and in a county in which building and the household comforts requiring carpentry was rapidly expanding.[42] So the range of occupations represented in the criminal class of tradesmen and craftsmen was wide, and its concentration was largely centered around what might be expected to be its counterpart in the whole of society. The number of women who committed crimes is easier to assess. Presumably the population was divided approximately evenly between the sexes, but only 10% of the crimes committed in Essex were by women.

The distribution of felonies among some groups, namely gentlemen, husbandmen, tradesmen, craftsmen, and women remained constant throughout the reign. But not all: The portion of crimes committed by yeomen fell from 18% in the first third of the reign to a mere 5% in the last third, and that of laborers rose from 42% at the beginning to more than 50% by the end, a striking shift in criminal statistics that rests upon the social, economic, and demographic changes to be discussed later on.

Another important point which the distribution of felonies among social status groups reveals is that different groups were prosecuted for different types of felony. Oddly enough, nearly a fifth of the women charged with felony had committed a violent crime, suicide and infanticide being the most frequent, indicating, it seems, not so much the brutality of their nature as the desperation of their lot. Gentlemen were equally prone to brutality, but more because of social code, tainted as it was by the warrior's creed, than because of economic deprivation. About 20% of them committed crimes of violence.

Crimes of violence diminished as social status declined. Eighteen percent of yeomen, 9% of peasants, 8% of tradesmen and craftsmen committed crimes of violence, while laborers brought up the rear with a low 4%.[43] This inverse ratio of social class and number of violent crimes (excepting

[41] The Assize Files contain a large array of occupations and crafts that are blurred in the total amorphous tradesmen and craftsmen category.

[42] E.R.O. Publication, *Elizabethan Essex*.

[43] See Appendix I.

the "women" category) upsets the commonly held notion of lower-class violence, at least for the last half of the sixteenth century. Despite these varying percentages, it should be stressed that violent crimes were always a minor element in the total crimes committed by all social groups, while more than half the felonies in all groups were larcenies.

The total number of felonies and the legal, sociological, and geographical patterns into which they fall are difficult enough to portray. To explain what these configurations mean, however, is an even more onerous task, because the figures and their distribution are the product of an intricate interweaving of sixteenth-century economic developments, changing social values with respect to law and order, shifting demographic configurations, and the impact of improved recording and intensified reporting, a mixture impossible to sort out with statistical precision. Nonetheless, it is at least safe to say that intellectual, social, and economic conditions in Essex that prevailed during the reign of Elizabeth made the county a rich breeding-ground for crime. Religious strife was encouraged by the expansion of cosmopolitan London in the west, and by the radical Anabaptists who came across the channel from the Low Countries in the east and settled in the southeast.

In addition, Cambridge University was just across the border to the north. Its extreme puritan atmosphere and general intellectual ferment was bound to have an affect on its southern neighbor, and it did. Nearly every Essex JP was educated there, and Emmanuel College, Sir Walter Mildmay's radical Puritan center, housed many future Essex parish clerks. It is not surprising, then, that the county which sponsored Lollardy in the fourteenth century should embrace Presbyterians and nurture the separatist movement in the sixteenth. Moreover, just across the North Sea Channel, there was even more religious revolution. So strong were the spiritual waves flowing from the storms of that fanatic century that a colony of Anabaptists from the continent was swept onto the southern shores of the county, and a group of radical protestant Dutch immigrants landed in Colchester where they helped the woolen industry grow in the northeast. Even though most American school children know that religious fervor sent many people to North America to set up a pure religious state, they probably do not know that many of them came from Essex.

This intellectual and religious ferment was forcefully felt, both because it was truly a religious age when preaching was a welcome innovation in church activity and because a rising literacy rate made it possible for expanding numbers of persons to read the writings of a burgeoning company of religious pamphleteers. Its effects were the more profound because the growth in literacy affected all ranks in society. These were the days when Puritan preachers faithfully believed in education for improvement of the poor and disadvantaged as well as the rich, and, unlike the seventeenth century when learning became suspect and literacy emerged as a class phenomenon (the province of the privileged), the teaching and writing touched all social levels more or less equally throughout Elizabeth's reign.[44] This is beautifully captured in the encounter between two peasants who got into a brawl in a village pub over the nature and validity of transubstantiation.[45]

Having said that religious feeling in the county was strong and that people from all ranks in society were participating in religious debate, still it should be stressed that the movement touched only a minority of the total population. Most men and women did not actively take a part in the Puritan and other current strains in the church disputes. And it is impossible to divide up the county into Catholic, Puritan, and Anglican factions. In the first place, such categories were not rigidly defined, and few men or women in the shire let their spiritual predilections or practices be known. To be sure, the faith of some important persons was public. The Petres were Catholic, but not staunch ones; the Riches became in-increasingly Puritan; the Mildmays, to all intents and purposes, were Anglicans. The Quarter Sessions Rolls tell of religious disputes among persons in lower social ranks—though not many—that reveal some Puritan and some Catholic feeling. Lists of recusants show that as the century wore on more people in the shire were disillusioned with the Church of England, and the ranks of those who refused to attend church grew larger as Elizabeth's reign advanced. But this information does not include the precise distribution of religious belief in Elizabethan Essex—it only shows that some Catholics, several Puritans, and many Anglicans inhabited the territory.

Along with the unsettling effects of religious controversy came economic crisis. The overriding economic fact in sixteenth-century history was inexorable, at times even rampant, inflation: prices rose more than 500% between 1500 and 1600.[46] Since nearly every Englishman got his livelihood from the land, most men tried to squeeze more money out of agriculture in order to beat the obstinate rise in prices. Basically, a landholder had three options if he hoped to realize more profit from his fields: He could raise more of the same crops he was already growing, which usually required improved farming methods; he could switch from grain production to more lucrative animal husbandry; or he could increase the rents or other fees his tenants owed him. In short, farmers, prodded by the pressure of inflation, were forced either to become semicapitalists or to

[44] The data on literacy is from the unpublished research of Professor David Cressey of the Claremont colleges.

[45] E.R.O. Q/SR.

[46] Elton, *England Under the Tudors* (London, 1955), Ch. 4.

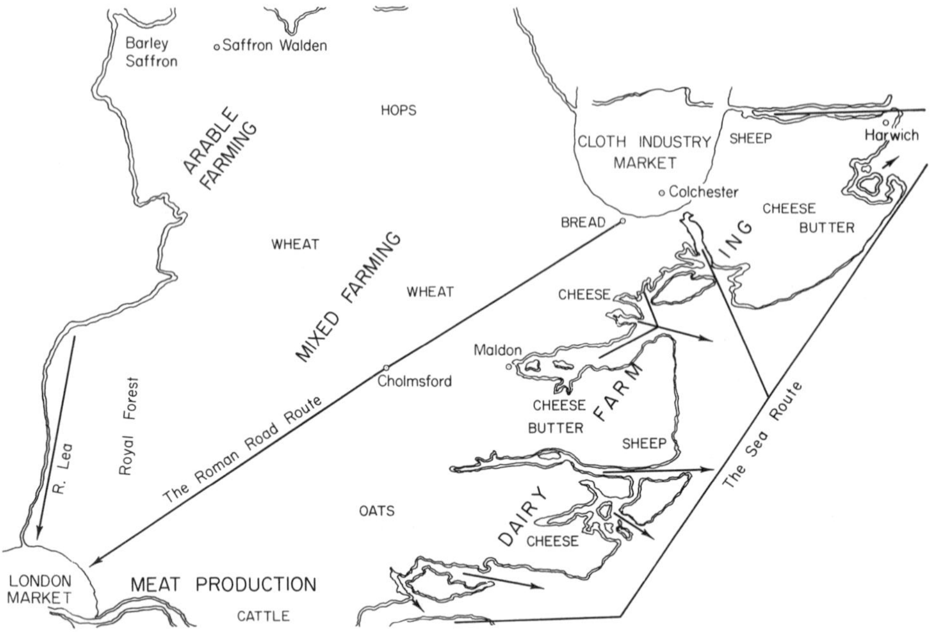

Fig. 3. Economic divisions of Essex, c. 1600: (1) types of farming; (2) principal products; (3) chief markets for produce; (4) main trade routes. [From Felix Hull, *Agriculture and Rural Society*, 1950.]

be destroyed. Fortunately, in Essex, if they could produce more than they needed, ready markets were to be had for the taking because of the proximity to London, the county's growing population, and the rise of Colchester's clothing industry.

To an enterprising landholder profits were within easy reach, but they depended on the availability of land and ready capital to buy it. Happily, Essex had an abundance of both. Merchants from London, fat with new money, and courtiers, rich with the fruits of Henry VIII's bounty (actually payments for serving him so well at court), found vast tracts of monastic lands for sale in Essex. With superlative administrative and business talents, they were soon able to buy out less enterprising men in the county and transform subsistence farming into surplus commercial agriculture. Essex was literally invaded by men who had recently made private fortunes from service to the Crown or from commerce. In fact, more than three-fourths of the shire's gentry came either from the court at Westminster or from businesses in London, not from Essex. In this manner, more than 200 "foreign" families swelled the ranks of the Essex gentry from 1530 to 1560.[47] Upstart county magistrates like Petre, Mildmay, and Riche pushed aside ancient landed Essex families such as the de Veres (Earl of Oxford), the Bourchiers (Earl of Essex), and the Radcliffes (Earl of Sussex), and set themselves up as rulers of the county's administration and leaders in its social hierarchy. Even lesser men at times moved in on old landed families. Roger Harlaikendon, the Earl of Oxford's steward, for example, bought the Earl's estate at Earls Colne and, within a few years, was accepted as part of the Essex gentry as well as becoming a respected and active member of the county bench.[48]

The impact of these men on judicial administration will be discussed later,[49] but their effect on economics and society at large was also significant, touching as it did the daily lives of ordinary people the whole country over. Indeed, it is ironic that their activities in county life outside criminal law enforcement probably had a greater influence on the number of felonies committed and reported than did their duties performed as JPs. This was because they so extensively revolutionized the way land was held and managed that they catalyzed a fissure in old social relationships and hastened the breakdown of traditional institutions, replacing personal ties with money and countywide administrative units for the more parochial manor, both of which deeply disturbed the community's stability and created a climate in which crime could grow.

Elizabethan Essex landholders were proficient in creating new forms of profit. One was market farming, an enterprise to which more and more farmers were turning, including the large landowners. The Petres in a single year, 1556, realized the enormous profit of £610 in produce alone.[50] Other landlords leased their land in huge tracts for others to manage. These lessees in turn sublet to tenants who did the actual farming. Thomas Golding, for instance, leased more than 900 acres (approximately 35% of the parish of Belchamp St. Pauls) and then sublet it out to farmers who cultivated it.[51] The actual farmer was responsible for maintaining the condition of the property. These new capitalist farmers were, according to one writer of the time,

> good husbands and know . . . well how to improve their lands to the uttermost . . . so that they take their farms into their own hands as their leases expire and either till themselves or else let them out to those who will give more; whereby the yeomanry of England is decayed.[52]

[47] Hull, *Agriculture and Rural Society*, p. 265. Note also Fig. 3 which shows economic divisions.

[48] See Chapter III.

[49] *Ibid.*

[50] Hull, *Agriculture and Rural Society*, p. 314.

[51] *Ibid.*, p. 315.

[52] Thomas Wilson, *The State of England 1600*, Camden Miscellany, Vol. XVI, ed. F.J. Fisher (1936).

The combination of market farming and large-scale land leasing strongly suggests that the moving force behind farming and letting land was profit.

Large-scale leasing and commercial farming were not the only indications that Essex was shifting to a money economy. Two other developments in the county clearly point in the same direction. Markets and fairs had been held for centuries in every manor in the county. In the 1500s, and particularly during Elizabeth's reign, however, a change took place in both. Manor fairs gave way to county fairs located in the major economic centers of the shire.[53] Markets, too, declined in number as a few key locations came to manage most of the business. Chelmsford, for example, served the mixed farming center, while Colchester predominated in the cloth-producing northeast. Consolidated markets and fairs bought at the expense of manorial economic organization indicates how strongly economic decay had set in on Elizabethan Essex feudal society, bringing with it social and economic repercussions, not all of them desired or desirable.

Taking economic regulation away from the manor was not meant to put it at the disposal of the free market. Quite the contrary: Tudor economic policies were extensively paternalistic, even if they were locally administered. Price and wage controls were by law in the hands of the JPs, who were supposed to determine market regulations as well as prescribe what jobs were lawful and who could have them. But this was only theory. In practice the magistrates, who controlled enforcement and were themselves usually engaged in profit-making agriculture, rarely observed the rules they were supposed to enforce. Sir John Petre, a leading JP from Essex and Deputy Lieutenant for the county, carried on a large private trade outside the market.[54] The constant flow of cases that involved engrossing (selling above market price) and forestalling (waiting until prices were high to sell goods), such as that of William Crane, a peasant, indicted for engrossing 20,000 pounds of butter worth £300—surely enough to satisfy his community's total demand[55]—are proof enough that business was not confined to authorized markets and fairs but was carried on in the most profitable way for the sellers—and it was a seller's market. Even when trading took place within fairs and markets, there were complaints that it did not stick to prescribed rules. One Essex rector was deeply disturbed because fairs were being held on Sunday, and people instead of "hearing any one word of the Gospel of Christ preached give themselves over to buying and selling."[56] Apparently, when business was available, the Lord had to wait until profit seekers had reaped their rewards.

[53] P.R.O. *Star Chamber* 8/253.

[54] See Chapter III and E.R.O. D/DP 06 (Petre family archives).

[55] E.R.O. Q/SR 131/88.

[56] Hull, *Agriculture and Rural Society*, quoted on page 154. Dr. Hull has found that shippers who carried goods along the water routes of Essex were also springing up, even though no

Rising population was another element that affected both the number of felonies recorded and the actual number of crimes that took place in Essex during Elizabeth's reign. Determining crime rates for the period must be speculative because complete demographic information has not yet been compiled for the county.[57] Based on a very rough estimate a 33.3% population *growth* during the reign (from about 60,000 people in 1558 to about 80,000 in 1603),[58] the overall crime rate in the county doubled. It rose from seven felonies for every 10,000 people in 1559 to 14 per 10,000 by the end, with a peak of 36 per 10,000 in 1598. The result is similar when 5-year moving averages are used. Beginning with 9 for every 10,000 in the first 5 years, the rate at the end was a little over 20 per 10,000 people. Although it is dangerous to compare two radically different time periods like modern Britain and sixteenth-century Essex, especially in view of the growth of modern police agencies and new and contrasting reporting techniques, it is helpful to look at certain twentieth-century crime statistics. In 1902, the crime rate in England was 24.9 for every 10,000 people; by 1965, it had risen to 95.4, a much higher overall ration of felony to population and a much greater growth in modern Britain than in Elizabethan Essex.[59]

In late Tudor Essex as well as in twentieth-century England population increase had something to do with rising numbers of felonies, but it should be emphasized that both periods demonstrate that population explosions did not keep pace with the crime explosion. This was because expanding population had an effect far outweighing its numbers. What happened in the early modern period was that the rising population exerted a pressure on the existing food supply that had significant and varied effects. In the first place, it had a great deal to do with the rising price of food, an increase, it should be noted, that far outstripped contemporaneous rises in the price

---

one called them such. He also discovered that many men who made their living by shipping goods were styled yeomen, esquires, gentlemen, clothiers, and even found one widow engaged in it [pp. 193–194].

[57] The Cambridge group led by Professor Peter Laslett has at last turned its attention to Essex, and with the help of Mr. F. G. Emmison, former Essex county Archivist, the parish registers are being scrutinized, but the results, unfortunately, are not yet available.

[58] The basis for these figures is the muster rolls, lists of men available to serve in the armed forces during the wars in which Elizabeth engaged. They were supposed to include all men between the ages of 16 and 60 who were resident in the county parishes. Taking Roger Schofield's suggestion that a multiplier of four be used, I have multiplied the number of men in the muster rolls by four and have thus derived the figures cited here. Of course, they are subject to serious criticism since the efficiency of the information gatherers definitely improved as more and more musters were called, and naturally not all men eligible for counting actually found their way into the muster figures. Nonetheless, they give the maximum figures that population increased.

[59] F. W. McClintock, *Crime in England and Wales* (London, 1968).

of manufactures like woolen cloth. Furthermore, it influenced the falling real wages of workers in the county. The law of supply and demand seemed to have been working very well and very much to the laborer's disadvantage. Food was scarce; therefore, the demand for it was high and its prices ever climbing. The supply of labor was growing; the demand for it, therefore, was shrinking and consequently wages were falling. The rising price of food and the falling price of labor were crucial elements in the shift to commercial agriculture in Essex. Profits, as we have noted, were readily available to those who could grow food for the market, and many enterprising men in the county were only too willing to exploit the situation to their immense profit. Unfortunately, though it gave landowners more profits, the attempt to shift the county's resources in the direction of more food was not entirely successful. Commercial agriculture may have made profit-seeking landholders rich, and new farming methods, good husbandry, and variety crops may have prevented widespread starvation, but they did not solve the general food shortage of the sixteenth century—a shortage that was aggravated both by the proximity of London with its much faster growing population making repeated and swelling demands on the county's food supply and the unlucky concurrence of a long string of bad harvests in the 1590s. What with the crude methods available to improve production, the aggravation of London's expanding needs, and nature's unwillingness to cooperate, it is no wonder that the food shortage became a subsistence crisis which caused, in part, the number of crimes in Essex to outdistance the growth in its population.

The effect of these social and economic developments were far-reaching. They revolutionized county society and put a new type of man at the top while hastening the shift of economic life from subsistence farming to commercial agriculture. But what of ordinary people? What did it do to them? It made some poor men rich, but most common people suffered a great deal. Though Essex was called the English "Goshen" and was generally thought by contemporaries to be a prosperous county, half the landholding population could not survive simply by working their own land. They had to have extra work. Nearly 48% of the landholders in the rural parts of the county held less than five acres of land, an amount considered insufficient to support a family, whereas in the clothing industry areas 53% had subminimal plots. Even in the most prosperous part of the county, the central region, more than 25% of the population was at the poverty level.[60] And the laborer's lot was getting worse. In the first place the number of laborers was increasing in the total population in the countryside. One estimate makes the percentage of laborers at about

[60] Hull, *Agriculture and Rural Society*, pp. 471–473.

one-third of the whole in 1540 and about 47% by 1640.[61] This part of the rise in number of felons from the laboring poor was due to the increase in their actual numbers. Indeed the comparison between these rough national percentages for that total populace and the specific figures for Essex county felons[62] are so close as to be uncanny. But, it would be wrong to rely solely on the rise in actual numbers of laborers as the explanation for their increase on the court rolls though, to be sure, the rise is of fundamental significance. Two other factors played their part as well, though they cannot be quantified. The position of the Elizabethan laborer was definitely declining. Some, it is true, bettered their position, but the vast majority were gradually falling behind the rest of the population. Those lucky enough to hold onto the diminishing supply of land saw their plots decrease in size. The Quarter Sessions Rolls tell many sad tales such as this one: John Weaver, a Danbury laborer, had been living in a house with such "lamentably high rent" he could not support his wife and five children. So he had rented an outhouse "and thereto attached a wooden chimney." The whole thing violated the law requiring a real house and four acres attached, but with 13 friends testifying to his honesty the court granted him a license to keep living there.[63] It should be added that the court was frequently presented with petitions for licenses to build on plots of one acre or so, none of which were denied. These small holdings usually encroached on the common land of the area, thus decreasing pasture, wood, and wasteland for the rest of the community as in Langham, for example, the "parish being of late years much enlarged and increased by reason of new buildings remote from the parish church."[64] More important, however, were the expansions by prospering farmers, yeomen, and gentlemen eager to increase productive lands. Hardly a quarter session passed without numerous complaints of encroaching on the common land, land badly needed by poorer peasants to pasture their few stock, hunt for wild animal meat, and get firewood.

Worst of all was the totally landless proletariat, of whom there were growing numbers. They had only their labor to sell, and it was going at a cheaper rate all the time. Moreover, as the number of landless workers unattached to any lord in the personal sense or any land in the legal sense swelled, the attitude toward them shifted—they were no longer part of the community that deserved a place and safe keeping but were rather considered merely as employees to be bought for the time being, only to be discarded when they were no longer needed. As a result of this shift

[61] Thirsk, *Agrarian History*, pp. 398–399.
[62] See Appendix III.
[63] E.R.O. Q/SR 22/67–68.
[64] E.R.O. Q/SR 155/31.

in attitude the evils of society were all laid at their doorstep, and the general notion that they were a scourge encouraged their disproportionate prosecution in court just when their declining economic position drove them to steal in order to live. What commercialization all over the county, urbanization in the southwest near London, the clothing industry in the northeast and the general increase in numbers had done, therefore, was to produce an almost modern agricultural, urban, and industrial proletariat that depended for survival on wages alone.

Had no famines come along to raise the price of bread or had wages kept pace with prices, then this half of the population could have survived. Unfortunately, neither dearth nor inflation stayed away. The effects of a bad harvest can be seen in the little parish of Heydon. In 1564, which was a good harvest year, 19 people were able to give poor relief and did, 10 could give nothing but survived without help, while the remaining three needed to be relieved. In 1568 (a year of bad harvest), more than half the parish went on relief, while a full quarter lived at poverty level. In Chelmsford during the dearth of 1596 "many men, women, and children go out of the town-a-begging . . . and . . . there is neither work nor victuals unless they beg for it. . . ."[65] Neither did inflation help laborers, since prices increased between 1533 and 1593 by 240%, while wages rose only 175%.[66] Thus, on top of the specific problems that bad harvests created, there was the steady and relentless pressure of a shrinking buying power, unseen but felt by nearly all ordinary people in the shire.

Economic hardship in the 1590s drove expanding numbers of desperate people to steal in order to live. Since only figures for the whole country are available, it is impossible specifically to connect grain prices and recorded crime in Essex, but they do appear to have fluctuated at approximately the same rate. For example, in the early and mid-1590s when prices were skyrocketing, the number of thefts also soared. These developments and figures, especially when seen in connection with the rhythmic pattern of criminal behavior, therefore lend credence to the conclusion that men committed crimes due to pressures created by economic deprivation and social dislocation, not because they were in the "business" of crime.

The connection, therefore, between social and economic conditions and the number of thefts seems clear.[67] But it is impossible to sort out the

[65] E.R.O. Q/SR 135/21.

[66] Hull, *Agriculture and Rural Society*, p. 360.

[67] The link between poverty and crime has been extensively investigated in a book edited by William Bonger entitled *Criminality and Economic Conditions*, trans. Henry P. Horton (New York: Agathon Press, 1967). The studies included are not exactly analogous in that many of them deal with modern society, but the criminals involved are persons living at subsistence level, that is, in an economic condition in which even a slight rise in prices could

actual increase in crime that these upheavals spawned[68] from the other influences that were reflected in the swelling criminal court records. One of the most significant, but also unfortunately elusive variables that bore upon the shifting statistics of crime was the attitude of society toward lawlessness. The rise in crime simply had to be linked to shifting public opinion. Whether or not the attitude toward lawlessness was a response to growing crime or whether it was spawned by the mentality of new men running the county, the mentality of individuals who were dedicated to order and efficiency in general and who had strong educational training in obedience as well, critically affected the felony curve for the period, no matter how difficult to measure. This will be examined in Part II, and further discussion of it must be postponed for now, but its weight should be always in the forefront of viewing and evaluating criminal statistics during the reign of Elizabeth.

For now, we turn to other elements in the makeup of the crime curve of Elizabethan Essex.

First, recording variations and reporting fluctuations made their mark on the crime figures. It is not surprising that few recorded crimes would have occurred in the dairy farming belt in the southeast or in the open fields in the north, because both were sparsely populated. What needs explanation is the high frequency of crimes in the mixed farming area in and around Chelmsford in the center of the county, the near absence of them in Colchester in the northeast, and the fluctuation that characterized the outskirts of London in the southwest. One would reasonably expect that urban and industrial areas like those around London and Colchester

---

bring on acute economic suffering, if not actual starvation itself. The conclusions of every relevant study in the work point out that crimes against property go up when prices go up and they descend with declines in prices.

[68] See the following: C. H. S. Jayewardene, "Criminal Culture and Subcultures," *Probation and Child Care Journal* (1963), 2, pp. 1–5; Manuel Lopez-Rey, "Economic Conditions and Crime with Special Reference to Less-Developed Countries," *International Annuals of Criminology* (1964, Pt. I), pp. 33–40; Secretariat paper, Third United Nations Congress on the Prevention of Crime and Treatment of Offenders, "Social Change and Criminality," United Nations, Stockholm, 1965, A/CONF. 26/1; Shlomo Shoham, "The Approach of the 'Culture-Conflict' Hypothesis to the Criminality of Immigrants to Israel," *Journal of Criminal Law, Criminology, and Police Science* (1962), 53, pp. 207–214; and Herman J. Venter, "Urbanization as Crimenogenic Factors in the Republic of South Africa," *International Review of Criminal Policy* (1962), 20, pp. 59–71.

Such sociological studies are useful in suggesting how the historical evidence in this study can be interpreted. Most are based upon information drawn from developing countries that face the impact of rapid industrialization and commercialization brought on by Western cultural invasion. Though they are not the same, the situations are analogous in that the sixteenth-century subsistence farmer who had to come to terms with commercialized agriculture and its accompanying money economy faced deep psychological shock just as do underdeveloped peoples when they must cope with modern Western life patterns of work and leisure.

would have continuously high crime figures while rural areas would have had considerably lower ones. This is especially true since Colchester and the southwest were the most densely populated parts of the county, while the center of the county was only moderately so. The reasons for what at first seems to be a puzzling pattern lie both in the effectiveness of law enforcement and the degree of reporting as well as in demographic factors, though perhaps more of the former two than the latter one. Living near to London made it easy for criminals to slip across the border into the city and get lost among its teeming nameless faces. This was especially true as the period progressed and the population expanded. Toward the end of the reign, the parish of West Ham (just on the London border) complained that many criminals were crossing the line into Essex where, if caught, they became a charge on the townspeople, because parishes were financially responsible for transporting suspects found within their village to the county gaol in Colchester—a hefty distance since it was the opposite end of the shire.[69] In fact, however, more criminals were going the other way—out of Essex into London—as the decreasing number of felonies recorded in West Ham after 1586 shows. In Colchester the problem was one of records, not geography. The borough had its separate Quarter Sessions, where felonies that occurred in its boundaries were indicted and its special gaol deliveries where they were tried, thereby making it appear in the county records as if no crimes were committed in the city.[70]

Better reporting partially produced the heavy concentration of crimes recorded in and around the county town of Chelmsford, and here we come to what may be the most important single factor in explaining the increased rate of crime in Essex, the question of attitude toward crime and will to prosecute. It is important to realize that anyone who reported a crime in the sixteenth century engaged in an expensive operation. Victims or witnesses were rarely, if ever, paid for coming to court to prosecute or give evidence in a felony proceeding. They had to come to Chelmsford (where more court sessions were held) at their own expense to press charges personally. Their presence in court was required due to the rules of oral argument.[71] Under the circumstances, an injured person who had to pay his own travel costs, feed and lodge himself during the period of the indictment, and then return to Chelmsford several weeks later to testify at the trial might well decide it was not worth the money or effort, especially since he had to help pay the suspect's transportation as well and probably would not

[69] E.R.O. Q/SR 13/43.

[70] The borough records were not tallied for this study, but a superficial survey of their content makes it clear that the courts in the city had primary criminal jurisdiction over misdeeds taking place there.

[71] See Chapter II.

get his goods back anyway. Because of this, people living near Chelmsford were much more likely to take the chance of catching and bringing a culprit to justice than those residing in the outlying parts of the shire. Furthermore, both Sir John Petre and Sir Thomas Mildmay resided in the neighborhood. The two most powerful magnates and the most active JPs during Elizabeth's reign, their efforts unquestionably had a profound impact on the degree of law and order which was achieved in the center of the shire.

In conclusion, it should be stressed that even though it can be said that the level of theft measured by the felony statistics virtually skyrocketed over the 45 years of Elizabeth's reign, and that from these statistics a fairly clear picture emerges of rising nonviolent felony spawned by a mixture of rising prices, lower wages, and the proletariazation of labor in the countryside, only a portion of the story, however, has as yet been told. The rate of crime recorded was not only a matter of economic hardship and social dislocation or demographic and geographic factors or accidents of recording and reporting. It was also the result of a tension in society between the established authorities, that is, the men in power and, one would suppose, some of the victims of crime on the one side who yearned for order (or in the victim's case at least revenge), and on the other side, the large sector of the community that was not willing to make the necessary sacrifices to make the law operative. The amount of dedication to law and order is a matter first of society's attitude toward lawlessness and second the machinery set up to translate that public sentiment into legal reality, both of which, it must be realized, affected the amount of crime recorded in the county. The felony statistics, therefore, reflect not only an increase in actual crime, but also a combination of delicate interacting forces of public opinion and legal machinery. To those forces involved in society's response, so critical yet so elusive, we must now turn if we are to understand fully the statistics of crime in early modern Essex county.

PART **II**

THE CRIMINAL JUSTICE SYSTEM

The evidence about the system of criminal justice is more abundant than that for crime and criminals, even if it is more difficult to use because of its bulk. Schedules of JP attendance, lists of jurors, calendars of constables and bailiffs as well as gaol delivery calendars and registrations of prisoners kept in the Colchester Castle gaol are voluminous, and they all help to reconstruct the personnel of the law enforcement machinery. Furthermore writs, warrants, letters, and memoranda add a depth of detail impossible to find in the indictments by themselves, and through these rich sources it is possible to relate the statistics of crime to the system that created them.

The law enforcement agencies worked through an intricate interplay of officials, victims, courts, and legal procedure. A burgeoning staff of zealous JPs drawn from the ranks of the county gentry stood ready to cut out the festering sore of lawlessness from the ailing body politic.[1] Meanwhile, a blossoming bureaucracy ably handled the upper classes' growing preoccupation with law and order and ordinary people's growing demand for protection against the effects of lawlessness by keeping the machinery of justice running.[2]

Responsibility for enforcing the law, however, was not limited to judges and JPs; it lay in the hands of "all good men." In line with this philosophy, ordinary men in the shire were constrained to act as jurors. These neighbors in the community in the form of the grand jury made the initial decision about whether or not to try a suspected felon and, acting as a trial jury,

[1] See Chapter III.
[2] *Ibid.*

sealed a suspect's final fate—gallows or freedom—as well as the distribution of his property, if he had any. Also drawn from the ranks of ordinary good men were the constables who carried the burden of physically bringing wrongdoers into custody.[3] Finally, without the cooperation of the people who were the objects of crime, the efforts of JPs and their helpers would have been worth little, since almost every recorded felony came to the attention of the authorities because a victim told them about it and charged a suspect with the offense.[4]

[3] *Ibid.*

[4] See Chapter I.

CHAPTER II

CRIME, SOCIETY, AND THE LAW

The need for order is imperative in every community, but it is particularly acute as societies grow more complex and where relationships become subject to rigid rules that are intended to produce optimal harmony amongst a host of conflicting individual interests. As social matrices become more intricate, as social and economic changes hasten, discord becomes more prevalent and crime rates go up, as we have already seen in the case of Elizabethan Essex.[1] At the same time that crime increases, however, another critical development occurs: The level of tolerance for disorder diminishes. Within society there is a growing demand for order, that is, attitudes toward lawlessness harden. Such a shift in attitude took place in Elizabethan Essex, as we shall soon observe. This transformation also had its effect on the period's crime figures. But law and order was not easy to achieve, and translating desire into reality was fraught with problems. That it was expensive, time consuming, difficult, and unrewarding both for the victims of crime and the officers of the law, we have noted already. But there is more. At every stage in the criminal justice process—in the detection of crime, in the reporting of offenses, in the formal charge, indictment, trial, and conviction of the defendant and even to the time of execution of sentence—the amount of crime brought under control depended on the combination of two highly volatile forces: public sentiment and the manipulation of legal rules.

The level of lawlessness in early modern Essex can only be gauged by the records that the law-enforcement machinery produced. But the pro-

[1] Donald W. Cressey and David A. Ward, *Delinquency, Crime and Social Process* (New York, 1969) pp. 60–66.

duction of more records does not only mean that there was more crime; more numbers also signify a greater desire for order and consequently increased and more efficient enforcement of the laws. To complicate the meaning of crime figures even more, the choice of whom should be prosecuted was replete with bias against certain segments in society. So, to be sure, we cannot accept the statistics at their face value and must still ask some difficult questions: Exactly how efficient law enforcement was, did it become more efficient as time passed, was there a shift in attitude toward crime, and against whom was the criminal justice system most likely to be directed. All these questions in turn demand some attention to the amount of community cooperation with the enforcing agencies, public prejudice against certain sectors in society, personal and class discrimination by the officers of the law, and the extent to which the legal machinery can be abused by the suspect himself. If there is one constant that can be assumed, it is that the accused will endeavor to save his skin by any means available to him, and during the early years of Elizabeth's reign, both public opinion and the technicalities of the law conspired to help him avoid prosecution. Only slowly and hesitantly as the period progressed did those who broke the law (or more accurately, were charged with having done so) confront a growing social hostility and rules that grew more difficult to circumvent—a change that resulted in more prosecution and more convicted felons.

Underlying the whole criminal justice system was the problem of punishment. The efficacy and morality of punishment as a means to social control was debated by sixteenth-century educated laymen and jurists, just as it is today. Some writers questioned the humanity of harsh punishment. The popular writer Thomas Dekker, who was himself a bitter critic of "scamps and ne'er-do-wells," nevertheless complained that: "Many lost their lives for scarce as much coin as will hide their palm, which is most cruel." He was obviously referring to the draconian penalty of death as punishment for the theft of a single shilling.[2] Even Sir Edward Coke, who thought punishment was often laxly administered, concluded that it was

> . . . a lamentable case . . . to see so many . . . men and women strangled on that cursed tree of the gallows; . . . in a large field a man might see together all . . . in one year throughout England come to that untimely and ignominous death, if there were any spark of grace or charity in him, it would make his heart to bleed for pity and compassion.[3]

A few tender-hearted men may have writhed under the inhumanity of laws written in blood, but most Elizabethans believed that revenge was a proper aim of punishment and that social order depended on the brutal public reminder that crime does not pay. That is why the gallows stood in

[2] A. V. Judges, *The Elizabethan Underworld* (London, 1930), p. viii.

[3] Quoted in Sir James F. Stephens, *A History of the Criminal Law of England*, Vol. I (London, 1882) p. 468.

the center of Chelmsford on a main thoroughfare[4] and why, as late as 1771, when John Howard, the prison reformer, visited the county, the prisoners "were brought upon a chain through the heart of the town, where numbers of the country people flock to see them and attend them from the gaol up to the courthouse."[5] William Lambarde, Kentish JP, urged his countrymen to use cruelty to keep their neighbors on the law's straight and narrow path[6]; Sir Edward Coke argued that "forasmuch as many do offend in the hope of pardon, that pardons be very rarely granted"[7]; and even the kindly Essex pastor, William Harrison, wished terrible punishments on wrongdoers, ones which would "prove more bitter than half an hour's hanging."[8] These were mere verbal admonitions, but as we shall see, it was not unheard of for Essex JPs to punish, in various ways, men merely "for example's sake."[9] Whatever writers said or local officials did, however, the common law was clear on the point: Convicted felons must hang, save only petty thieves (those who stole less than 12d.) who were to be whipped until the blood ran down their backs.

The comments of upper-class Elizabethans, worried by the fear of social revolution and the loss of their property are deceptive, however, and the draconian felony laws are misleading, because neither reflects what actually happened to individuals who committed crimes. An enormous attrition in the number of suspected felons brought to public notice took place from the time an offense was committed and a convict was hanged, a fact that drastically diminishes the impact of the brutal felony laws of the sixteenth century, measurably lightens the weight of some humanitarian-minded critic's evaluations and partly explains the calls for brutal punishment by worried country gentlemen and Westminster judges.

The escape of prospective convicts began with the failure of many, perhaps most, victims to use the criminal justice system to redress their injuries. It is critical to remember that these people were villagers who lived in close daily contact with each other, many times sorting out their problems on a personal level, reflected to some extent in the number of assaults registered at manor courts and in Quarter Sessions. We do not know the code of the ordinary person in early modern Essex, but we do know that "they" (said in a suspicious way) was the term reserved for the authorities, and we can reasonably assume that knowing your neighbor's personality—

[4] E.R.O. *D/DM* P1.

[5] E.R.O. Publication, *Law and Order in Essex*.

[6] William Lambarde, "Charges to the Juries," in Conyers Read, *William Lombarde and Local Government* (Cornell, 1962).

[7] Quoted in Sir James F. Stephens, *A History of the Criminal Law of England*, Vol. I (London, 1882) p. 468.

[8] William Harrison, *The Description of England* (Ithaca, N.Y., 1968), p. 194.

[9] Numerous instances in E.R.O. Q/SR 1–160.

and the records show that almost all persons charged with felony were neighbors of their victims—reduced the total number of persons brought to official notice. Furthermore, those who finally reported crimes and named possible offenders had to overcome enormous pressures within the community and probably were able to do so only out of anger or the desire for revenge and, as the period progressed, out of a growing fear of crime due in particular to the loss of a dwindling supply of food and necessary items. Even assuming the desire to report a crime, victims often did not have the skill to do so. Justice Waldgreave, for example, requested the Clerk of the Peace to draw up an indictment for one complainant because "he is but a simple man." Moreover, many victims (and some officials too) feared reprisal from their neighbors if they reported a crime. And with good reason in an age when suspects often beat policemen who tried to arrest them to bloody pulps and frequently successfully sued their accusers for malicious prosecution or false imprisonment.[10] Other sufferers had qualms about the shame they were sure to endure if they publicized their woes, particularly if they were the object of sex offenses. Most women did not relish walking down their village streets if they had been sexually abused, especially in a society prone to assume that her invitation and not her partner's licentiousness prompted the assault in the first place. The records are virtually bulging with examinations laying out in the minutest of detail the acts leading up to sexual intercourse that resulted in the birth of illegitimate children in Elizabethan Essex, and there is not a single one in which the woman's contention that she was forced into the sexual act was taken seriously. Of course, there must have been promiscuous women then, just as there are now, but to assume without question that lewdness and licentiousness was a natural attribute of ordinary country women was grossly wrong. It was bound to make the victims of rape keep their violation a secret rather than risking certain public reprobation and, judging by the few accused rapists ever convicted, losing even the satisfaction that the offender might be punished for his wrongdoing. Buggery was similarly stigmatized: Both the offender and the victim were subject to heavy social and religious censure, which made even unwilling participants in unaccepted sexual activity pause before exposing their assailants and themselves to public degradation.

Most victims were too practical to report crimes to the officials. They knew the certain work and possible futility in attempting to bring culprits to justice. Charges had to be registered with the neighboring JP, after which the complainant was bonded to appear and prosecute the accused. Furthermore, the complainant was compelled to go in person to Chelmsford to frame an indictment before the grand jury and testify

[10] See Chapter III.

at the defendant's trial, which often meant two journeys, since trial usually followed indictment by several weeks. All of this actually spelled time away from work and money out of pocket since victims had to pay their own way to court and support themselves while they were there. Finally, losses were seldom restored because offenders had often already disposed of stolen goods. One has to ponder long the wisdom of a criminal justice system that is based not on private restitution but public retribution. How much more willing our ancestors as well as ourselves would have been to search out a wrongdoer if the end of that search would produce replacement or at least repayment for property stolen and restoration of loss in injury, instead of public trial and possible execution. When this great shift was taking place during the early medieval period (that is, the movement away from private remedy to public trial) there were good social, political and economic reasons for it, but they had long outlived their usefulness and the price society paid was to have the almost impossible burden of trying to instill in ordinary people the very abstract notion that it was their duty to report crime and that somehow society in general would benefit if they performed it. Failing that instruction, then the enforcement of law had to rest upon the desire for revenge, the sometimes latent, but always present pleasure in witnessing or at least imagining violence. This latter was clearly the most promising. Private violence was censured in stronger and stronger terms, whereas feeding the public's appetite for it at the public trough was steadily encouraged, and indeed has not really stopped yet. Even the urge for revenge often went unsatisfied, however, because a hanging felon was an unusual sight in those days of lax jurors and legal loopholes.

The strength of the judicial system and the amount of confidence an honest citizen had in it were inextricably intertwined. The courts could not punish offenders if honest folk did not report them, and victims of crimes would not turn in suspects unless they felt quite certain they would be punished. One Somerset JP's estimate that four-fifths of all crime went unreported because ordinary people in the shire would not turn in their neighbors was undoubtedly not based on modern statistical analysis, and allowing for his class bias it was perhaps an exaggeration as well,[11] but it nonetheless highlights a serious limitation in the administration of justice and must be considered in measuring the value of the criminal statistics. For instance, dipping into his reservoir of unreported felony, either because of hardening attitudes or more efficient enforcement, might well produce

[11] Stated in Rowse, *The England of Elizabeth*, p. 348, n. 1. This was a prejudiced view, since members of the ruling class had a penchant for overestimating the amount of lawlessness on the part of their "inferiors." It is, nevertheless, a helpful reminder that what we see in the court records is only the tip of a very large iceberg of crime, most of which is forever hidden from view.

a striking rise in the *registration* of crime, but would not represent a whit of increase in the actual crime rate, a fact that would give anyone pause before attempting to read too much into swelling felony figures for the period.

Let us now look at those who actually entered the criminal process and see how many prospects for the gallows were lost along the way. Once a crime was reported, it became the constable's responsibility to bring the suspect in for examination. Since their efforts were not always successful, at this point in the criminal justice process many potential convicts were lost, but because so much of this crime escapes the record keepers, it is impossible even to estimate how many prospective convicts were lost due to constable's failures to bring them into custody.

Even when the constables succeeded in their efforts to round up suspects, many escaped trial after they were brought into custody. A full 33% of all persons imprisoned on suspicion of felony were freed by proclamation because no one came to court to prosecute.[12] This was due both to the rules of oral pleading, which required that the victim or witness come to testify in person,[13] and the necessity for having the JP who conducted the preliminary hearings be there to shepherd the case for the prosecution through the courts.[14]

The attrition did not end when a defendant finally got to trial. Even if the victim reported him, the constable caught him, the witnesses came to testify and the JP prosecuted him, he still might well go free if the jury did not convict him. So the jury too played its part in determining the number of felons who ended up on the gallows. Four types of jury operated in the Tudor system of criminal justice. The hundred jury (one for each of the 19 administrative units in the county) decided if sufficient evidence existed to indict suspected criminals from their own neighborhood and passed them to the grand jury, either to be charged formally or to be dismissed from further action. If the grand jury found enough evidence to indict an accused person, a trial jury was convened to resolve the question of innocence or guilt. The fourth type of jury, that of matrons, was called together if a woman who was found guilty by a trial jury claimed she was with child. The matron jury's duty was to discover if this was true, though no hints remain disclosing their methods of discovery. If she was pregnant, the benefit of her womb entitled her to postponement and sometimes total avoidance of punishment.

The functions of these four kinds of jury were easily distinguishable, but the social base of their members was not clearly defined. It is commonly thought that grand jurors were drawn from the lesser gentry, that hundred

[12] See Appendix II on gaol delivery.

[13] See Chapter I and earlier cited, pp. 38–39.

[14] See Chapter III.

jurors were yeomen, and that trial and matron jurors were recruited from the "baser sorts" of people.[15] Such a neat division simply did not exist in fact. On the Epiphany Quarter Sessions grand jury for 1570, five men were hundred and trial jurors, three were grand as well as hundred jurors, and three others were both grand and trial jurors; merely three were grand jurors exclusively.[16] The hundred juries from Barstable and Chafford in 1589, moreover, were drawn from a wide social spectrum, embracing a gentleman worth £40 in land and two peasants who owned no property at all worth mentioning, whereas the remaining members had wealth ranging from 20s. to £6.[17] Out of the 42 grand jurors at the Hilary and Trinity Assizes in 1588, there were only five who were gentlemen, one an esquire, and five yeomen, while the remaining 31 were nonfreeholders of various types.[18] Thus, jurors were drawn from all ranks in society, and the individuals served quite indiscriminately on all kinds of juries; that is, the grand jury had about it no apparent social exclusiveness, nor did the hundred and trial juries suffer any particular social stigma. It is also interesting that no one questioned the ethics or the legality of trial juries trying defendants whom they themselves had indicted as grand jurors. John Waylett, for example, sat as a grand juror on several occasions when he was a trial juror at the same session.

The social status of jurors was then clearly mixed, but such egalitarianism was not officially sanctioned. A statute in 1585 complained that sheriffs allowed "better men" to stay home for a price and commanded those officials in the future to return only grand jurors for the Assizes who were worth £4 per annum in land.[19] The Essex JPs tried to extend this requirement to Quarter Sessions, but their efforts were sporadic, and they finally abandoned the idea. In 1567, they issued a writ that called for juries made up of 40s. freeholders[20]; in 1589, the requirement was raised to £4,[21] in 1594, it was reduced to 40s. again,[22] and after upping it in the summer of 1602 to £4, in the autumn of that year it was permanently lowered to 40s.[23]

[15] Almost all introductions to printed Quarter Sessions records take this view. It is probably based on the later history of jurors, but it is not true of Essex during Elizabeth's reign. See for example, G. Ogden Williams *Caernarvonshire Quarter Sessions Records*, Vol. I, "Introduction," Caernarvon, 1956, lxxxviii–lxxxix, and works cited in n. 4, lxxxviii. For an interesting summation of the status of jurors in the eighteenth century, see Sir Richard Phillips, *On the Powers and Duties of Juries* (London, 1811).

[16] E.R.O. Q/SR 32/40 and jury lists in the following and preceding rolls which included their names.

[17] E.R.O. Q/SR 102/6 compared with E.R.O. D/DP 04.

[18] P.R.O. Asz/35/30/1; 35/30/2.

[19] 27 Elizabeth, cap. 6.

[20] E.R.O. Q/SR 31/39.

[21] E.R.O. Q/SR 110/18.

[22] E.R.O. Q/SR 128.

[23] E.R.O. Q/SR 159/1.

While these efforts were being made both at Westminster by statute and in the county by JPs' writs, ordinary subjects sometimes also complained about the sufficiency of jurors. Brentwood townsmen reported that petty constables repeatedly returned to the grand and hundred juries unskillful persons who either could not or dared not present disorders in the parish, and requested that only men worth over £3 in goods be permitted to serve.[24] The JPs obliged them with a court order to that effect.[25] Such complaints were, however, rare and indicate that only in higher circles was there much discontent with the quality of jurors or an inclination to do anything about it.

Jurors varied greatly in the amount and regularity of their participation, and they could make as much or as little of the job as they chose. Some men made careers out of jury duty. John Waylett, a Widford yeoman, served 66 times in 15 years, indiscriminately accepting, or perhaps pursuing, places on the trial, hundred, and grand juries, finally working his way up to foreman of the county grand jury in 1575.[26] Nicholas Petcrewe, on the other hand, was summoned to serve three times and sat only twice in his life.[27] Between these extremes was John Choppyn, who was called once a year for 10 years, and though he sat a few times on the grand and trial juries, he limited his activities chiefly to Dunmow hundred.[28]

It was in the interests of both efficiency and justice to secure an adequate supply of jurors. Problems arose when insufficient numbers of qualified persons arrived in court, because the law required that at least 12 individuals be present to serve. The problem was particularly acute in outlying hundreds in the county where it was hard to find enough candidates willing to make the long and expensive trek to Chelmsford. Of course, absentees were fined, but this did not help overcome the immediate obstacle, which was the possible illegality of jury actions due to lack of numbers. The law in these circumstances allowed justices to bunch up panels until they had 12 men on them, thereby permitting several hundreds to make their charges together. But this took time and caused delays, because enough prospective jurors had to be called to make up the legal number, and they needed time to compare notes and decide which charges to make. Since men from different hundreds did not know the circumstances of a case, they had either to acquaint themselves with the details very quickly or, what was more likely and much more of a threat to justice, simply take the word of the one or two jurors from the hundred wishing to make the charge. To expedite

[24] E.R.O. Q/SR 73/73.

[25] E.R.O. Q/SR 74/67.

[26] Jury panels in E.R.O. Q/SR 60–105.

[27] *Ibid.*

[28] *Ibid.*

proceedings and aid the cause of justice, it was obviously necessary to avoid this bunching of juries.

One means used to achieve this goal was to step up the number of men summoned for jury duty. In 1570, 82 or an average of 27 men per panel, were called for grand jury duty; by 1589, it had reached 162. The attempt to expand the number of grand jurors was not successful when the total summoned is compared with those who actually appeared. In 1570, an average of 20 jurors per panel actually attended court; in 1589, only 21 came; and by 1602, the average had dropped to 19. Efforts were more successful in the hundred juries where the problem was far more acute. In 1570, 455 were summoned; in 1589, it rose to 609; and by 1602, it had reached 703. More impressive was the number who wound up coming to court. In 1570, 236 appeared; 303 in 1589, and by 1602, 446 came—an average rise from 7.6 to 10 jurors per hundred (see Table 5).

TABLE 5 *Jury Panel Summaries from Selected Years*[a]

		Juries from the Body of the County ("Grand Juries")			
		Summoned		Appeared	
Year		Number	Average	Number	Average
1570		82	27.0	59	20.0
1589		164	54.0	87	21.0
1602		52	52.0	75	18.7
	Number of panels	Hundred Juries			
1570	31	455	17.7	236	7.6
1589	36	609	17.7	303	9.0
1602	44	973	22.0	446	10.0

[a]These samples were drawn from the Quarter Sessions Rolls for the relevant years.

Not all jurors were "good men and true." In 1577, James Chapman, Bailiff of Chelmsford, was fined for taking 2s. from a husbandmen and 4s. from a yeoman in return for a promise that they would not have to serve as jurors either at Quarter Sessions or gaol delivery.[29] The most notorious case of chicanery involved the attempt to frame an Essex gentleman, Thomas Wyniff, who was charged with stealing a horse. David Bennet and John Twede, both yeomen, were each imprisoned without bail for one month and fined £5 and £10 respectively for their efforts to procure

[29] E.R.O. Q/SR 68/28.

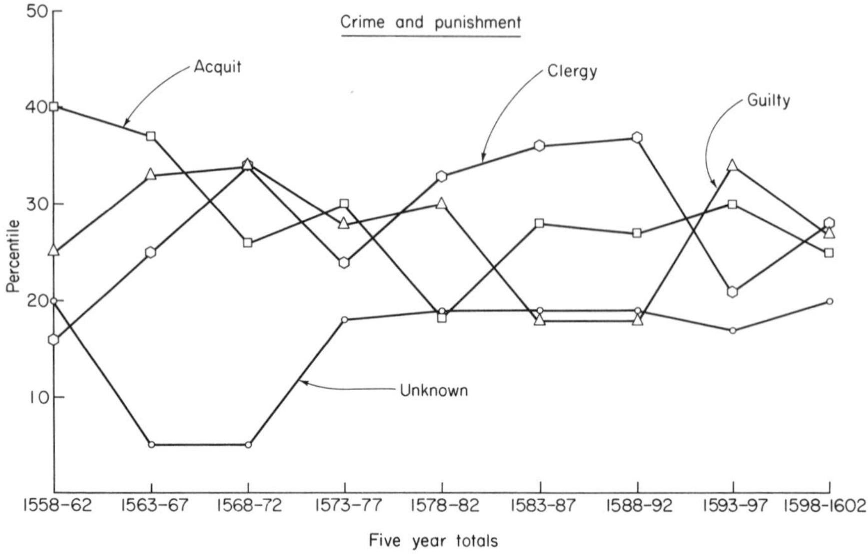

Fig.4. This graph depicts the proportion of offenders who were dealt with at the Assizes during the Elizabethan period. In order to smooth out the erratic annual patterns, total cases for five-year periods were used. Note the sharp drop in clergy and the steep corresponding rise in the proportion found guilty during the famine years 1593 to 1597.

seats on the grand jury to indict Wyniff.[30] Obviously, the influence of the gentry could still be felt, and jurors might still "punish the leastest, and favor the greatest." Influence by the gentry in the legal process was definitely in operation during the period, but it is difficult to measure precisely to what degree the enforcement of the law of felony was affected by it. John Throughgood, a yeoman in the Queen's household, paid Joan Haughton to accuse Richard Stanton of felony on one occasion[31]; Paul Davy, a Stanway butcher was put in gaol without bail for a fortnight because, although the court pressed him, he refused to prefer an indictment they wanted him to frame[32]; Justice Gawdy, one of the Assize judges gave strict instructions to the inferior JPs that "I am informed the matter to be very foul and fit to be strictly and thoroughly examined." Taking no chances, he ordered them: " . . . do not proceed with him at Quarter Sessions but bind him over to the next Assizes and in the meantime I will take order to have the matter thoroughly examined."[33] All of these were cases of gentlemen determined to get somebody and they probably did. Corruption

[30] E.R.O. Q/SR 68/3, 80.
[31] E.R.O. Q/SR 137/56.
[32] E.R.O. Q/SR 128/70.
[33] E.R.O. Q/SR 152/30.

and direct interference by the upper classes was, however, as, we shall see, in the case of constables' and jurors' misbehavior, exaggerated in the court rolls. Furthermore, the stern treatment given to Bennett and Twede, though it might smack of Wyniff's power, nonetheless indicates that malfeasance was not always tolerated. Imprisonment by itself exposed them to death, due to the awful conditions prevailing in Colchester Castle gaol, while fines of £5 and £10 were onerous in those days.

It is impossible to know how many suspects were dismissed by the grand jury, because many of the decisions are lost. In determining whether or not sufficient evidence existed to indict a suspect (send him to trial), the grand juries were supposed to endorse *billa vera* (true bill) on those they formally charged and *ignoramus* (we do not know) on those they dismissed. Due probably to the cost of parchment (required for all formal documents) and the labor of drawing up legal instruments, the clerk waited until the grand jury found a bill true before drafting the final parchment indictment, a practice which lost for history any record of charges which were dropped before trial.[34] Nevertheless, much can be gleaned from the remaining "true bills." They are an invaluable index and have sent across the intervening four centuries an unmistakable message—grand juries were indicting more and more people. The community, in the form of this body, was thus increasingly willing to use the judicial machinery to crush what it considered to be growing social disorder.[35] Thus can we see clearly here how the rising number of indictments means at least two things. Without denying that crime was on the rise, the number of felonies recorded in the books was obviously due as well to the growing determination of the grand jury to squelch it—a determination that caught up in the system a larger proportion of the total criminal population.

The next point when the system of justice lost a large portion of its prospective defendants followed indictment (see Fig. 4). Fully 15% of all persons indicted for felony simply did not appear for trial. Although some suspects died before court was held, the great bulk of nonappearances was due to disregard for legal procedures, suggesting that some men in Elizabethan Essex still believed that justice was a private matter to be settled between man and man in their own way (see Figs. 5 and 6). And if it does not signify an attachment to an earlier social code of self-help, it still meant that some men could and did take the call of the criminal process lightly.

The degree to which different elements in society took advantage of

[34] A large bundle of *ignoramus* bills is extant for the early seventeenth century in Essex. All of them were written on paper and stored separately from true bills, which indicates that the procedure was similar in the sixteenth century, but that no bundles of such informal documents have survived.

[35] See Chapter I and Appendix I.

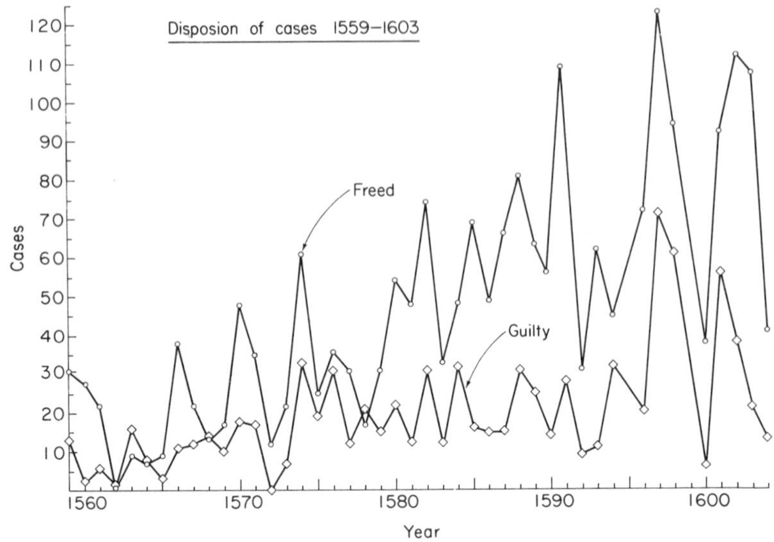

Fig. 5. Disposition of cases, 1559–1603.

these weak links in the chain of criminal justice varied considerably (see Fig. 7). Gentlemen, as might be expected, flouted the system with alacrity both because they could get away with failure to appear, and because ordinary people who had the courage to report their social "betters" initially often failed in the strength of will it took to go forward and face them in

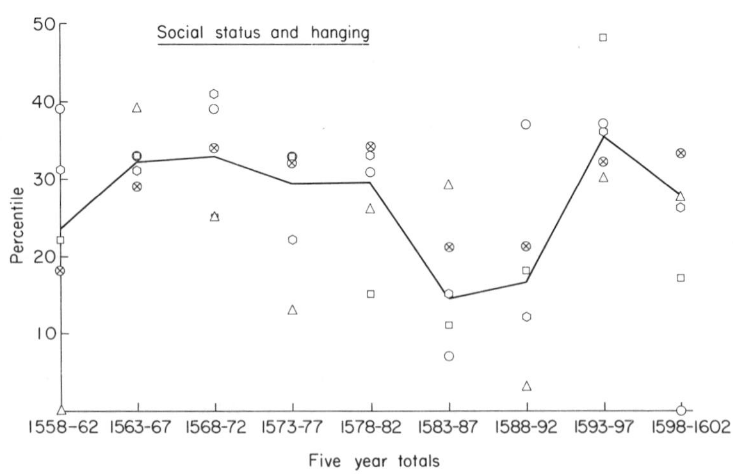

Fig. 6. Social status and hanging.

person in order to prosecute them. And who could blame them—the ordinary people in the shire were beholden to the gentry—they held lands from them, they spun their wool into cloth and did their odd jobs, which often meant the difference between starvation and survival.[36] It took a powerful will indeed and probably financial independence as well for men like John Twede, a peasant, to attempt to get a gentleman like Thomas Wyniff—and he a member of the gentry's lowest rungs—indicted.[37] We will never know if Twede's punishment was for stacking the grand jury or for daring to attack one of his "betters."[38] By the end of the Elizabethan era, gentlemen were escaping trial at the shockingly high rate of 79% and nothing was done to stop it. Nearly every name on one extant writ of outlaw—the last, if futile effort of the law to bring offenders to justice—was that of one of the county's petty gentry, a pathetic reminder that the law could not even touch the upper classes' lowest ranks, if they wished to cast it aside. In general, it seems, they came to court when they wanted to do so and not otherwise.[39]

The remaining names on the writ of outlaw previously mentioned were yeomen, another group which frequently avoided coming to court for trial. Between 1558 and 1568, 19% of the yeomen indicted never faced public trial; by the closing years of Elizabeth's reign they were avoiding legal process at the rate of 43%. This was the largest rise in the evasion of the law registered by any class in society, an advance that takes on added significance when the dramatic decline in total number of yeomen who were charged with crimes during the period is taken into account.[40]

Husbandmen opened the period with a 17% escape rate and ended it with 27%—a substantial 10% rise. Behind the peasants came the tradesmen and craftsmen, who escaped at the rate of 9% at the outset and 17% at the end. The lowest amount of evasion was, unsurprisingly, among laborers and women who registered a consistent 15 and 13% respectively.

At the next stage in the criminal process, the trial, petty juries released another group of prospective hanging felons by acquitting defendants who had already been indicted by the grand jury (see Figs. 7 and 8). Twenty-nine percent of all defendants were freed outright because juries found them not guilty. The total average is misleading, however, because the proportion definitely declined as the period progressed. In the beginning decade, 36% were acquitted; by the end of the reign, the average dropped to 27%. And again the distribution among social classes was selective. Though in

[36] E.R.O. D/DP 18–22.
[37] E.R.O. Q/SR 68/80.
[38] *Ibid.*
[39] E.R.O. Q/SR 83/46.
[40] See Chapter I.

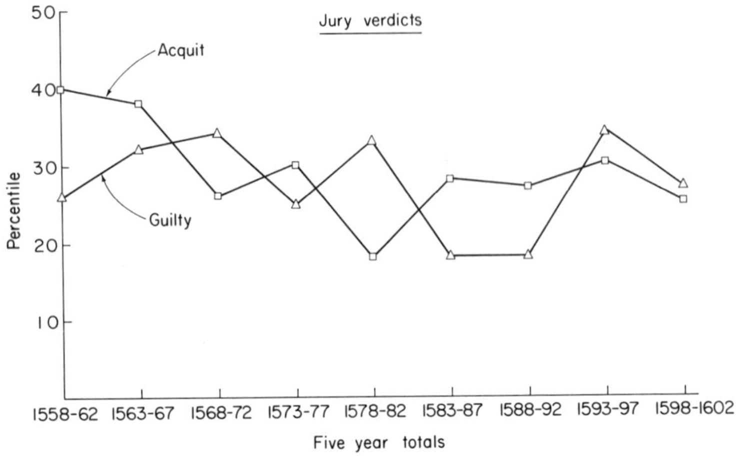

Fig. 7. Jury verdicts.

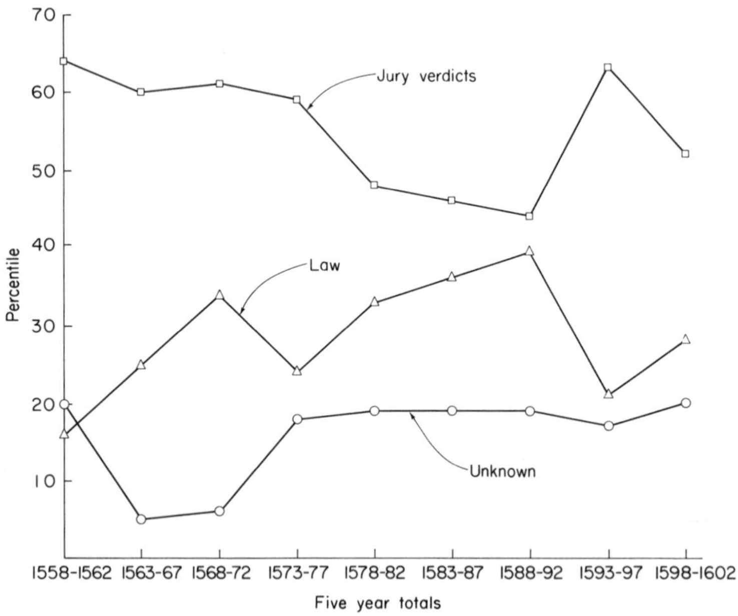

Fig. 8. This graph depicts the relative weight that three forces played in the disposition of felony cases, 1559–1503—the social representatives in the jury, the power exerted by the judges or the law, mainly benefit of clergy, and finally the weakness in the system in bringing offenders to justice (the unknown). Note the sharp rise in the power of the jury in disposing of cases during the famine years and the corresponding falling off of the law's interference to keep offenders from reaching the jury's final pronouncement.

overall numbers it was fairly even, ranging from 26% for yeomen and husbandmen to 27% for laborers and 29% for tradesmen-craftsmen, women registered a striking 48% acquittal rate. Furthermore, and in striking contrast to total averages, the shifts within social class groups during the period varied considerably. Gentlemen suffered the greatest losses, falling from 40% in the first third of the reign to 14% in the closing 15 years. Next came husbandmen whose losses dropped from 39% in the opening decade to 12% in the final one, a decline of 27%. Laborers came next, losing 17% (from 43 to 26%). They were followed closely behind by yeomen who dropped 16% (from 35 to 19%). Women fell 15% (from 63% in the opening decade to 48% in the final 10 years). Tradesmen-craftsmen lost the least, dropped only 8 points from a remarkable 34% to a healthy 26%. It should be stressed that jury verdicts do not always reflect the actual innocence or guilt of defendants; juries did not often serve as instruments of truth, but rather public opinion about how much violence they *thought* prevailed in the community. In that respect, the trend in verdicts is important, because it demonstrates the local society's growing willingness to police themselves. Disturbed by what they felt was a crime wave of swelling magnitude, juries reacted to it by hardening their refusal to bow before their betters and stiffening their resolution to show little mercy for their neighbors. This was especially true during the 1590s, when economic hardship hardened them against their neighbors. During that period they registered more guilty verdicts than at any time during Elizabeth's reign, showing little sympathy for their poor countrymen's plight. And here again we see graphically illustrated the melding of at least two components in the criminal statistics—the rise in crime and the waxing energies devoted to suppressing it. The striking confluence of guilty jury verdicts and the denial by the court of benefit of clergy, especially during the 1590s (see Figs. 5, 6, and 7), is strong evidence that both the rulers of society (the judges) and the representatives of it (the juries) were cooperating to stamp out crime, an alliance that could not help but raise the number of criminal cases brought to public notice and therefore inflate the number of recorded crimes.

Society's failures to report crime, witnesses' negligence in prosecuting offenders, grand juries' dismissals of charges, and trial juries' acquittal rates all contributed to the escape of prospective candidates from the hangman's noose. Equally important, the chances that ordinary people in the shire would escape were increasingly unlikely; though to be sure even the gentry was beginning to be drawn into the law's net. Despite evidence that all juries were stepping up their efforts to reduce the number of suspects who avoided the law's ultimate penalty, ironically the law itself stood in the way of high hanging rates. By various means available to anyone who had a lawyer clever enough to take advantage of them, hanging was reduced to even slimmer proportions. Since the number of lawyers available to help suspects grew as more and more men studied law at the Inns of Court, it is to be expected that legal loopholes would be fully exploited.[41]

In the first place, indictments had to be framed in absolutely precise terms or they were thrown out of court. There are numerous examples like the following one in the court rolls of the time: The indictment was found insufficient because it used only the word "plough" without saying what kind of plough it was—an oxen one or a hand one or some other kind.[42] That defendants in criminal trials were not allowed counsel may well have been technically correct, but the evidence of picking weaknesses in indictments and of exploiting other minutiae in criminal procedure is convincing proof that many suspects had legal counsel, if not at the trial itself, at least before or afterward. And it did them a lot of good, as the number of cases dismissed due to a failure to comply with procedural rules clearly demonstrates. The rigid rules of pleading were a tricky path to follow and worked mainly in the favor of clever men, just as it hurt poor and ignorant countrymen. It was not often that help came their way in using the law for their own benefit, and the request by a JP that the Clerk of the Peace help prepare bills of indictment for "this poor man" who was ignorant of legal technicalities is virtually unique.[43]

Pardons provided another way for men found guilty by a jury to go free. The law of pardons was highly technical, but briefly, two types were available. The first was general and was granted by the Queen and Parliament; it did not need to be pleaded and was allowed at the judge's discretion. The other was special, that is, it issued to a specifically named person and required special pleading by him in court. It is difficult to tell under what circumstances judges allowed general pardons, since laconic notes such as "certain causes moving the judges" are the only guides left in the Assize files to interpret the construction placed on them. Special pardons, on the other hand, were the results of purely monetary efforts; they were available to anyone with enough money to pay the price to get one. Of course, it was not simply a matter of money, since it took a good deal of skill to draft and plead them successfully.[44] The cost and difficulty in managing them in

[41] It is now perfectly clear that enrollment at the Inns swelled immensely as the reign of Elizabeth progressed, a growth probable never matched either before or since. Though it is unclear exactly what happened to most of these students, it is safe to assume that larger portions of them went home to reap the benefits that a growing local legal administration provided for bringing personal profit for acting as attorneys to the waxing number of defendants in felony cases who knew enough to look out for wily lawyers deft in using legal niceties to save their lives—for a price, of course.

[42] E.R.O. Q/SR 26/17.

[43] E.R.O. Q/SR 40/23, 51.

[44] See "Pardons" in Giles Jacob, *Law Dictionary* (London, 1809) and "Pardons" in Sir Edward Coke, *Third Institute* (London, 1837).

court probably accounts for the reason so few were pleaded in Essex—the amount never exceeding 1% of the total cases. Even general pardons were sparingly used. Lord Coke claimed that the general pardons of 1559 and 1571 were the most sweeping in history, but only 12 persons gained from them in Essex.[45] It is striking that no social elitism attached to pardons, particularly in view of their cost. Furthermore, judges were often willing to wait for them, sometimes for more than one term. They usually granted a delay until the defendant had the time to raise the money to obtain one from Chancery. The reason is obvious: The Crown was patient when a profit was waiting.

Insanity and infancy also excused convicted felons from hanging, but were rarely pleaded in Essex. Only occasionally does one find beside the name of a child notes such as "excused, girl aged 10," or "freed, boy of only 10."

In addition, pregnant women were also freed. Technically it was supposed to be only a temporary respite until the child was born, but in fact women who successfully pleaded the benefit of their belly rarely appeared for trial on future occasions. One girl used the excuse for two years, and in the end went free entirely.

Benefit of clergy was the largest loophole in the law through which convicted felons slipped to freedom from hanging. By Elizabeth's reign, the privilege had already had a long and distinguished history. It began when William the Conqueror separated church from state courts, a division which spawned a rivalry between the two institutions and which the conflict between Henry II and Saint Thomas Becket only dramatized. Until the fifteenth century, benefit of clergy flourished and even expanded. All persons in holy orders and even inferior personnel (doorkeepers, for example) could commit felonies free from the danger that they would be held by royal officials or tried in secular courts.

A clerk proved his status by the ability to read, by his dress, and by his tonsure. Literacy, in the beginning, was only a supplementary proof, but during the fourteenth century, it was sufficient evidence in itself, thus opening the doors to lay use of its benefits. So widespread had it become that one writer complained that "book learning could run to meet the prodigal son and snatch the fugitive... from the gates of death."[46] By the end of the fifteenth century, actual literacy had become a mere form, even blind men escaping death by reading,[47] a development sarcastically summarized in the fifteenth-century play, *Mankind*: "Mischief is a convicte for he could

[45] Coke, *Ibid.*, p. 234.

[46] C. B. Firth, "Benefit of Clergy in the Time of Edward IV," *English Historical Review* (1917), 32, pp. 175–191.

[47] *Ibid.*

his nekverse." (Neck verse was the part of the psalm from the Bible that convicts had to memorize in order to get the privilege.) So lax had the requirements become that men were allowed time to learn the verse if they could not recite it on the first try. By Elizabeth's reign, then, the successful plea of clergy did not indicate literacy, and the ability to read was not, as the Essex rector Harrison would have it, "devised to train the inhabitants of this land to the love of learning."[48] The final abuse to which benefit of clergy was subjected came under Elizabeth when all pretense was set aside and convicted felons were no longer turned over to the church official, but instead were freed at once, subject only to one year's imprisonment at the judges' discretion.[49]

As clergy expanded to include more people who stood to profit from its historic rights, the application of those privileges was restricted by statute to fewer circumstances. The Tudors were largely responsible for this attempt to restrict its use. In 1487, persons "lettered" but not in holy orders could have the benefit of clergy only once[50]; in 1496, servants who murdered their masters were denied the privilege[51]; and by Edward VI's reign, the list of prohibited offenses extended to murder, buggery, highway robbery, theft of chattels from a church, and burglary when any person in the house was put in fear in the course of the felony. During the reign of Phillip and Mary, the prohibition was stretched to encompass accomplices in all the above-mentioned felonies.[52] In 1565, taking goods from another's person, even if it did not amount to robbery, was excluded,[53] and in 1596, rape and all burglaries, irrespective of whether anyone was in the house or not, were taken out from the protection of the privilege.[54] Finally, in 1597, theft of more than 5s. in a dwelling house during the day was added to the list.[55] What all of this amounted to was that only minor theft remained within the benefit's scope and then only if it were a first offense. What the law was doing in a roundabout way was using ancient custom to establish a hierarchy of felonies whereby in minor cases first offenders were treated lightly.

These restrictions on clergy were rules formulated by Parliament and the Crown, but they did not do much to change actual practice in Essex,

[48] Nor can it be used to measure literacy in society as Professor Lawrence Stone has attempted to do in "The Educational Revolution in England, 1540–1640," *Past and Present* (July, 1964), 28, pp. 41–80.

[49] 18 Elizabeth, cap 7.

[50] 4 Henry VII, cap 14.

[51] 12 Henry VII, cap 7.

[52] 4 and 5 Philip and Mary, cap 4.

[53] 8 Elizabeth, cap 4.

[54] 18 Elizabeth, cap 7.

[55] 39 Elizabeth, cap 15.

since legal procedure there was never confined to the narrow bounds in which the government tried to contain it. By judicial practice the first-offender rule was expanded to allow a multiple offender to use it, provided he committed all of his offenses in a short enough time span so that all of them were tried at one court session. Thus it is not unusual to find a long string of indictments against a single person with *legit* or *clericus* inscribed on all of them. What the offender did in these cases was to wait until he was found guilty on all the charges and plead his clergy. Someone in the county questioned this procedure, but the Clerk of the Peace assured the doubter that "if there be many indictments against one man for which he may have his clergy yet the certificate (clerks had to send lists of those granted benefit of clergy into the Queen's Bench) of one will serve for all."[56]

Thomas Lawrence's case was doubtless the cleverest manipulation of the privilege to free a defendant.[57] Lawrence had been indicted for breaking and entering a dwelling house from which he stole £5 in July, 1581. He was found guilty the following year and pleaded his clergy. Thereupon the court examined his left thumb and discovered that it was branded according to a statute of Henry VII's reign, which required all lay first offenders who pleaded benefit of clergy to be branded on the ball of the left thumb with "M" for murder, "T" for theft, and so on. Since he was a second offender, the court denied the privilege, but he was remanded to gaol to await his attorney's proof that he was entitled to clergy (did they mean holy orders?). He did not appear again until March, 1584 when the court remanded him once again, this time because the judges doubted "if they could judge him a second time for the same offense" (they had passed judgment on him at his first trial). Finally, after surviving four long years in the Colchester Castle gaol, he was granted a new trial and was acquitted outright. The case illustrates an agile exploitation of benefit of clergy, but considering that Lawrence endured four years in Colchester Castle, unquestionably he paid a heavy price for the theft in which he indulged.

Skillful use of legal technicalities in prescribed felonies was not the only value benefit of clergy bestowed on convicted felons, because in practice it was never limited to the crimes that statutes defined for it. Though most men employed it in simple theft, which the law definitely allowed, it was also pleaded in every other common law felony in existence from violent murder to highway robbery and horse stealing, all of which the law forbade. When statutes were not flouted outright, a kind of sixteenth-century plea bargaining went on between defendants and their counterparts on the bench. In return for a guilty plea, murder was occasionally reduced to homicide, burglary to mere breaking and entering, and robbery to stealing, all of

[56] E.R.O. Q/SR 160/6a.

[57] E.R.O. Q/SR 79/135, 145; P.R.O., Asz. 35/24H, 26T, 27T.

which changed the crime from a nonclergyable to a clergyable one, thus allowing judges to permit clergy and set the convicted man free—at least until he committed another offense. It is difficult to figure out exactly how this worked, since attorneys were not technically allowed in court, though as we have seen in Thomas Lawrence's case as well as several others at the indictment stage, lawyers must have had clients who were criminal defendants. Whatever may have been the role of lawyer, the reduced charge following a guilty plea occurs too frequently in the records to discount its importance. What cannot be known is whether the jury did it out of mercy, whether the judge coerced the defendant into it, or whether a clever lawyer organized it. Most important of all, why was either judge or jury moved to do it? The likely answer is that judges and juries did at least seek to manipulate the law so that the individual and his punishment matched. It is striking that during the bad years of the 1590s we find not only more guilty verdicts but also less pleas of clergy allowed, again strongly indicating that the attitude of both judges and jurors was hardening toward crime and that a law-and-order mentality was working, to the misfortune of criminal defendants. This in turn points up the more general implications that officials attitudes had for criminal statistics: Records of crime may tell as much about the system that produced them as they do about deviant behavior itself.

Despite shifting attitudes, the extensive use of benefit of clergy both within and without statutory bounds made it a salient obstacle to convicts winding up on the gallows: 697, or 28%, of all guilty defendants were freed because of it. Moreover, during most of the period, the use of the privilege was on the increase, rising from 21% in the opening decade to a high of 37% in the years 1558 to 1592. As already noted, it finally tapered off in the closing decade, but still amounted to 24% of all final case dispositions. It was not, however, equally employed by all social classes. Not a single gentleman claimed it, which is not surprising, because so few of them came up for trial anyway. Yeomen at first exercised it sparingly, a mere 9% of the convicted pleading it in the beginning of the reign. By the end of the period, however, it rose to an average overall of nearly 20%. Even more husbandmen took advantage of it: 29% of them successfully pleaded their clergy during Elizabeth's reign. Tradesmen-craftsmen and laborers used it most extensively, nearly one-third of them successfully avoiding punishment by means of the privilege. Women, who could not claim benefit of clergy at all, in its stead had the advantage of their womb, an immunity which helped 20% of all women convicted of felony to go free during Elizabeth's reign. Technically, a woman's belly was only supposed to be a temporary respite, lasting only the term of her pregnancy. In practice, however, women who were reprieved once were able to continue their advantage through several court terms and ultimately they disappear from the records altogether. Now, it is possible that these female convicts repeatedly got themselves with child to avoid the noose, but that is unlikely. It is also possible that the reason for their ultimate disappearance from the records did not mean that they went free but rather that the clerk did not record their ultimate fate. But, alternatively, it makes sense to suggest that they were put to bail for the birth of the child and never appeared again, and this seems to be the soundest explanation for a good portion of the women's mysterious omission from the calendars after one or two court terms.

The 640 people in Essex who were finally sentenced to hang during Elizabeth's reign must be seen against this immense and biased attrition that took place between the time a crime was committed and the final pronouncement of the death penalty. But even then the figures are inflated, because they represent the *maximum* number of individuals hanged as a result of trial at the Assizes during the reign. This is because the total quoted embodies many doubtful cases. In some the clerk noted only the jury's verdict without making clear whether or not the defendant was "judged," an indispensable prerequisite to sentence. Many indictments show only the clerk's note, "susp.," an abbreviation for "to be hanged" written at the time of judgment was passed. They did not always reach the gallows, as the appearances of some men who were thus sentenced at later trials on different charges clearly demonstrates. It is, of course, impossible to determine how much these discrepancies between actual hangings and jury verdicts and clerks' notes affected totals, but it is clear that the figures represent the upper limits of persons hanged. Assuming the numbers are accurate (and we know they are inflated) and that jury verdicts mean the convict was guilty (and we know this is untrue), the number of criminal suspects who wound up at the end of a noose averaged 14 every year. In percentages of the total defendants in felony cases, the proportions were also considerable, ranging from a low of 18% in one 5-year period to a high of 34% in another, the average for the whole working out to a 27.5%—certainly enough to impress upon the spectators who flocked to watch the public hangings following every court session that at least sometimes crime does not pay.

As was to be expected, a social bias was present in hangings. Fewer gentlemen faced death than other groups in society, but since hardly any appear in the records, the 10% average is based on too slight a number to be meaningful statistically. The average for women is next lowest, 21% having been hanged. The other classes were relatively similar, ranging from 28% for yeomen and laborers to 27 and 25% for tradesmen-craftsmen and husbandmen respectively.

Totals, however, are misleading because some significant shifts over time took place. Yeomen fell from an average of 36% in the first decade of

Elizabeth's reign to 18% in the last 10 years, a dramatic halving of the portion of yeomen hanged. Women, on the other hand, climbed from 20% at the outset of the reign to 29% by the end. Laborers, though, suffered most at the hands of the law: From an average 22% in the opening decade, the proportion swelled to 32% in the closing 10 years, an increase in actual numbers from 20 to 136. The rise is the more dramatic because laborers were least prone to commit violent crimes.

The same inverse relationship between social class and severity of punishment existed as between social class and violence of felony.[58] Thus, those convicted of violent felonies received, on the whole, the lesser punishments, not only an indication of the well-known hierarchial nature of society and the willingness of the community to permit a greater license among the upper ranks than was tolerated among the humbler people, but also of the hardening attitude toward the swelling ranks of landless laborers and their illegal acts, an attitude especially prevalent during the famine years of the 1590s.

It is no coincidence that more guilty verdicts, fewer clergy allowances, and more hangings all happened concurrently. All stem from the community's fear of uncontrolled crime, a fear that the already too small supply of food would be distributed by means outside the normal channels of the market. In other words, the people with a great deal of property—represented by the judges and JPs, who made the decision about whether or or not to allow clergy—and those with a little bit—represented by the "good citizens" on the juries and worried people throughout the county—were all afraid that poor people would take food or property they could sell in order to buy food in any way they could. So the law, jurors, and community joined ranks to stop the attempt.

No food riots supported public fear, but in the autumn of 1595, when the famine was well underway and had taken its toll, Thomas Bynder, complaining "that everything was dear," threatened that "there were some made shift as long as they could and that if victuals did not grow better cheap some would be plucked out of their (the town's victuallers) houses" and that "twenty victuallers would be hanged at their gates."[59] It is important to note that Bynder was a smith and not a laborer. We do not hear the latters' speeches, if they made any, but the multiplying numbers of thefts recorded during these years seem to bear out at least jurors' and the judges' fears if not the reality that the lower orders were distributing the county's wealth in their own way, by stealing it. In 5 years of the famine, 1593 to 1597, the number of gentlemen and yeomen defendants stayed roughly the same, and the number of peasants actually decreased. In

[58] See Chapter I.

[59] E.R.O. Q/SR 131/35.

striking contrast, the numbers of workers and women, almost certainly worker's consorts, doubled during the same years, the former climbing from 179 to 266 and the number of women from 30 to 63.[60] Of course, the insoluble problem of how many of these worker defendants were in court because of increase in their *actual* criminal behavior and how many were prosecuted due to the community's prejudiced *belief* that they were criminals is still there. All that can be said is the combination of a real rise in crime by poor workers and the community's fear of it both played their part in the growing felony statistics.

Further demonstration, if any is needed, of the inequality of prosecution and punishment was the policy of imprisonment prior to trial for felony. All gentlemen and most yeomen were immediately put to bail and did not have to await their day in court in gaol. Poor peasants, day laborers, and women, on the other hand, were routinely held in prison until their law day, a severe punishment in itself. Justice Morrice recognized the hardships involved when he asked that one man be set free and suffer no further prosecution for his misdeeds, since he had already been incarcerated for 6 months awaiting trial. During this time the man had lost not only his wages, but had also put his family under heavy deprivation. On another occasion, Justice Harris requested that since one Griffith "lie in gaol all winter and is very weak, please have Baron Clarke [an Assize judge] be favorable to him for his deliverance."[61] Not only did a man flirt with death in gaol and lose his livelihood during his stay, but the likelihood that he would come out with any goods remaining to his name was slight even were he acquitted. Prisoners had to support themselves while they were incarcerated, and gaolers usually did not free a man or admit him in the first place without considerable surety that he would be able to pay his keep. If any money was left from his room, board, and the fees to go through trial, the remainder was surely sucked up by graft by the gaoler's cronies or by the clerk's staff. It is not surprising, in view of this, that jurors invariably found that convicted felons had *nulla bona* (no goods) by the time they had been judged guilty.[62]

Lord Coke thought "that we have found by woeful experience that it is not frequent and often punishment that doth prevent like offences," and concluded that "those offences are often committed which are often punished."[63] Surely the Essex records show that the deterrent power of brutal

[60] See Appendix III, Tables 30 and 31.

[61] E.R.O. Q/SR 112/80.

[62] Jurors had to determine the value of the prisoners' goods so that the Crown would have an accurate accounting of valuables forfeit to it due to the law requiring all convicted felons to forfeit their chattels to the Crown.

[63] Coke, *Third Institute*.

punishment fell short of total success, especially in times of economic distress. Despite all the limitations on the law's efficacy, however, a subtle and almost imperceptible shift was taking place in Essex law enforcement that the famine of the 1590s brought into clear relief. A new attitude toward crime, especially the lawlessness of the growing number of landless laborers and the need for its control was creeping into the community—a development reflected in the shifts in crime reporting, jury behavior, and manipulation of legal loopholes already mentioned—and a shift that clearly affected criminal statistics, however real was the growth in crime itself. But the shift was in itself of great significance. It is not only evident in the waxing number of felony indictments, in the swelling ranks of jurors whose attitude toward criminals was hardening, and in the judges' growing reluctance to grant benefit of clergy, but it is also discernible and perhaps best studied in the men who ran Essex county and their helpers and in the judicial machinery that had to adapt to the growing demand for law and order. And that story must now be told.

CHAPTER III

THE JUSTICES OF THE PEACE AND THEIR HELPERS

The rule of law is a fiction. Only men can rule, because submission to law hinges on the belief, adhered to by policemen and judges who enforce it and men and women who submit to it, that law is a universal code which all must heed if public peace is to be secured. This belief is never embraced wholeheartedly. As is well known, law is a social instrument, sometimes used for the good of all, sometimes solely for the benefit of the few. Some men invariably treat law as their personal weapon to attain private ends, thus causing a friction in attitudes about the fibre and destination of the law. How officials view law, as binding code or personal weapon, determines the procedures they follow in executing it. Since Elizabethan JPs were chiefly responsible for leashing in violence and rooting out lawlessness in their county, it is important to elucidate their theories of law, which in turn determined their administrative styles. Although Tudor justices rarely immortalized their thoughts in writing, luckily two of them did, thus exposing how their varied jurisprudential assumptions led them to divergent legal decisions.[1]

The two justices, Lord Morley and Mr. Leventhorpe, backed by their liveried retainers, met on the moatside of Morley's estate in Pelham in Essex on an early spring morning in 1578. The purpose of their encounter was an attempt to end, or perhaps to triumph in, a dispute over a bastard sired by one of Lord Morley's men and about to be born to one of his maids. Smith, the prospective father, had packed the girl off to Ashwell

[1] All of the following account is based on E.R.O., *Manor of Hatfield Broad Oak*, Steward's Papers, D/DHt M49. I am indebted to Mr. Arthur Searle for this reference.

parish in Leventhorpe's jurisdiction, where townsmen quickly fired her back because they feared she would deliver the infant there and they would have to support it. Smith had then appealed to Lord Morley, who granted him a warrant to send her back to Ashwell again—a warrant that Leventhorpe steadfastly refused to honor. Morley was doubly piqued, since Leventhorpe had also rejected "in good conscience" a private agreement in which Smith promised to pay the girl the enormously generous sum of £2 a week maintenance because it was not drawn "as the statute doth appoint."

"Why what will you make of it," Morley asked, "since it was but between a single man and a single woman?" Leventhorpe's response was a statement of principle: "Sin and wickedness . . . deserve punishment and chastisement and according to law the offenders should be whipped." Morley then demanded to know what law gave leave to bestow such cruel punishment upon two youngsters who made love at no one's expense. Leventhorpe replied at length, laying bare his deep convictions about

> . . . the law of the prince and God's law upon which the prince's law is grounded. We have also the laws of the realm whereby to punish them, which refers it to the discretion of the judges and we think good to whip them.

Outraged, Morley pointed out the economic inequality built into such high-mindedness:

> Yeah, with like discretion you take up poor travelling men by the way which by reason that they be far from their country and friends are not able to bring testimonial of their credit and behavior and therefore do send them back to gaol. And there, forsooth, one of their ears bored through, who often times is more honest a great deal than the justices who sent them thither.

Morley ended this outburst with a threat and then returned to the case at issue and announced that Smith was one of his own tenants and beyond Leventhorpe's jurisdiction. Unruffled, Leventhorpe retorted, "Let him keep his woman then out of our country and suffer him not to lay her great belly here to be a trouble and a charge . . . for surely if he do he will be punished." Since Ashwell was in Leventhorpe's jurisdiction, Morley had little choice but to back down and agree to keep Smith's girl away.

Animosity erupted again when Lord Morley had a mind to tear up several victuallers' licenses because the men who held them had broken down his hedges. Now Leventhorpe was outraged because Morley thought he could manipulate the law to serve his private ends:

> . . . they being though poor men yet free men would desire to have the benefit of Her Majesty's laws who if there were of them that offended in hedge-breaking . . . there was a law to punish them for it. But let us not, my lord, . . . punish one wrong with another.

Ironically, it was Leventhorpe's rigor and not Morley's pliability that brought about justice.

The rift between the two magistrates was deep. Morley had mastered scarcely any law, even the statute that condoned whipping vagabonds eluded him; Leventhorpe, on the other hand, could quote it chapter and verse. To Morley, law was property, inherited like a title and his to exploit—to flatter his vanity, shore up his rank, succor his henchmen, and destroy his enemies. Leventhorpe clothed it with divine attributes capable of leading dutiful followers into willing submission and injected with an immutable and all-embracing essence—a body of precepts which men might discover but never create, which they could never alter and from whose power they could never escape (a brooding omnipresence in the sky). While Morley's worldly and pragmatic notions had their merits—Smith and his maid had injured no one by their lovemaking and were fully willing to pay for its consequences—Leventhorpe's ethereal conception worked injustices—after all, the vagabond statutes sent innocent men to gaol while corrupt justices who landed them there remained at liberty. The better, if also the more arbitrary, position was Leventhorpe's. Morley's view had a fatal flaw: What the young lord called justice—taking away a man's living because he broke down a hedge—Leventhorpe exposed for what it was, revenge.

The two justices' discord was rooted in varied sources. They were personal rivals vying for stakes in land in the northwestern corner of the county. Lord Morley was young, only the year before succeeding to his title, while Leventhorpe was middle-aged and a seasoned JP. Religion also intruded on their legal philosophies. Lord Morley would soon head up a prominent Catholic family, while Leventhorpe had strong puritan leanings. It would be risky, however, to link Morley's laxity to his Roman Catholicism and Leventhorpe's zeal to his puritanism, since dedication to the rule of law ran the religious gamut. For example, devout Catholic Sir John Petre, nonreligious Sir Thomas Mildmay, and ardent puritan Lord Robert Riche all worked closely together to bring law and order to Essex, remaining at the same time close personal friends. Incidentally, for the record it might be noted that Catholic Petre labored harder than puritan Riche, and uncommitted Mildmay outdid the lot.[2]

Disparate social backgrounds added a further discordant note. Morley sprang from a long line of aristocratic blood (he was the twelfth lord of that name) and was far enough removed from his humble origins to cultivate the art of aristocratic posing, of which an integral part was an unsophisticated approach to law because old families in Essex still believed that "noblemen born, to learn they have scorn." Leventhorpe was of a

[2] See Appendix III.

different stripe. Inheriting neither title nor money he gathered all that he had by hard work. Manly prowess, gaudy display, and the "art" of living were not his fortes; rather it was knowledge, diligently sought and intelligently applied that he wanted, because he believed that it would lead to both private fortune and public order. Morley and his kind may have had more dash and flare, but they did little work in controlling lawlessness. Morley attended only two Quarter Sessions in his life, and another of the old Essex nobility, the Earl of Oxford, though he mustered 80 liveried retainers to accompany him to the Queen's court in London, never came or brought any of his representatives to Quarter Sessions in Chelmsford. Indeed, by Elizabeth's accession, the old nobility's role in law enforcement had faded away, and the real work was left to men of Leventhorpe's bent.

Three county families dominated the county bench during the late Tudor period. William Petre, founder of the first family, was a Devonshire tanner's son who went up to Oxford and received a doctorate in civil law. He eventually secured a position at court from Thomas Cromwell, under whose tutelage he learned much about the "business of government." By 1536, he was made Master in Chancery and managed to obtain a place on the commission to survey monastic lands in Essex, a position which he exploited with ruthless efficacy to gain not only a post at court, but to amass great chunks of land in Essex as well. Later he was made Secretary of State, but shared his time in that office with his county duties as *Custos Rotulorum*, which he used to establish the magnificent series of court records in Essex that eloquently testify to Thomas Cromwell's powerful impact on the minutiae of administration.

Richard Riche, whose father was a London merchant, founded the second family. After studying law, he entered royal service and became another of the Tudor workhorses who placed duty to his sovereign above everything else. Securing Thomas More's conviction as Solicitor General, he was later appointed Chancellor of the Court of Augmentations. In this office he not only substantially enhanced the Crown's revenue, but also gathered up an impressive £18,000 in Essex land, which made him at least one example of Tawney's "rising gentry."[3]

Thomas Mildmay, whose father ran a market stall in Chelmsford, founded the third family.[4] So thoroughly did he perform his duties as a commissioner to survey monastic lands in Essex that Henry VIII made him Auditor of the Court of Augmentations. Busy as he was at the King's work, he did not suffer his private affairs to go wanting, building what was a virtual empire in land around the county town.

All three magnates lined their purses with riches siphoned from their

[3] Hull, *Agriculture and Rural Society* (1950), p. 234.

[4] E.R.O., *Wills, Bishop's Commissary* [Essex and Hertfordshire Jurisdictions], D/ABW 25/92.

administrative posts, even if they did not leaven their cultural curiosity with the intellectual ferment of the times—they were practical men, secretaries, chancellors, and auditors, mindless of theology, philosophy, or literature. That they were catapulted into lucrative positions and succeeded in hanging onto them through Henry VIII's religious revolution, Edward VI's protestant intemperance, Mary's egregiousness, and Elizabeth's pragmatic moderation does not so much display religious hypocrisy or political expediency as it bespeaks their real talent—the business of government. The lesson of the fathers' success was not wasted on the sons, who continued to dominate the Essex bench throughout most of Elizabeth's reign. The older men instilled in their heirs a marvelous training and a deep respect for details. They were the first Essex landowners ever to survey their manors, and they did the job so well that every chimney, window, and story in every village cottage on every village street emerges sharp, clear, and colorful. Sir John Petre, one of these magnates, not only explodes the mirage of a dirty sixteenth-century dandy—he changed his clothes daily, had his linens washed weekly and pine shavings strewn on his floor fortnightly—but also was the archetype of the efficient manager who succeeds in any age. He consolidated his landholdings, introduced new farming methods, and compelled his tenants to do the same, thus making better use of meadowland and arable pasture as well as demanding that they preserve the soil on their plots.[5]

Enhanced social status followed quickly on the heels of money accumulated through effective business methods. William Petre's father was a tanner, but his son became Baron Petre of Writtle; Thomas Mildmay's grandfather hawked goods in the Chelmsford market, but his grandson, the Earl of Fitzwalter, hobnobbed with nobility; Richard Riche's father was a London merchant, his son a baron, and his grandson won (perhaps "bought" is the proper word) the Earldom of Warwick. These whirlwind successes may or may not lend support to the thesis of rising gentry and falling aristocrats, blooming court servants and fading country bumpkins. But they are clear illustration that industry is a highly rewarding virtue, and that they were close enough to their business and administrative origins that they brought hard work, pragmatism, and executive ability to the process of criminal justice in the county. Unlike their fathers, they did not cast their ambitions beyond the county, but rather concentrated their energy on local affairs. Though they were called upon occasionally to help in a royal request, it was always confined to Essex. Sir John Petre collected the 1588–1589 subsidy, but was responsible only for his local hundreds.[6] Sir Thomas Mildmay was commissioned to round up suspicious aliens,

[5] Hull, *Agriculture and Rural Society*, p. 238; E.R.O., D/DP A17–22.

[6] E.R.O. D/DP 04.

but only on Essex shores.[7] Similarly, their private estate-building did not interfere with effective public service. They attended Quarter Sessions and Assizes regularly; sat at home in the evenings to hear complaints about lawbreakers; examined suspected felons; and carefully watched their neighborhoods for signs of disturbance. Even in seemingly trivial clerical tasks, they did not waver in their duty. Sir Thomas Mildmay, *Custos Rotulorum*, for example, changed the clerk's "matter" to the more precise legal term "cause in controversy" on one draft court order and in closing added the cryptic note, "This I hold to be the meaning of the court."[8]

The county magnates and their families dominated the bench, but they alone could not enforce the law. One hundred nineteen JPs drawn from the lesser gentry, though they did not hold vast estates and fortunes, nevertheless loomed large in the persistent struggle to trammel the forces of violence in Essex. It is as important, therefore, to know their background as it is their social betters, since they were critical in making up the fibre of judicial administration.

Every JP had to have some income from landed wealth, but averages mean nothing since individual variation was so extreme, even though an old statute set a minimum cut-off point of £20 income a year from land.[9] Lambarde noted that inflation made it necessary that JPs "livings be . . . increased accordingly,"[10] but the range in fact was tremendous, descending from the inordinate opulence of the county magnates down through justices who barely made the statutory minimum and even on down to those who fell below it.[11] A wide sector in the Essex upper classes participated, then, in law enforcement and though the great personages prevailed in ceremony—Sir Thomas Mildmay presided at Quarter Sessions; Lord Riche led the court processions; and Sir John Petre acted as Deputy Lieutenant—in the formidable toil and prosaic drudgery which keeping the peace entailed, smaller landholders and local notables both did an equal measure.[12]

The sources of these magistrates' wealth originated in diverse quarters. Service to the Crown, as already noted, made the magistrates rich. Trade provided the means to buy land for those like William Cardinal, an ardent puritan who did not turn his energies to religion or magistracy until he had bought up a considerable estate in land near Dedham with money garnered from the flourishing Colchester woolen industry. Hard work, particularly among the less wealthy justices, seems to have been the

[7] P.R.O. SPD 12/148/34.
[8] E.R.O. Q/SR 117/64.
[9] 18 Henry VI, cap. 11.
[10] William Lambarde, *Eirenarcha* (London, 1589), pp. 37–38.
[11] E.R.O. D/DP 04.
[12] See Tables 8 and 9 on page 82.

common denominator. Roger Harlaikendon started as an efficient steward to the Earl of Oxford and eventually bought him out at Earl's Colne. Thomas Rawlens and John Sames were yeomen, who only two years after they each contributed £50 to the royal loan of 1588, were appointed to the Commission of the Peace.[13] The link is clear—any freeholder, if he had enough money, could buy his way onto the bench. Lest the impression that the office was a sinecure be created, it should be stressed that the emphasis on wealth was probably not ill-placed, since JPs were unpaid, and poverty would have laid them open to the enticement of bribery and surrounded them with the unsavory odor of corruption.

Historically, education was also a prerequisite to membership on the county bench, and statutes had long attempted to set the standard that justices ought to be "gentlemen learned in the law." It was easy enough to know Elizabethan gentlemen: "they come good cheap in England," since anyone who "can live without manual labor and . . . will bear the port, charge and countenance of a gentleman" could be one.[14] What it meant to be "learned in the law," however, was diversely interpreted. A few JPs were professional lawyers, but they always played a minor role in county law enforcement and, as the period progressed, an ever-declining one. At Elizabeth's accession, a lawyer was always present at Quarter Sessions, but by 1600, none bothered to come.

Lack of professional lawyers on the bench does not necessarily mean the JPs knew no law. Forty out of the total 141 of them spent some time at an Inn of Court, even if they did not stay long enough to be admitted to the bar. Nevertheless, John Petre's three-year stint at the Middle Temple suggests that they did not know a great deal.[15] He came up to London when he was 18, and though study occupied some of his time—he attended autumn and spring lectures and the Reader's Feast during his first year—outside activities far outstripped his devotion to the law. He was an accomplished lutist and an avid sightseer, two tempting distractions to fulminating about legal precedents. All in all, he spent little time at the Middle Temple that year, arriving late in October, leaving for Christmas holidays in early December, not returning until late January when he quickly escaped to the Duke of Gloucester's on "business for my father." Easter holiday took up most of April, May was spent at court in Greenwich, and, except for a fortnight in June, he spent the summer in Essex courting Justice Waldgreave's daughter. During the second year, his studies waned, even from the first year's moderate pace. He attended neither lectures nor Feast, though he bought *The Pleas of the Crown* and *The Office of the*

[13] E.R.O. D/DP 06.

[14] William Harrison, *The Description of England* (1968), p. 114.

[15] E.R.O., D/DP A17.

TABLE 6 *Justices' Education and Profession*

Year	New JPs	University No.	University %	Inn of Court No.	Inn of Court %
1562–1571	44	11	25	21	47
1572–1581	26	6	23	10	38
1582–1591	33	9	27	13	39
1592–1601	33	11	33	9	27

Justice of the Peace; meanwhile his outside activities stepped up, dancing and hunting having been added to sightseeing and the lute. In the spring of his third year, he was permanently distracted—he got married. In his three years at the Temple he showed no inclination to move up the professional ladder, taking part in no moots (mock arguments prerequisite to being admitted to the bar) and taking no advantage of collegiate life in the Inn to develop important professional contacts—he ate nearly all his meals alone in his chamber or outside the Temple altogether. It is clear that Petre was no lawyer in the professional sense, but this did nothing to hinder his long and distinguished career on the county bench, suggesting that formal training in law had nothing whatever to do with his appointment or his advancement in that capacity. That the number of JPs who attended an Inn of Court fell from something more than half to about a quarter of the membership during Elizabeth's reign further indicates that a legal education was of minor importance in making local judicial appointments.[16]

University education was a different matter, actually increasing during the period from 25% at the outset to nearly one third by 1600.[17] Some JPs were in fact distinguished scholars. Sir Thomas Smith was not only a doctor of civil law, Regius Professor of civil law, and the author of several books (including the classic work on the sixteenth-century constitution, *De Republica Anglorum*), but he was also an active magistrate, attending Quarter Sessions, taking bonds to keep the peace, and examining suspected felons. Naturally, he was unique, and to treat him statistically would both diminish his individual stature and distort the amount of education typical of Essex JPs, most of whom were amateur scholars just as they were unprofessional lawyers, attending university only casually without attaining any degrees.[18]

Religious training appeared among JPs later in the period. In the early

[16] See Tables 6 and 7.
[17] See Table 6.
[18] See Table A–43.

TABLE 7 *Quarter Sessions Attended by Professional Lawyers*

Name	Position	Number of sessions attended 1562–1571	1572–1581	1582–1591	1592–1601	1602
William Ayloff (1562–1590)	Justice Queen's Bench	5	—	—	—	—
William Bendlowes (1562–1564)	Barrister Sergeant	4	—	—	—	—
Anthony Browne (1563–1564)	Justice Queen's Bench	2	—	—	—	—
William Cardinal (1562–1584)	Barrister Reader	2	5	1	—	—
Thomas Meade (1568–1595)	Sergeant Justice Queen's Bench	4	7	1	2	—
Richard West (1564)	Justice Queen's Bench	1	—	—	—	—
Thomas Gente (1572–1591)	Baron of the Exchequer	—	20	8	—	—
James Morrice (1573–1593)	Barrister Reader Attorney for the Court of Wards	—	13	7	1	—
Robert Clarke (1582–1595)	Baron of the Exchequer	—	—	19	1	—
Edward Hubbard (1582–1598)	Clerk in Chancery	—	—	1	3	—
Edward Grimston (1591–1602)	Master in Chancery	—	—	—	4	1
John Tyndall (1593–1598)	Barrister	—	—	—	6	—
Total		18	45	47	17	1
Average number of lawyers per session		.54	1.29	.77	.25	

years, no churchman was in the Commission, but in 1586, the Bishop of Colchester appeared at Quarter Sessions and from that date actively participated in law-enforcement activities. Between 1594 and 1603, three more clergymen entered the Commission. Though it is difficult to explain why this occurred when it did, surely it casts doubt on the notion that it was the Stuarts who returned to the practice of calling upon men of the cloth to take part in secular judicial proceedings. From Essex experience it would seem they only furthered policies begun in Elizabeth's reign.

Varied degrees of wealth and education should not be allowed to obscure the basic ties which bound members together, bonds tight enough to give rise to a true community of magistrates. All of them were local men who were interested in managing Essex affairs and were bitterly disappointed when their sons did not want to do the same. Christopher Chibborne, the Lord of Messing Manor and energetic JP, was distressed when, after he sent his son to Cambridge and Lincoln's Inn, the young man went off to the Low Countries where he was "corrupted by worthless spendthrifts" instead of coming home to Essex to live a more productive life.[19] Furthermore, the Essex bench, on the whole, was *nouveau riche*. Fifteen families had received their coats of arms as recently as 1552, 25 not until 1558, while 15 appeared as late as 1612, and some never did: 37 of the total 102 families on the Essex bench during Elizabeth's reign were not armigerous.[20]

Community within the governing class was reflected most strongly in close family ties. Five Mildmays, four Darcys, and three Riches held office during the period. The bonds of marriage were even more abundant, the following only one of many possible combinations: Justice Roger Amyce (Justice Israel Amyce's father) had one daughter who married William Cardinal, whose daughter married Justice Henry Appleton, who was Justice Eustace Sulyard's stepson, whose sister married Justice William Ayloff.[21]

This community of men, magnates no less than minor gentry, had a solemn duty to control violence in Essex and had at their disposal vast powers to help them do it successfully. Combined in their office were the roles of policeman, detective, public prosecutor, and judge; every stage in criminal law enforcement depended on their active participation. They kept the peace, arrested offenders, conducted preliminary investigations, committed suspects to gaol or put them out on bail until trial, managed the case for the prosecution at the Assizes and presided over indictments at Quarter Sessions. In addition, sometimes they heard felony cases and passed judgments on convicted criminals.

Keeping the peace, that is, maintaining law and order, was carried out using primarily two bonds: one called the recognizance "to keep the peace" and the other "to be of good behavior." The offender promised to appear in court to answer for his misbehavior, failure of which resulted in his forfeiting between £5 and £20, depending on the JPs severity. This for-

[19] P.R.O. *Star Chamber 5*.

[20] Walter C. Metcalfe, ed. *Visitations of Essex*, Vols. XIII-XIV (London, 1904).

[21] *Ibid.*

feiture had to be secured by two "substantial" persons who promised to pay the money if the bonded person defaulted, and again it was up to the justice to decide who was "substantial." Furthermore, JPs had wide latitude in interpreting what was "breaking the peace" or "good behavior," which, for example, embraced all of the following: Reginald Meade for threatening to kill Robert Brooke,[22] William Boltwood for conspiring to commit murder,[23] Joan Dawson for assaulting her friend,[24] William Luckyn's whole family for squabbling with their neighbors.[25] Lambarde argued for a broad construction, including within its purview men who merely "contended in hot words"[26] and limited it only by the claim that an actual breach of the peace, however small, must have taken place.[27] Justice Leventhorpe went even further, issuing a recognizance when "the peace was *nearly* broken."[28] Even these limited restrictions did not apply to bonds of good behavior, which could be issued when a man did not "demean himself well in his port or in his company,"[29] such behavior being determined by circumstances like "the number of a man's company or the weapons he carried, or if any man in such company be of ill-fame or if he frequent a bawdy house or use suspicious company."[30] It seems superfluous that Lambarde should have found it necessary to conclude his discussion of a good behavior bond with the suggestion that it "should not be restrained to narrow bounds."[31]

Recognizances were generally effective and became an increasingly popular means of social control used during the period. Most persons bound over actually appeared in Court; few found legal loopholes to avoid doing so. The following isolated case is a lonely exception that clearly proves the rule. A peasant, Robert Cokerill, found this out when he petitioned no less a man than Lord Chancellor Bacon for a peace bond.[32] Cokerill complained that he was peacefully traveling down the road when a gentleman, Edward Glascock, suddenly appeared and boxed him on the shoulder and shouted, "Take thee that!" Cokerill defended himself with his whip and escaped. But not for long. Laying in wait for him further up the road, Glascock beat him again as he passed, this time with a "long pike staff." Once again Cokerill escaped, this time into his house. Glascock,

[22] P.R.O. SPD 12/157/92.
[23] E.R.O. Q/SR 75/1.
[24] E.R.O. Q/SR 109/49.
[25] E.R.O. Q/SR 107/2.
[26] Lambarde, *Eirenarcha*, p. 76.
[27] *Ibid.*
[28] E.R.O., D/DHt M49. Italics added.
[29] Lambarde, *Eirenarcha*, p. 116.
[30] *Ibid.*
[31] *Ibid.*
[32] E.R.O. Q/SR 30/1.

however; would not give up. He hid outside Cokerill's house for days waiting a further opportunity to attack. After he tried, but failed to come to some private agreement with Glascock to keep the peace, Kemp issued the warrant, but Glascock simply went to Justice Golding and got a *supersedeas* (an order overruling Kemp's warrant). These legal maneuverings did not end the hostilities. Glascock attacked Cokerill yet again, this time with a sword and buckler. Under the circumstances, it is not surprising that Cokerill moaned that Glascock either "was not sufficiently bounden to keep the peace or else that he hath scant regard thereunto."

Naturally, as Cokerill's case indicates, lawlessness occurred despite peace-keeping activities, and the law responded accordingly. When a crime was in progress and a JP saw it, his authority to act was clear. He could immediately arrest the wrongdoer and order bystanders to help; if the culprit refused to obey or bystanders failed to help, both were subject to immediate and unchallengeable imprisonment. Even when the crime was not committed in a justice's presence, he could break into an offender's house to catch him in the act. Justices Harvey and Maxey, being "credibly informed of some evil activities of the Earl of Surrey's servant," went to his house and demanded entry. Failing to get permission, they knocked down the door, found some weapons which they seized, and sent him to gaol to await the next Quarter Sessions where he was duly fined.[33]

Justices also conducted preliminary hearings into crimes they did not see committed, even though their actions rested on questionable legal authority. The Commission of the Peace limited their hearings to those taken in a jury's presence. Two statutes passed in Philip and Mary's reign authorized them to examine felons, but the purpose of these laws was to make it easier to collect evidence, not to widen the justices' powers. Furthermore, they contained specific limitations that these examinations be held in open sessions and that they take place before two justices. This strongly suggests that the statute intended them to be formal judicial proceedings. Legal technicalities aside, Elizabethan Essex JPs regularly conducted preliminary investigations into treason, felony, and misdemeanor. Lord Riche and Sir Thomas Mildmay examined one Mother Dawe for treasonously claiming the Queen was pregnant with Dudley's child.[34] Christopher Chibborne and Peter Tuke took John Walker's examination for manslaughter,[35] and innumerable examinations for lesser offenses could be cited.[36]

The atmosphere of these preliminary hearings was not always judicious,

[33] E.R.O. Q/SR 93/35.
[34] P.R.O. SPD 12/13/21.
[35] E.R.O. Q/SR 160/68.
[36] E.R.O. Q/SR 1–160.

and many like the following had about them a definite air of the inquisition. Justice Harvey said he "knew" that Edward Turnbridge was a robber and a thief and was indicted and imprisoned for the same, despite Turnbridge's claim that he desired to "be damned body and soul if he were guilty." Justice Harvey assured his fellow JPs "that in less than a quarter of an hour after" he got through with him he "confessed all to be true."[37]

Justices had to discover lawbreaking before they could conduct these far-flung investigations. Three means of uncovering information about crime existed. Sometimes the Privy Council told them to look into a matter, as when Cecil wrote to Francis Barrington about a constable's misbehavior.[38] On occasion, justices themselves reported a crime, as when Geoffrey Nightingale and Thomas Lucas initiated a search for evidence in a theft of three bulls.[39] Most often, however, the victim reported the injury to the JP nearest his home. The JP's clerk then took the informer's testimony down in writing and bound him to appear in court to prosecute the offender. Professional informers were active also; John Petre paid a spy to come to court and give evidence.[40]

JPs required ample power to compel appearance if they were to do a successful job at preliminary investigations, but the authority to do so was looked on with suspicion by some legal writers. Coke claimed that the judges in Henry VIII's time decided that "a justice . . . could not make a warrant to take a man for felony, unless he be indicted thereof, and that must be done in open sessions of the peace."[41] Lambarde wrote that justices sometimes examined suspects on a third person's word, but he contended that it was illegal to do so.[42] Despite these warnings from eminent jurists, Essex JPs issued warrants to appear as a matter of course throughout Elizabeth's reign. That they were not formal parchment documents suggested their recent origin, but the word "warrant" was common and the language used to draw them up was standard, thus indicating they were routinely issued. The local constable took the warrant and on its authority brought the suspect to the justice's house. Sir Thomas Mildmay scribbled one on a small scrap of paper, ominously summoning Thomas Asser to appear "at my house this Sunday evening to answer for your misdemeanors."[43]

Once the accused's presence was secured, the JP, unaware of modern distinctions between prosecutor and judge, threw all of his power and

[37] E.R.O. Q/SR 143/23.
[38] B.M. *Egerton MS* 2644/61.
[39] E.R.O. Q/SR 115/28.
[40] E.R.O. D/DP A18.
[41] Coke, *Third Institute*, pp. 176–178.
[42] Lambarde, *Eirenarcha*, p. 168.
[43] E.R.O. Q/SR 115/27.

talent into getting evidence. Israel Amyce, for example, referred to a suspect he was examining as one who had "committed" a crime, rather than waiting for a decision on that issue in the preliminary hearing.[44] Gathering up all the incriminating information he could get from Suffolk as well as Essex, he boasted to his fellow justices that he would bring all kinds of damaging evidence to the next Assizes.[45] His zeal smacks much more of a committed public prosecutor working for a conviction than it does of an impartial judge weighing all the information. Some justices were actually paid to act as prosecutors. For example, two of them received £15 for "finding and successfully prosecuting" libelers in the borough of Colchester.[46] Sir John Petre gave a servant 20s. for providing evidence, 12s. to the undersheriff for a writ of summons, and a shilling to a bailiff for giving evidence against three rabbit thieves.[47] To illustrate how important a justice was as a public prosecutor, if a justice who conducted the preliminary investigation was not at the Assizes to manage the Crown's case, the suspect usually went free. Thus, the JP may have been a judge in his Quarter Sessions, but he was often an advocate at the Assizes.

A powerful weapon in every stage of law enforcement was the JP's authority to commit suspects or put them to bail. If anyone refused to cooperate, the JP could demand surety. If the offender could not secure it, or did not bring what the JPs considered satisfactory sureties, the suspect could be committed to gaol at the justice's pleasure. A stint in the gaol in Colchester Castle frequently meant not only loss of livelihood and liberty, but due to regular outbreaks of gaol fever, it could also result in loss of life.[48] When Sir Thomas Lucas put two uncooperative people in gaol "for example's sake" he clearly demonstrated how extensively the power to imprison was used.[49]

Summary conviction was the most striking of the JP's power to control violence. Without formal proceedings or a jury to decide innocence or guilt, Sir Edmond Huddelston put Hercules Turner in the stocks because on Huddelston's own knowledge Turner had "misused the watch and was a common disturber of the peace."[50] Justice Capel sent a tanner, Robert Fuller, to the Colchester gaol because, despite Justice Maxey's "most friendly admonitions," he continued to steal rabbits, apparently for his craft.[51] Sir Edmond's and Mr. Capel's willingness to certify their actions to

[44] *Ibid.*
[45] *Ibid.*
[46] E.R.O. *Morant MS* 41/97.
[47] E.R.O. D/DP A21.
[48] P.R.O. KB9, coroner's inquests into prison deaths.
[49] P.R.O. *Acts of the Privy Council 1576–1577.*
[50] E.R.O. Q/SR 131/33.
[51] E.R.O. Q/SR 77/60.

Quarter Sessions is convincing proof that such summary decisions were not illegal. Seen against the justices' duties to preside at Quarter Sessions or prosecute at Assizes, which were, after all, only periodic events in one town, these out-of-court powers were much more awesome because they constantly touched everyday life in ordinary people's neighborhoods. Every man knew that a justice lived close by who was carefully watching his actions and who had the wherewithall to punish him or make him mighty uncomfortable if did he not respect the law.

It is important to note that the whole process of law enforcement in preindustrial Essex was intensely personal, even if it seemed dangerously partial. Nonetheless, the way in which the system worked—and I might add to a large extent still does—is through knowing someone. And for good or ill, most JPs knew the people in their neighborhoods. They were their tenants, employees, servants, and customers. Such close contacts were bound to give them firsthand information about the suspect, even if it was distorted by personal bias. It often worked for the ordinary person's benefit, as when the Earl of Bedford asked that the JPs consider a poor woman with a lame husband's case favorably for the old couple,[52] or when Thomas Lucas told Justice Sames not to prosecute a suspected horsethief whom Justice Lucas knew "to be a good man for more than 12 years and the man who charges him a lewd fellow."[53] Of course, knowing a man could do him harm as well. Francis Harvey "knew" for 20 years that Edward Turnbridge was a thief and robber and threw him in gaol on that knowledge.[54] In listing the JPs' powers and setting out their qualifications for office, it should be stressed that the most important quality and the most operative element in their job was this personal knowledge of their territory and the people who lived in it. And it is significant that as population grew; as the nexus of the relationship between the rich and the poor changed from a personal one to one of cash; as economic conditions worsened, even though the community was still small enough for the JP to know many people personally, the growing numbers of landless laborers were sure to be much less known and much more the object of the justices' suspicions. Thus they received a diminishing degree of sympathy and influence that would have lightened the strict operation of the criminal law which the JPs controlled.

Justices used their powers more and more vigorously as the period progressed, probably in response to the social-demographic change overtaking Essex (see Tables 8 and 9). In the first decade, 44 JPs came to 166 Quarter Sessions (an average of eight justices per session), whereas in the last 10 years,

[52] E.R.O. Q/SR 55/35.
[53] E.R.O. Q/SR 132/47.
[54] E.R.O. Q/SR 143/23.

TABLE 8 *Attendance of Justices at Quarter Sessions*[a]

No. of JPs	No. of Sessions attended	Average attendance
1562–1571 (22 rosters): 44	166	8.0
1572–1581 (35 rosters): 38	331	9.4
1582–1591 (37 rosters): 61	384	10.3
1592–1601 (37 rosters): 66	496	13.4

[a] These figures are based on the available attendance figures from the Sessions Rolls. The number beside the years shows the total number of rosters available for the 10-year period.

TABLE 9 *Number of Active JPs*[a]

Year	Term	No. of JPs	Two-year totals
1559	Hilary	42	
1559	Trinity	50	
1560	Hilary	50	
1560	Trinity	(no roster)	
			142
1570	Hilary	(no roster)	
1570	Trinity	39	
1571	Hilary	37	
1571	Trinity	42	
			118
1580	Hilary	40	
1580	Trinity	40	
1581	Hilary	39	
1581	Trinity	39	
			158
1588	Hilary	40	
1588	Trinity	40	
1589	Hilary	42	
1589	Trinity	26	
			148
1601	Hilary	48	
1601	Trinity	68	
1602	Hilary	52	
1602	Trinity	69	
			237

[a] Active JPs were those whom I know to have been at least present at one Quarter Session during their membership in the commission. The rosters were taken from P.R.O. Asz. 35/1–44. Numbers were drawn from a 10-year sample spread over the 45 years of Elizabeth's reign.

66 JPs were present at 496 sittings (average attendance climbing to 13.4 per session).[55] Out-of-court activities swelled from a mere 30 bonds to keep the peace in 1570 to 286 filed in 1602, an increase of 1,000% in little more than 30 years. The numbers of documents filed by individual JPs was obviously somewhat inflated by the steady improvement in record keeping that took place during the period,[56] but it would be wrong to attribute too much of the rise to this cause. It is wiser to consider the waxing numbers of total JPs who took part in law-enforcement activities as the root cause of the swelling record of out-of-court activity, though to be sure it must be slightly discounted by better record keeping.

Naturally, all justices did not work at full capacity or with equal intensity, Sir Thomas Nicolls did virtually nothing, came to court once, and took no part in extra-sessional peacekeeping. Others did not come to court, but worked at home instead. Justice Henny investigated, examined, and sent a suspected murderer to prison, but never attended a Quarter Session in his life. Most JPs, however, came to court regularly and did their share of extra-sessional work as well. Most of the lesser justices acted in small geographical areas, because they preferred to concentrate their efforts close to home. The county magnates, on the other hand, scattered their efforts. Sir Thomas Mildmay, for example, covered practically every hundred in Essex.[57] As the new century dawned, however much individual diversity, more justices were working harder to stamp out lawlessness in the county.

The majority of magistrates were industrious, but their energy was not always tempered with restraint in the face of due process. Obviously men armed with so much power were bound to overuse or even abuse it sometimes. It should be noted here that the criminal process is at least a two-dimensional phenomenon. On the one side is the idea that the individual should be protected against an all-powerful government, especially in damaging criminal prosecutions. On the other is the idea that crime must be controlled and that in order to accomplish this, particularly during times of high crime activity, an efficient machinery must be in operation, one which will catch up in the criminal justice system as many lawbreakers as possible in the quickest possible amount of time. These two sides to law enforcement vary in intensity, but one thing is certain—during times when society fears a crime wave the administrators of justice will not tarry for individual liberty. Lambarde sensed this in expressing his fear that justices might turn their houses into private courtrooms. Occasionally, this happened in Essex. Justice Bury spoke of recognizances he took but

[55] See Appendix III.

[56] See Chapter IV.

[57] E.R.O. Q/SR 1–160.

did not send to court because he had already "disposed" of them, presumably at home; Lord Riche ordered a man discharged because he had already "released" him. How many justices, by threats off the record, intimidated ordinary people no one knows, especially at critical times like the 1590s. That Justices Bury and Riche candidly certified their actions without penalty or reprimand suggests that they were perfectly legal; but since they took the trouble to do so indicates they were also exceptional.

Justices sometimes used their office to further personal causes and secure private gain. Justice Bendlowes put his clients' business first at Quarter Sessions, while Baron Clarke, one of the Assize judges, was tempted at least twice into corrupt behavior. Two men on their way to him for a felony examination were given the following bit of advice by a friend: "If you look to have favor do what I did—carry a fat capon now and then and put a red capon close in his hand." William Cardinal, a devout puritan JP, was prosecuted in Star Chamber for retaining some of his hundred's taxation.[58] Most justices, under ordinary circumstances, seem to have had deep respect for due process of law. Justice Harrys voluntarily refused to conduct the preliminary hearing of his servant charged with sedition because he might "favor him in the examination." (Lord Morley might not have been so scrupulous.) Justice Waldgreave ordered a prisoner set free because he was committed to gaol on nothing more than the "bare information of him that charges him." Sir Thomas Lucas did not carry out a threat to search a house without a warrant, but rather tried instead to get the owner to give him permission to do it without one. Justice Morrice made the most eloquent plea for due process of law in criminal proceedings. In it he drew heavily upon history and, in particular, on the clauses of the Great Charter and claimed that to forego common law procedures guaranteeing open accusation, presentment, and indictment before a grand jury were "a course not tolerable in any well governed Estate of Commonwealth."[59] These and other instances like them suggests that JPs usually exercised their power with discretion.

The ardent struggle of country gentlemen to bring law and order to Essex was largely conducted under the auspices of the versatile and far-flung powers embraced by the office of justice of the peace. But gentlemen justices, no matter how sedulous they were and despite the weapons they held to give their assiduousness expression, were only one piece in the mosaic that comprised the system of Essex law enforcement. Without lesser men to help them, the JPs could never have achieved the amount of success they did. The constable was one indispensable adjunct to the JPs'

[58] P.R.O. *Star Chamber*, 5.

[59] "A Remembrance of Certaine Matters Concerning the Clergy and Their Jurisdiction," Cambridge University, *Baker MS*, 40, Mm11, 51 Fol. 105.

effectiveness. Shakespeare has stamped an unhappy image on the Elizabethan policemen, and unfortunately, Dull's stupidity, Dogberry's foolishness, and Elbow's corruption have become legendary, thus giving a very bad impression of what the Elizabethan constable was really like, and more serious writers, like the Essex antiquarian William Harrison, have not helped the image. Harrison tells the story of a parishioner who raised a hue and cry against a felon, only to encounter the constable who looked him squarely in the eye and said, "God restore your loss, I have other business at this time."[60] That historians have done little to alter this dark picture is demonstrated by the author of one textbook in which all of the following pejoratives are found in his description of the Elizabethan constable: uneducated, untrained, incompetent, failure, sheer ignorance, and stupidity.[61]

The constable was an indispensable officer in law enforcement, and how well he performed his duties is of prime significance in weighing the success of maintaining order in the county. He was elected at the leet court by "honest men" in the parish to serve a 1-year term, and his duties on both the criminal and civil side of the law were immense. Generally, his job was to keep the Queen's peace. He was sworn to maintain peace by preventing its breach, stopping it when in progress, and punishing its violation.[62] His chief responsibility was to repress felony by arresting suspects, seizing their goods, and bringing them immediately to a JP or directly to gaol. Furthermore, he was the JP's agent in serving warrants and was armed with the power to commit to gaol anyone who resisted its service. Finally, he drew up a list of all the honest and legal men in his parish who were eligible to serve as grand, hundred, and trial jurors. No account of law enforcement is complete which fails to give the constables credit for their role in peacekeeping. After all, judges of Assize who visited the county but twice a year might admonish local authorities to do their jobs, but most felons whom they tried were present only because some constable had pursued and caught them. Justices of the peace might sit in their parlors and demand surety or take examinations, but it was the constable who executed the warrant and escorted the offender into the JP's presence.

Doubtless not all constables were worthy of their positions. Libbeus Ebbes took a ld. bribe for excusing prospective jurors from duty[63];

[60] Harrison, *The Description of England.*

[61] Edward Cheyney, *A History of England*, Vol. II (New York, 1948), p. 408. For a more recent but almost identical view, see Thomas G. Barnes, *Somerset Assize Orders 1629–1640*, Appendix III.

[62] William Lambarde, *Of the Duties of Constables* (London, 1602), p. 10.

[63] E.R.O. Q/SR 59/2.

Christopher Broadstreet refused to serve a JP's warrant[64]; Richard Asser was mysteriously summoned to Sir Thomas Mildmay's house[65] "this Sunday evening to answer for your misdemeanors[66]"; John Wall set John Hope free for a price[67]; John Churchman kept part of his parish rates[68]; and Christopher Thurgood was negligent in keeping the Queen's watch.[69] Where examples of outright misfeasance are lacking, stories of the constable's ineffectiveness conveniently take their place. The constable of Coggeshall was unable to get three parishioners to keep the watch[70]; Aveley men refused to obey a constable's order to give lodgings to a night wanderer[71]; and the constables of Chafford returned weak and ineffectual jurors.[72] According to some cases, criticism, even more than misbehavior and weakness, was the constable's lot. Sometimes it was only verbal abuse, as when Hercules Turner shouted insults from the stocks where Halstead's constables put him for tearing up a warrant.[73] More often, they were the brunt of physical violence. Francis Smythe stabbed the constable of Blackmore for keeping Smythe's friend in custody in the church.[74] John Abel (a JP!) assaulted the Lexden constable, and two of Abel's cohorts beat the official with their fists when he tried to take them into custody.[75] They were also the objects of lawsuits. Hercules Turner sued the Halstead officials in the Exchequer for false imprisonment, and George Dibney demanded that the Colchester constables who came to search his house stand forth and give their names so he could sue them for illegal entry and promised that he would be successful just as he was the last time he brought a similar action.[76]

Corruption and stupidity make good copy, and court records, since they are by nature repositories of information touching corruption, evil, and brutality, have led writers to read general misbehavior into these concentrated collections of individual wrongdoing.

On the whole, constables did their jobs well; for every tale of bad a story of good and effective petty officials can be found in the records. Thomas Emery served Chelmsford well, so well in fact that he was reelected

[64] E.R.O. Q/SR 151/91.
[65] E.R.O. Q/SR 76/54.
[66] E.R.O. Q/SR 76/18, 77/2.
[67] E.R.O. Q/SR 37/46.
[68] P.R.O., *Star Chamber* 5/C77/14.
[69] E.R.O. Q/SR 36/37.
[70] E.R.O. Q/SR 110/56.
[71] E.R.O. Q/SR 73/58.
[72] E.R.O. Q/SR 73/72.
[73] E.R.O. Q/SR 121/41.
[74] E.R.O. Q/SR 106/28.
[75] E.R.O. Q/SR 26/3.
[76] E.R.O. Q/SR 121/41; *Morant MS* 41/71–76.

to the post 10 years in a row, paying uncollected taxes out of his own pocket and allowing his own affairs to go unmanaged in order to do the crushing work of the constabulary.[77] The JPs were well aware of his worth, and it took them nearly a year to grant his well-deserved request to retire from his onerous task.[78] Justice Harrys praised John Hasteller highly for his valuable aid in enforcing the law and demanded that other members of the bench give him all possible support so that similar "officers well affected . . . should be encouraged and not discountenanced."[79] Isolated examples of good behavior are not the only evidence that a considerable number of constables were good and faithful servants of the law. Even in the biased records at hand, less than 2% of the cases in the Quarter Sessions involved constables who behaved criminally. This figure creates a very different picture from that of the bumbling, impotent, and corrupt Dogberry, Dull, and Elbow.[80] One should beware of arguing from omission, especially in records where omissions are to be expected. On the other hand, it seems safer to take the court records at their face value than to rely upon upper-class complaints and playwrights' jibes in order to evaluate the constables' performance. It is well known in any age that gentlemen and scholars will not find the policeman doing his job to their satisfaction. Law enforcement that falls short of total perfection will usually upset the "gentler" sort, and policing society to any degree will nearly always bring cries of encroachment on individual liberties from the "scholars." The constable, moreover, was not the scamp who was only a cut above the culprit he was expected to discipline, as he has usually been depicted. Lord Coke was correct when he noted that the only difference between the two officials was in the territory which they supervised—the petty constable looked over the parish and the high constable over the hundred. Nor was the social base of high and petty constables clear-cut. Twenty-seven constables appeared on subsidy lists for 60 parishes, and their worth ranged from 20s. to £4 in land and from £3 to £12 in goods. Seven of the parishes had petty constables of at least yeomen status, and in about a quarter of the parishes they were men of considerable substance. The remaining 46 parishes (roughly three-quarters of the total) had constables drawn from the lower rungs in society.[81] These figures amply demonstrate that the petty officials were drawn from all sectors in society.[82]

Rather than dwelling, then, on the few times that constables failed in their duties, it would be more fruitful and more accurate to record the

[77] E.R.O. Q/SR 40/18.
[78] E.R.O. Q/SR 41/41.
[79] E.R.O. Q/SR 94/15.
[80] See table in Appendix IV on court cases in Quarter Sessions Rolls.
[81] E.R.O. D/DP 04. See also chapter on JPs for the accuracy of these schedules.
[82] See tables of criminal social status in Appendix III.

growing number of times they succeeded. Take recognizances, for example. In 1570, only 30 were filed; in 1580, there were 64; in 1589, 126; and by 1602, the number reached 286. Without constables to call in the persons named in these documents, this impressive growth would have been impossible. Similarly, every offender who stood trial was the result of a constable's labors. This official had to go out and physically bring the suspect in, and every named defendant in the records is due to his efforts, even though no direct proof remains, because constables were not bound to certify their actions in court.[83] These men drawn from all ranks in society were able, then, to give the people in Essex the kind of protection society needed and the amount of enforcement it wanted. That does not mean that many crimes did not go unreported or that many criminals did not go unpunished. The amount of law enforcement that satisfies any community is a relative thing. And it varies from time to time and within various segments of society. It is obvious that Elizabethan gentlemen had different standards for order than did their poorer neighbors. But in a society that provided the machinery for justice and manned it, at least in part, with ordinary people, it is safe to assume that the Queen's lesser subjects used their neighbors and the machinery of justice as much as they thought they needed it. And that is what is more important. To read a general dissatisfaction out of the gentry's complaints, especially the complaints of a gentry whose standards of order were rising, is to make a dangerous jump. That is why it is so difficult to sort out the elements in the criminal statistics and it is why so much emphasis has been placed in this study on the meaning of those statistics in relation to the system of law enforcement rather than on their importance in determining the actual level of crime in the community.

Constables were only one arm of the JPs. The other was the burgeoning ranks of the clerk and his staff without whom the orderliness of new and growing court business would have been impossible. Bureaucracy was rough hewn in Elizabethan Essex, and bureaucrats' work makes dull copy. Nonetheless, improving and extending the Queen's law hinged on how well they did their work. Justices demanded that justice be widely

[83] This is not quite true, since we are overlooking two important categories of officials. The watchman, under the constables' supervision, surely helped in these operations, but little evidence of them remains to tell of it. The sheriff and his staff were also indispensable parts of the law-enforcement machinery in the county. They are dealt with at length elsewhere, and to duplicate that work here would be useless. The bailiffs, on the other hand, have not been accurately described anywhere. The reason for their absence in this study is that bailiffs and constables often tended to be the same people and therefore performed the same duties—summoning and bringing in jurors. The one important duty that remained to bailiffs was to serve judicial writs. In this dimension their conduct and treatment seemed to parallel so closely that of their fellow local officials, the constables, that it seemed needlessly repetitious to spell it out in detail here.

administered, but only the clerks and their staffs could supply the wherewithal to meet their wants. Only they had the requisite skill to draw up the myriad of technical instruments crucial to stepping safely through the treacherously meandering path of the law's process. They saw to it that writs of summons were in proper form, made sure no fatal flaw in an indictment gained for a wily attorney the anxiously awaited chance to pounce on a means of escape for his client, and supervised the drafting on documents of the critical final disposition of cases. Moreover, they gathered up letters, orders, and a host of correspondence flowing to and from Westminster and from place to place within Essex; they arranged papers so that when justices and judges assembled for Quarter Sessions and Assizes they could move with dispatch; and they stored the records to avoid destruction and to facilitate lawyers' use of them.[84]

The Clerk of Assize was the most prestigious of bureaucrats. Royally commissioned, some of the awesomeness of the Westminster judges to whom he was attached rubbed off on him, and he lorded his influential place over the Clerk of the Peace and even the justices at times. John Glascocke, Clerk of Assize, curtly reminded the Clerk of the Peace as well as the JPs that they were not supposed to bother him with minor criminal matters, but were to dispose of them in their own Quarter Sessions.[85] His haughty tone was directed to none other than John Carrowe, who was appointed by the great county magnate Sir William Petre. It apparently had its effect, because trespasses and misdemeanors rarely appear in the Assize files after that.

One family and chiefly one man monopolized the Assize clerkship from 1558 until 1603. John Glascocke shared the office with his yeoman cousin John Lindsell until the latter died in 1558. Glascocke then bought Lindsell's moiety for £50[86] and held down the position by himself until 1597, when his son-in-law John Meade, who had been Associate Clerk since 1580, replaced him.[87] Neither Glascocke nor Meade was noted for ancient lineage; Glascocke secured a coat of arms only in 1571,[88] and the Meades not until 1634.[89] Nonetheless, both had superior academic and legal

[84] E.R.O. Q/SR 1–160. These conclusions are based on the clerk's notes and the various handwritings on the documents, too numerous and subject to codes difficult to cite specifically or at length here. For an excellent similar study for Caroline Somerset, see Thomas G. Barnes, *The Clerk of the Peace in Caroline Somerset* (Leicester University Press, 1961).

[85] P.R.O. Asz. 35. On all commissions of gaol delivery, it is possible to follow the appointments of Clerks of Assize, because they are always named immediately following the two judges. When associate clerks came to be a part of the Clerk's office, they too were listed, their names coming just after the clerk's. E.R.O. Q/SR 8/34; E.R.O. Q/SR 9/51.

[86] E.R.O. D/DU 23/70.

[87] P.R.O. Asz. 35/39/1.

[88] E.R.O. D/DP Z24.

[89] Walter C. Metcalfe, ed., *The Visitations of Essex*, Vol. 13 (London, 1878).

training. Glascocke attended Eton and then King's College, Oxford, and went on from there to become an Inner Temple Bencher, while Meade finished his Bachelor of Arts degree at Oxford and was later called to the bar of Lincoln's Inn.[90] Although Glascocke had purchased his office, his and Meade's distinguished careers conclusively prove that it was no mere sinecure; the dexterity to manipulate the law's intricacies and the talent to master its technicalities were imperative prerequisites.

The Clerks of the Peace were several cuts beneath the Assize Clerks. The Queen did not grant them royal commissions; the *Custos Rotulorum* picked them, and they held office at his sufferance. John Carrowe admitted as much when he bluntly wrote that he owed everything to William Petre, the *Custos* who named his Clerk of the Peace.[91] Furthermore, though they were of the same social status as the Assize clerks, their professional training was substantially inferior. All the Clerks of the Peace had attended an Inn of Court, but none was ever called to the bar, and none, save George White, obtained a university degree.[92] Nonetheless, the Clerk of the Peace held a weighty office; in his charge was nearly all criminal process up to trial. Included were the writs of summons and the indictments, the latter of which he turned over to the Assize clerk just prior to the opening of Assizes.

The dimensions of the Clerk of the Peace's power were several. Naturally, he was the master of his own staff, and this source of authority waxed in strength as his personnel swelled in numbers. For instance, in 1556, John Carrowe, the first of the Elizabethan clerks, had one ad hoc deputy and possibly two scribes.[93] Richard Brown, the last man to hold the office in Elizabeth's reign, had acquired by 1600 at least 13 underlings who drafted indictments, calendared offenders' names, and sorted, filed and recorded recognizances, presentments and other legal instruments.[94] Moreover, every justice of the peace had personal clerks who were beholden to the Clerk of the Peace, if only indirectly. These personal clerks, usually private servants, wrote up the examinations taken and drafted the

[90] J. S. Cockburn, "Seventeenth-Century Clerks of Assize—Some Anonymous Members of the Legal Profession," *The American Journal of Legal History*, Vol. XIII, No. 4 (October 1969), pp. 315–332, 320.

[91] P.R.O. S.P. 11/5/3.

[92] John Venn and S. A. Venn, *Alumni Cantabrigiensis*, Cambridge, 1922–1927.

[93] This statement is based on the handwriting on the documents in the Quarter Sessions Rolls and on the signatures found at the bottom of writs in the records for the early years. Only Carrowe's name was on the writs and only a few recognizably different hands appeared on other documents.

[94] Again the handwriting is an important clue to this staff. Fortunately, however, underlings by now had become much less shy in identifying themselves. Clerks who drew up indictments often initialed and sometimes even signed them while deputy clerks almost always put their names to court orders and other legal documents.

recognizances issued between sessions at the home of individual JPs. Because they received fees for writing such documents, and since the Clerk of the Peace was responsible for collecting the money, he could, if he so desired, refuse to release accused persons until they had paid all costs, including the ones of the private clerks. Thus, the Clerk of the Peace had a potentially powerful means to control the lesser, private secretaries to the JPs.[95] A number of pleas from JPs asking the clerk's help in collecting their servants' fees point to how powerful his position was in this respect, and it expanded as the number of justices and their activities stepped up.[96]

Sometimes the clerk's strong arm was felt, for good or ill, even by the justices themselves. In one instance, Justice Harrys asked the deputy clerk to use his influence with Assize Judge Clarke to get a prisoner released.[97] On another occasion, Justice Bury, who had been in Henry VIII's bedchamber and who had sat on the county bench for nearly 30 years, nevertheless had to make apologies to the clerk for sending in recognizances on paper (they should have been written on parchment) and pathetically asked "his loving friend" (meaning his social equal, the clerk) to excuse him from Quarter Sessions because he was "old and lame."[98] The clerk did not always grant requests from the justices, even when the great county magnates made them. In the margin of a request from Sir John Petre to issue alehouse licenses to several applicants, the deputy clerk boldly noted: "one license granted, the rest denied."[99]

The clerk's mastery over the fate of all who had occasion to come before the court was unquestionably the most potent single dimension to his authority. He and his staff set up the schedule of business and determined the order in which persons presented, indicted, or otherwise charged were called for the disposition of their cases.[100] A suspect's position on that list determined his fate, because, as we have already noted, witnesses bound to frame indictments sometimes grew impatient or tired and went

[95] Justices' private clerks had an interesting development during this period. In the early years, they were almost always spoken of as "my man" but toward the end of Elizabeth's reign they became with greater frequency "my clerk." This transition from the informal "my man" to the formal "my clerk" is a graphic illustration of the institutionalization of the bureaucratic side of law enforcement.

[96] See tables in Appendix III on JPs and their attendance at Sessions. See also tables of the number of recognizances and other instruments filed by JPs.

[97] E.R.O. Q/SR 112/8.

[98] E.R.O. Q/SR 48/26.

[99] E.R.O. Q/SR 160/5.

[100] On nearly all documents in the rolls, the Clerk's staff has numbered the presentments and indictments before the Session in the order in which they are to appear. Then, during the court session, he marked through those cases in which a final disposition was made.

home. Hence, suspects went free by proclamation because no evidence was available on which to prosecute them. Jurors also often left court early, thus making it impossible to try every defendant.[101] Individuals at the bottom of the list, therefore, stood a good chance of escaping the law because those who were not called at the session for which they were scheduled to appear had a curious habit of disappearing from the records forever. Once or never seemed to be the rule governing the trial of those charged with crime in Elizabethan Essex, and however eager JPs were to establish order, the abyss between hope and fulfillment in law enforcement remained wide open, and the clerk was instrumental in deciding who would fall in the gap.

Power was a magnet, especially to members of the lesser gentry, but alone it was insufficient to draw men into the legal bureaucracy. Money, too, was alluring. More than any other local official, the clerk profited from justice by raking in enormously lucrative fees from the multifarious documents he wrote up throughout the legal process. Summonses, three of which every defendant was entitled to have, cost half a crown, and since most people took full advantage of the law's delays by not appearing until the last possible moment, the clerk could generally depend on the issuance of three summonses and the weight of three half crowns in his pocket.[102] Since the persons named in a single writ could number as many as 40, the total profit from them alone was a fat one. Moreover, clerks were not above saving on the price of parchment. They did not always bother to draw up separate writs for every summons, but rather used the old ones over and over, merely erasing the name of the writ (*capias* for *venire facias*, for example) until the parchment wore too thin to write any more on it.[103]

Expenses did not stop when a defendant finally arrived in court. He had to pay 2s. to be indicted for a misdemeanor, 13s.4d. to be charged with felony, and 2s. to plead not guilty. Even going free had its price; it cost 5s.4d. to discharge a recognizance and 4s.4d. to be acquitted in a criminal offense. It is impossible to determine accurately over the whole period how many of these fees were actually collected, but John Petre's sheriff's account book shows that most of the justice's profits were realized during the year he held the office, and it indicates further that clerks took their own fees from the fines collected from convicted criminals.[104]

[101] B.M., *Landsdownce MS* 49, folios 59–60; P.R.O. Asz. 35, Calendar of prisoners.

[102] B.M., *Landsdownce, ibid.*

[103] Too many writs to cite specifically here bear this pattern of erasures with, incidentally, the names of those who appeared on the former writ struck through.

[104] E.R.O. D/DP 058. At the end of each accounting is the interesting but admittedly inconclusive statement "total received in court by the Clerk of the Peace and in part settlement *valdorum* justices of the peace and their clerk."

Furthermore, since JPs customarily gave the clerk the 4s. per diem allowed by statute to every member of the bench, what fees the clerk did not otherwise receive were adequately recouped in this gratuity, which was a rising one since more justices sat in court more often and sessions went on for more days at a time as the period progressed.[105] It is beyond hope to put a precise figure on the Elizabethan Clerk of Peace's income, but for the sessions held during Petre's year as sheriff, Richard Brown brought away more than half the total collected. This amounted to a total of £36 15s.2d., but it should be noted that this amount was only in "partial satisfaction" of his fees. Naturally, he had to share this amount with his staff, and, of course, he had income which these figures do not reflect, but they give some notion of the lucrative post this bureaucrat held.

Power and money were enticing spoils luring men to seek posts in the clerk's office, but desire by itself did not get them jobs. Special skills were required for even the lowliest place on the staff, and only literate men had the necessary technical equipment to master them. Fortunately, local men from the growing number of schools in all parts of the county and from all ranks in society were "learn[ing] the latin tongue" and acquiring "a good secretary hand."[106] The clerk's office tapped this deepening pool of highly skilled personnel to perform the many clerical tasks of the courts-writing, sorting, filing, and organizing. The thickening and better-organized Quarter Sessions Rolls that evolved during the late sixteenth century in Essex are eloquent proof of the growing numbers of these literate men who were entering into the clerk's staff. In addition to skill, a particular mentality was needed to do the meticulous work that bureaucracy required, and happily the eager justices' call for copious public records were readily met by this crew of anonymous scribes in the clerk's office who were perfectly content to share the profits of justice, but who demanded little of its power and none of its glamour. Here again we can see the critical nature of attitude on the criminal statistics. Without the mentality that made attention to detail an end in itself, the figures would have differed markedly. The obviously growing bureaucracy and the mentality that produced it does not lead to simple explanations about its origins. It is easy to assume that the pressure of increased crime forced a reorganization of the structure and functioning of law enforcement, and to some extent that may well have been true. But it is not the whole story, and we have our modern counterpart to prove it. Machinery does not drop like manna to answer the cries of hunger of society for law and order. If it did, then our almost broken-down modern criminal justice system in America would have come out of its doldrums long before now,

[105] P.R.O. S.P. 11/5/3.

[106] *Victoria County History of Essex*, Vol. II (London, 1907), p. 509.

and more people would have paid attention to Chief Justice Warren Burger's astonishing statistic quoted in a recent address to the American Bar Association—more money is spent on an American bomber than on the whole federal judiciary. Thus does it appear that bureaucracies are not created, they are made; though once made, they seem to have an unsurpassed quality of longevity and an inordinate ability to grow and survive without external reasons for their continued existence.

Despite the justices' energy and the help of the constables and clerks, the court system itself remained the instrument by which the goals of society were realized, and it is now necessary to turn from men to institutions.

CHAPTER IV

THE EMERGENCE OF MODERN COURTS

Institutional effectiveness is at least a question of prestige both in terms of the social influence of the men who hold office and in terms of the ritual which surrounds high office. As Lord Burghley astutely remarked: "In pompous ceremony the secret of government doth much consist." The awesomeness of the law was recognized as the JP's greatest ally in maintaining good order, a point fully realized by Sir John Petre when the winter Assizes met at Chelmsford in March of 1594. A richly bedecked procession made its way up High Street on the 28th of the month. Twenty-three liveried bailiffs holding white wands led the two judges from Westminster, who were wearing scarlet robes, from their lodgings at *The Lion* to Sessions House. The event was of such weight that Sir John Petre dispatched six of his men to Chelmsford 10 days early in order to make certain everything was in order.[1] Assizes were hectic because judges had only two days to do an enormous job—read the latest royal proclamations, reprimand wayward officials, hear all the civil pleas which had accrued in the county since their last visit, and preside over the indictment and trial of all felons whom the JP's had made ready for them. If the civil pleas were finished on the 28th and if the arraignments were made and the indictments taken that evening, only 6 hours remained to try suspected felons. With the number of felons totaling 72, it meant that an average of 12 per hour had to be tried.[2] This staggering pace left little time for the prosecution and defense to "altercate" or for the jurors and judges to deliberate.[3]

[1] P.R.O. Asz. 35/36/1; E.R.O. D/DP A20.

[2] P.R.O. Asz. 35/36.

[3] Sir Thomas Smith, *De Republica Anglorum* (Cambridge, 1906).

Sessions House was a foul place to hold court. It was much too small to cram in the 200 witnesses, jurors, suspects, officials, and spectators who congregated for hearings, and though its location afforded maximum publicity for the law's proceedings (it was in the heart of busy downtown Chelmsford where county market and London traffic converged), dirt and bad weather blew freely in through its unwalled sides upstairs, while the noise rose from below where cattle and other wares were being hawked in the market stalls.[4] Furthermore, the Essex Assizes were not even profitable for the judges, because low-paid criminal cases far outstripped lucrative civil ones. It was no wonder that most eminent judges preferred to travel to fat Norfolk or agreeable Somerset and leave the overloaded Essex felony dockets for the greener and more jejune jurists.[5]

After their grueling work at the Hilary 1594 Assizes, the judges, Baron Clarke, an Essex man, and Sergeant-at-Law Drewe, went to Sheriff Mildmay's lodgings for a badly needed respite. There, at his expense, they drank and ate the evening away while Scottish pipers played for their pleasure.[6] It is doubtful, however, that they felt sufficiently paid for their work or adequately rested for the hard journey that lay ahead of them. They had only 14 days to hold the Assizes in the four remaining counties in the Home Circuit—Hertfordshire, Kent, Surrey, and Sussex—and the total alloted time for the whole circuit was only 17 days including travel time.[7]

A fortnight following the 1594 Winter Assizes, another procession moved up the Chelmsford High Street. This time the bailiffs escorted John Stern, Suffragan Bishop of Colchester; Sir Thomas Mildmay, *Custos Rotulorum*; Sir John Petre, Deputy Lieutenant; and nine of their less illustrious colleagues up to Sessions House where the justices of the peace held the Easter Quarter Sessions.[8] They were meagre affairs compared to the Assizes, and at them less money was poured into lavish display. Sir John Petre, for example, spent less than half at Quarter Sessions than he did at the Assizes.[9]

Quarter Sessions' business was not so weighty. At them, misdemeanors were tried, while felonies rarely got past the stage of indictment there. A clerk made this clear by noting on one bunch of felony bills that they were "indictments taken at Christmas sessions and certified to the Assizes" for trial.[10] Beginning in 1584, however, special gaol deliveries were held

[4] E.R.O. D/DGe M50; D/DM P1.

[5] Thomas G. Barnes, *Somerset Assize Orders 1629–1640* (Frame 1959) xiv; P.R.O., Asz. 35/3–45.

[6] E.R.O. D/DP A20.

[7] P.R.O. Asz. 35, dates of opening of the Assizes.

[8] E.R.O. Q/SR 12.

[9] E.R.O. D/DP A17–22.

[10] E.R.O. Q/SR 169.

in conjunction with Quarter Sessions. Gaol delivery commissions (literally the power to empty the gaols of felony suspects) were granted for the days immediately following Epiphany Sessions of that year and nearly every other year thereafter until the end of the reign.[11] Some JPs were caught by surprise at the announcement of these special hearings and asked to be excused from attending them or to be granted more time to gather up their evidence against the suspects they hoped to prosecute for felony. Their unpreparedness suggests that this development was an extraordinary one. Lest it should appear that the emergence of these special gaol deliveries signalled a usurpation by Quarter Sessions of the Assizes' jurisdiction over felony, it should be emphasized that two Assize judges invariably were in attendance, as their rosters show; that they were held on separate days; and that their records, though they were filed with Quarter Sessions, were wrapped up and bound by themselves. These facts leave little doubt that Westminster jealously guarded its prerogative to judge felony cases.

Displaying even less pomp and treating more trivial matters than the Assizes or Quarter Sessions were the leet courts (the technical name for the criminal side of the man's judicial powers).[12] At these sittings the steward of the manor presided, the ranking village elders acted as grand jurors, and tenants took over the role of petty jurors to try minor culprits. In countless villages throughout the county, the law, by means of these leet courts, reached down and touched people in every quarter of daily life—clean water and scoured ditches, safe roads and fair prices, peace and quiet, harmonious marriage, and even proper dress.[13] The Assizes, Quarter Sessions, and leet courts were not simply quaint vestiges of a medieval past, though to be sure they had some of that flavor. They were, as has been noted, sources of social entertainment and engines of retributive justice for crimes already committed, but in the largest sense they were something more than these. In essence they were attempts to deter crime through periodic and dramatic reminders that social misbehavior might result in anything from minor fines to public humiliation and even death.

All three tribunals had a respectable history by the time of Elizabeth's accession. Judges of Assize had ridden out from Westminster since the twelfth century. Technically, the Assizes were special sessions rather than courts. They were, literally, sittings for certain specified purposes and in theory, anyway, the judges' authority was only ad hoc. Each session required new

[11] See Table A-47.

[12] See Tables A-48 and A-49.

[13] See tables of Wethersfield and Ingatestone manors. The conclusions here are based on the manor court rolls from these two estates. I am indebted to Mr. K. C. Newton, Essex County Archivist, who made his calendars available to me and whose willingness to lead me through many technicalities in the rolls was an invaluable aid in my research.

commissions issued out of Chancery under the Great Seal and formally at least given only at the Queen's suffrance. The judges came into the county with at least four separate commissions. First was that which gave them their name—the commission to hold the possessory assizes (cases involving land tenure). This was followed by their other civil commission, that of *nisi prius*, which gave them power to hear civil cases not heard at Westminster in the common law courts there.

Judges of Assize brought three criminal commissions. First and most important was that of gaol delivery, which empowered them to empty all gaols in the county of their prisoners. What this meant in fact was that they tried felony cases, since usually the only persons committed to prisons were suspected felons, though in theory the power was broad enough to cover anyone. Curiously, and despite much legal learning on the commission of *oyer* and *terminer* (general authority to hear and determine criminal cases), none survive for Essex in the files. Perhaps this was because the Commission of the Peace already covered the cases included in the commission of *oyer* and *terminer*, though it is difficult to explain why so many have thought it should be present and yet in Essex it is missing.[14] Though highly technical and, in some respects, academic, the commission's theoretical nature should not obscure its importance in determining the outcome of some cases. Since judges' powers were formally only ad hoc, clever lawyers used this to get their clients freed whenever a judge was removed from a commission, as they usually were since they often only traveled a circuit once in succession, except for the few previously mentioned. The lawyers argued that the judges' authority was null and void as soon as he was taken out of the commission. By Elizabeth's reign, the problem was solved because in the time of Edward VI, a statute whose preamble warned that a number of criminals were escaping on such grounds provided that any act of a judge while in commission would carry on in effect after he was removed. This statute clearly established the permanence of the Assizes in fact, if it did not do so in law, since the commissions continued to go out each time the Assizes were held, even though their authority was binding forever.

The manor courts also had an ancient history, though the first records in Essex date from the thirteenth century.[15] Even the Quarter Sessions, youngest of the courts in the county, were well established by the mid-1300s.[16] Age alone did not make courts effective instruments of law

[14] See Barnes, *The Clerk of the Peace in Caroline Somerset* (1961), xiii, and Holdsworth, William, *A History of English Law,* Vol. I, Methuen and Company, Ltd. (London, 1969), pp. 274–285.

[15] E.R.O. Publication 51, *Guide to the Essex Record Office* (1969), pp. 90–93.

[16] 36 Edward III, cap. 12.

enforcement. It was the heavy emphasis laid on pageantry and the rigid adherence paid to form that heightened their potency in a period when gaudy ostentation and lavish display were important attributes of government.[17] From start to finish court days were exploited to publicize the mystical authority of the law and to dramatize the salient value of keeping the Queen's peace.[18] Preliminaries to the actual opening of the court were utilized to create the proper atmosphere: Dressed in special garb, the crier demanded, "*Oyez, oyez, oyez*" (Hear ye, hear ye, hear ye), held the judges' parchment commissions high (long and frightening catalogues of their sweeping powers), and read them out officiously. Dire warnings to spectators to remain silent on pain of imprisonment, firm reminders to officials that failure to answer roll call would be at their peril and sharp admonitions to jurors to be "good men and true" were also proclaimed for the benefit of the weak of heart or those who did not heed their betters. All of these exercises were no doubt meant to inspire, but more important they aimed at intimidating and terrifying subjects of the Crown into a fearful obedience to, if not a warm affection for, the law and the authority of magistrates. The aura of solemnity that open court produced made it the proper setting for disciplining wayward officials. Richard Hammond, an errant constable, discovered this to his sorrow when he was imprisoned until he was willing to apologize in Quarter Sessions for flouting an order of the justices. Dramatically underlining the dual role of the apology, the court stressed that Hammond's humiliation was not only for punishment, but also for "example's sake."[19] Hammond never disobeyed another order—at least none is on record—which suggests that in this case public humiliation must have been an effective punishment.

Pageantry and form did not mesmerize everybody in the county into categorical and cheerful submission to law. George and John Raye, sons of a Stanstead yeoman, for example, were bound to appear at Quarter

[17] Harrison, William, "Of Their Apparel and Attire," *The Description of England*, pp. 145–149.

[18] Anonymous, *The Office of the Clerk of Assize Together with the Office of Clerk of the Peace* (London, 1676). Together with the documents in the Essex Record Office and Public Record Office, this invaluable book was largely responsible for the section on procedure and formalism included here. Since it did not appear in print until after the Restoration, its validity for practices during Elizabeth's reign might appear suspect. Such, however is not the case. The book contains extremely detailed information for clerks and their notetaking, which is identical to practices used in Essex during sixteenth century. For example, the book instructs clerks to place above the name of defendants who plead not guilty and put themselves on the country, the words *ponit se*, or the abbreviation *po se*. That procedure exactly was followed in Essex. Many other examples would further demonstrate this. By implication it seems that procedures regarding pageantry and practices not so well documented in court rolls must also parallel descriptions in this important little book.

[19] E.R.O. Q/SR 85/22–22e.

Sessions for tearing up a warrant sent from a JP. They came to court with a *supersedeas* (a writ overruling the bond) which the court "reverently accepted." But the two young men exhibited not only an "arrogant, inconsiderate and slanderous bill of complaint" against the justices sitting there "in a place of justice but very unreverently demeaned themselves to the indignity of that place and the derogation of justice."[20] Moreover, the cascading rush of business and an overfilled Sessions House inhibited the desired impact of dramatic spectacle; long dreary roll calls bored participants; burdensome criminal caseloads made jurors lackadaisical; and pressing schedules wore on everyone's patience and tempted many who should have stayed to go home early. At the Hilary Assizes of 1594, 73 JPs, 120 jurors, 21 bailiffs, 2 coroners, 72 prisoners, and 24 persons bound to appear on bonds were called, that is, a total of more than 300 persons who had to be tallied and processed. The results of this pressure had a deleterious effect on jury deliberations. At the outset of the Assize, the grand jury heard and returned six or seven indictments at one time, but by the end, they were rushing back an astonishing 25. Many jurors did not even bother to stay until the end of court. Four jurors from Dunmow hundred, after they were sworn into a panel, went off and were unable to give a verdict, and though they were imprisoned for the remainder of the Sessions it did not help the expedition of proceedings or the dignity of the court to have them flagrantly defy its power.[21] One vexed Assize judge complained that so many jurors left during the second day that it was impossible to try all felons, thereby allowing some of them to go free because of the jurors' dereliction.[22] Nevertheless, pageantry and spectacle were integral parts of effective law enforcement in the county, lending valuable support to the mystique of law and expressing it in a medium palatable to county gentlemen and understandable to illiterate humble people.

Ritual is only one side of the story of the growth of law and order. More important is the general process of bureaucratizing which was affecting all sides of Elizabethan government, a process that was related to, if not caused by, the swelling business that came to felony courts. It was especially true as the period progressed, since the number of cases reach nearly overwhelming proportions in the hard times of the 1590s.[23] The administrative growth manifested itself in diverse dimensions. Court sessions were regularized over what they were in previous centuries. It is noticeable in the Assize courts which, though they had long been held twice a year, did not have regular meeting days or fixed abodes, until 1580 they

[20] E.R.O. Q/SR 122/55, 56.

[21] E.R.O. Q/SR 122/2a.

[22] B.M., *Landsdowne MS* 49, folios 59–60.

[23] See page 36.

met any day of the week in numerous towns spread about the county.[24] Gradually, however, they settled into a firmer schedule until by the 1590s they were sitting almost exclusively on Mondays and Thursdays in the county town of Chelmsford.[25] Meanwhile, Quarter Sessions finally became in fact what they were meant to be in law—*quarterly* assemblies. Early in Elizabeth's reign they were convoked no more than three times a year, but by 1580, four sittings was an almost unbroken rule.[26]

The same regulation was reflected in better records: Formal parchment instruments fulfilling bare legal requirements were the sole documents in 1559. Until 1571, for example, only JPs', bailiffs', and occasionally constables' names and nothing more were enrolled on the calendars (official lists). After that date, clerks' notes were added: The names of officials who were present in court were pricked, later absences were noted, and finally excuses for failure to attend and fines assessed against negligent absentees were added.[27] In 1574, the Clerk of the Peace started to gloss the hitherto bare presentments of offenses in the Quarter Sessions Rolls,[28] and after 1597, witnesses' names were always endorsed on indictments.[29] Besides supplementing old documents with new information, new categories of documents were spawned in the budding bureaucratic offices of the Clerks of Assize and Peace. Calendars that contained informative notes touching the nature of criminals' offenses and the names of JP's who committed prisoners to gaol came to be a common addition to judicial records.[30] Summaries of the courts' proceedings, which contained the names of persons tried or bound over, the disposition of cases, the names of officials who attended, and notes concerning those who were absent also became common additions. These summaries, which were informal and on paper, were not permanent supplements until about 1570, although they appeared sporadically as early as 1561. That new types of registers arose early and after a lapse became routine is further indication of the fundamental, if subtle and gradual, bureaucratic metamorphosis transpiring in late Tudor Essex. That the summaries were used as inner wrappers for Sessions Rolls is an ironic testimonial to their practical value. Meanwhile, systematic

[24] P.R.O. Asz. 35/3–22. Days and places of meetings were always included in the Commission of Gaol Delivery, making it possible to compile a fairly complete schedule of meetings. See Table A-45.

[25] P.R.O. Asz. 35/22–45.

[26] E.R.O. Q/SR 1–160. On almost every head sheet in the rolls the dates, days, and place of meeting has been written down, making it possible to reconstruct exactly the schedule of Quarter Sessions.

[27] P.R.O. Asz. 35/3–45.

[28] E.R.O. Q/SR 48.

[29] P.R.O. Asz. 35/39.

[30] P.R.O. Asz. 35/17/2, and then disappears until Asz. 35/22/H, after which it continues uninterrupted until the end of the period.

record keeping was injected into legal administration. Early in Elizabeth's reign, paper and parchment documents, jury lists and presentments, indictments and calendars were rolled up together helter-skelter and without any attempt to organize them into sensible arrangements. Bunching up parchment and paper was grossly inefficient. Parchment, by law, was the sole medium for expressing formal "matters of record," that is, they were the only source whose contents were legally binding. So necessary was parchment to make an act of court legally binding that one JP who sent in recognizances on paper accompanied them with an obsequious note apologizing to the Clerk of the Peace for doing it. Slowly the documents were sensibly arranged; formal documents were separated from rough drafts, jury lists were filed with their presentments, indictments and recognizances were divided into two bunches, and writs of process were grouped at the end of the roll according to the nature of the order contained in them.

The birth of the Essex Plea Roll was a singularly momentous departure in administrative–judicial history.[31] The term plea roll is not strictly accurate, since the document contains much more than a record of pleas before Quarter Sessions, including precepts to sheriffs, petitions, appointments of constables, etc. In other words, instead of the title the clerk gave it, *placita ad generalem quarrerialem sessionem*, it was actually a transcription of almost all important business dealt with at the Sessions of the Peace. This is in itself important because it shows how crude were the beginnings of bureaucratic development in Elizabeth's reign.[32] It was a pithy enumeration of transactions at Quarter Sessions and was much more sophisticated than the rolls themselves. Chancery hand was standard form in the Plea Roll, whereas it was not used in Quarter Sessions Rolls until late in Elizabeth's reign and then only on writs of process. But most trenchant, the data in Sessions Rolls could at best only be arranged according to type of document—indictment, presentment, writ, and so on—while the newer Plea Roll accomplished much more since it provided a complete, if only brief, record of the progress of each case through the judicial machinery. Each indictment entered was followed with all actions taken by the court in connection with it—summonses, remands, respites, and judgments.

Court proceedings, as well as the recording of them, were bureaucratized during the period. In earlier years no schedule of business was made, and persons bound to appear on bonds, defendants who were on trial, parishes that were presented for broken bridges or for housing bastard children were dealt with helter-skelter; but as the Elizabethan period progressed, advance preparations were worked out before the court met in order to set up the program of judicial activity. Presentments were

[31] E.R.O. Q/SPa 1.

[32] E.R.O. Publication 51, p. 892.

labeled and numbered,[33] indictments were disposed of in a set format,[34] recognizances were sorted, calendared,[35] and ultimately recorded in the Plea Roll. These administrative reforms enhanced the court's efficiency and it could, therefore, dispose of more cases in less time. The Plea Roll's introduction, therefore, was much more than a landmark in administrative history. It signalled an immense achievement in bureaucratic effectiveness.[36] No longer was it necessary to rummage through a hodgepodge of documents to trace a particular case or check on an individual defendant. Now, neatly written in the form of an easily accessible entry list, the Plea Roll made it easier than ever before to find and deal with more criminals, thereby adding immeasurably to the efficacious enforcement of the Queen's peace.

But old habits were not wholly replaced with modern methods. A plethora of ancient jurisdictions and traditional courts made this inevitable. Ecclesiastical tribunals were still very much alive and tried many similar cases as were heard at Quarter Sessions: sexual offenses, disturbances in church, and witchcraft to mention only a few.[37] Manor courts' jurisdiction, in turn, overlapped that of the Quarter Sessions—misdemeanors were tried and felonies were presented at both. To complicate the situation further, four economically important and heavily populated towns—Colchester, Harwich, Maldon, and Saffron Walden—were independent boroughs and held royal charters granting them the authority to set up their own criminal courts.[38]

Equally significant were the ad hoc tribunals set up from time to time during Elizabeth's reign. Special courts in any age generate suspicion, but sometimes they are necessary, especially when urgency requires immediate action. Three important cases of this nature were riot, which could

[33] E.R.O. Q/SR 158.

[34] E.R.O. Q/SR 160.

[35] E.R.O. Q/SR 156.

[36] Abstracting the substance of sessions onto a separate document did not begin with the Plea Roll. The practice really started when, in 1600, recognizances were numbered and a calendar made on which their disposition could be recorded. It was not, however, until Epiphany Sessions in 1603 that a bundle of recognizances, all numbered, were bound together with another document on top which had the note, "recognizances together with a panel of them attached." This panel is a list of all persons bound with numbers corresponding to those on the recognizances.

[37] Alan MacFarlane, *Witchcraft Prosecutions in Essex 1560–1680*, Ph.D. Dissertation, Oxford University (1967); J. Pascal Anglian, *The Archdeaconry Courts in Essex*, Ph.D. Dissertation, U.C.L.A. (1965).

[38] Borough court records were not used systematically in this study, but a cursory survey of Colchester's court rolls demonstrate clearly that their Quarter Sessions were at least as powerful as those for the county. Indeed, the lack of felony cases from Colchester tried at the Assizes strongly indicates they practiced what the Commission of the Peace stated in theory—the right to try felony at Quarter Sessions.

not wait until the next regularly scheduled court; forcible disseisin, which left a man without a home; and coroners' inquests, which involved a dead body that could not be preserved until sometimes several months hence when the Assizes were convened. Such situations were dealt with at hearings specially constituted according to long-established tradition and legislation.

Potentially more dangerous and requiring more explanation was quite another type of hearing. This type smacked of the dreaded *eyre* of medieval days and consisted of special sessions that had about them no particular sense of urgency. They were authorized by special commissions of *oyer* and *terminer* granted to local magnates, and it should be noted that these sessions were called throughout the reign of Elizabeth and sat all over the county. They followed the procedures of ordinary courts and possessed plenary power to dispose of criminal cases by issuing summonses, ordering officials to be present and jurors to be impanelled; while at the same time they were arresting, arraigning, indicting, trying, sentencing, and punishing defendants. These special commissions of *oyer* and *terminer* (unlike the general ones issued to Assize judges which granted authority to *try* all suspects) empowered the Commissioners to deal with a specifically named wrongdoer, in some respects hinting on the surface at being judicial bills of attainder, if such loose application of the term is allowed. According to this procedure, John Morgan was tried for barratry in 1564[39]; Thomas Sherwood for assault in a church yard in 1599[40]; John Leighton for burglary in 1567[41]; Thomas Winkfield for murder in 1599[42]; and Hugh Barker for sedition in 1601.[43] These cases, it should be noted, spanned the second half of the sixteenth century and ranged from minor misdemeanor to sedition.

Ad hoc sessions of *oyer* and *terminer* might suggest that the judicial system was readily susceptible to manipulation by powerful local personages who could call special sittings at their pleasure. Hugh Barker's case lends credence to this supposition. Barker was scheduled to appear at the Assizes, but 10 days prior to their opening he was tried before a special tribunal composed of leading county gentry. Ominous as this appears at first, further investigation proves that they were not such dangerous threats to established judicial authority as one might imagine. In the first place, they were infrequently held. More important, the central courts kept a watchful eye on them; all the cases mentioned above, for instance,

[39] P.R.O. K.B.9 637I/46.

[40] P.R.O. K.B.9 704II/244.

[41] P.R.O. K.B.9 615/1.

[42] P.R.O. K.B.9 6141/43–47.

[43] P.R.O. K.B.9 7111/18.

were "appealed" (literally removed into the court of Queen's Bench by a writ of *certiorari*), though unfortunately no record of the disposition of these appeals has been located.

Another bulwark against arbitrary proceedings was, however, the surprising amount of knowledge criminal defendants had of their legal rights, an awareness which at least some suspects had and one which, it seems, most JPs respected when faced with it. Two cases illustrate this point very clearly. In 1578, Sir Thomas Lucas, JP, several other officials, including a constable, came to the home of George Dibney in Colchester and asked permission to search his house for seditious libels.[44] Dibney demanded to know by what authority they came. Lucas answered, by the authority of the Commission of the Peace, but Dibney would accept no such vague basis for invading the privacy of his home. Sir Thomas then replied that they were credibly informed by certain individuals that Dibney had the libels in his house. Again, not good enough for Dibney—he demanded to know who it was that reported such lies. Lucas told him and Dibney angrily retorted that the man who informed against him was well known to be a knave and warned Sir Thomas sarcastically to avoid the evil informer's company, protesting that he thought the justice had better judgement than to rely on such an ill-famed man's word. Lucas was angry and forced his way into the entry way of the house just past the door and threatened to come all the way in. Dibney at this point demanded to know the names of those who had come so that he could sue them for searching his house without a proper warrant, reminding them all that the last group of officials who tried to invade the sanctity of his home were heavily fined in the Queen's court and severely dealt with by her Privy Council. Sir Thomas and his men backed off, responding to Dibney's right to keep them out without the proper papers—presumably a formal warrant to search the house based upon reasonable grounds.

Dibney's case might appear a weak one to point out in general defendants' awareness of their rights. After all, Dibney was presumably an educated man who had precedent to back up his demands. But his is not the only case of its type on record. On another occasion, two parish constables, upon hearing that some matters in a sector of the town where poor people lived were "much needful and worthy to be amended," went there to find out the trouble. In the course of their search they came upon Newcombe's house. Finding neither him nor his wife at home, the constables proceeded to search the house anyway. Later they told Newcombe they had done so, to which he angrily replied "What have you to do to search my house. You shall not come there. I am as honest as the best of you

[44] E.R.O. *Morant MS* 46.

all."[45] No record of whether the constables were penalized remains, but Newcombe's indignation, coming from a man in the lower levels of society, clearly demonstrates an awareness that should not be overlooked. On the other hand, it would not do to overestimate the knowledge of those who came before the courts, charged with crime, and the effect it had on the system. The upper classes still ran the courts and, in the end, the fairness of the judicial system rested more on gentlemen's committment to due process than to the awareness of poor people in the county that they had rights which protected them from arbitrary treatment. To be sure, both played their part in making England's criminal justice system a relatively fair one and perhaps one which was too lax, or at least much more lenient for its time in history than we have been willing to admit previously. In Spain, for example, there were apparently no defendant's rights. The local lord had total judicial power.[46]

Much energy was wasted and efficiency lost in maintaining this quagmire of parochial and special jurisdictions, and in catering to notions of due process especially since both individuals and institutions jealously guarded their "liberties." The Bishop of London sharply reminded secular courts that they had no business meddling in cases cognizable in his court.[47] Colchester's powerful recorder and patron, Sir Francis Walsingham, on several occasions told county officials to keep out of Colchester's affairs,[48] and Sir William Petre threatened to fine anyone a heavy £5 who dared to initiate a lawsuit elsewhere before coming first to his manor court at Ingatestone for preliminary screening.[49] Petre's order is an extremely important document, because it asserted that he had original and potentially exclusive jurisdiction over *all* tenants (presumably that included freeholders as well as lease and copy holders) and *all* cases, civil and criminal. For these reasons it is well worth quoting in full:

> No tenant of the manor or residing within the precincts of the view shall at any time hereafter implead or call in law any other tenant or resident for any matter of cause before that he has warned the lord of this manor . . . so that he may know his will, with the intention that the lord may determine the cause in controversy and make an end thereof, if he is able and so wishes; and if the lord is not able or does not wish to determine the said cause and make an end thereof in due time, then the plaintiff may commence his action and have his remedy elsewhere.

The Mildmays laid claim to even vaster powers for their manor of Writtle. They alleged total exemption from the Quarter Sessions jurisdiction,

[45] E.R.O. Q/SR 4/14.

[46] I am indebted to Professor Michael Weisser for this information, which he found during the course of his study of sixteenth-century Spain.

[47] E.R.O. *Morant MS* 45/75.

[48] P.R.O. A.P.C. 27 January 1576.

[49] E.R.O. D/DP M99 folio 13.

and though the claim was denied, the Writtle constables, in concluding their presentment at one court session early in the seventeenth century, brazenly vowed that "all other matters . . . we present at the court leet holden in the manor of Writtle."[50] A late seventeenth-century steward of Avesley manor looked back wistfully to early Elizabethan days when "for their pains . . . about their honest presentments and care of reformation of abuse" they had had a peaceful manor, that is, when the leet was active.[51]

Defiant language fulminating from the mouths of powerful personages like the Bishop of London, a member of the Privy Council and a prestigious local magnate, carried a good deal of influence and indicates that jurisdictional definition based on rational operation was not a total reality. It also suggests that attempts were being made to make it so—the Bishop, Sir Francis Walsingham, Sir William Petre, the Mildmays, and others would not have complained had not their rivals been defying them. It is striking, as well as ironic, that in these jurisdictional disputes it was the county Quarter Sessions that was attempting to encroach upon more parochial and traditional institutions—the manor, the Church, and the boroughs—and that the efforts were being made by men like the Petres, Mildmays, and others who resented the intrusion when it concerned their own private domains. An undated petition to the bailiffs of Colchester reveals how successful the county was in making headway in breaking through this cake of custom in order to bring more judicial territory under its control:

> The bailiffs and sheriff of Essex upon mere process without warrant . . . do arrest and imprison diverse persons as well freemen as other inhabitants of this town [Colchester]. We therefore humbly pray that all such bailiffs as shall hereafter dare to make such infringements may be prosecuted and that the rights of the town be vindicated.[52]

Love of spectacle and devotion to ritual was one part of what is simplistically called the Elizabethan mind—it was a part that looked back in time for its source. Another part, the love of detail, the urge to record and to preserve for posterity, is equally simplistically referred to as part of the modern mind. But both the use of spectacle and enhanced detailed record keeping served a critical purpose. They reflected the growing demands placed upon the law as an instrument of social control in a society where the population was growing, where the relationship between men, especially those prone to crime, was increasingly based on cash and not on personal ties, where there was a shrinking supply of food for these

[50] E.R.O. Q/SR 273/35.
[51] E.R.O. D/DTh M12.
[52] E.R.O. *Morant MS* 45/56.

rootless, landless people, and where at the same time the price of mere survival was above their heads much of the time, making acquisition of food, goods, or money through illegal means the only road to survival. A cycle was involved in the legal system. The institutions were at hand and seemed to be working; thus they were used. As the law was used to preserve social order, the machinery became larger and had to be formalized. In becoming formalized, it became both more public and more effective, which in turn enhanced its respect and its use.

It is difficult to assess the elements that went into making this process begin—how much was due to the men like Petre and Mildmay and the host of lesser men who devoted their skills and their time to law enforcement, how much was due to the industrious clerks and their staffs who brought to law machinery a new rationalization, or how much was due to society's changing attitude toward law and order. But one thing is certain: They all combined with the pressure of a growing army of landless laborers who threatened the little bit of food and goods that their fellow laborers owned or the abundance of it that their better-off neighbors stashed away, which helped produce a revolution in thought and procedure, and the emergence of a criminal court system which has survived almost intact to the present day.

CONCLUSION

THE LARGER PICTURE

Dissecting the statistics of crime and reconstructing the system of criminal justice in Elizabethan Essex adds another dimension to the enlarging contours of our knowledge of early modern society. The bulk of this study has shown that early modern criminals were drawn largely from the ranks of landless laborers and that theft was the crime for which they were most frequently prosecuted. Furthermore, we know that society as a whole grew less tolerant of lawbreaking, at least within this segment in society where workers became less personally tied to masters and more inclined to break the law to get the food they needed to survive. Moreover, we now know that the machinery used to prosecute these growing numbers of defendants, though medieval in origin, was bureaucratized, rationalized, and staffed with more and more competent personnel so that society's hardening attitude toward lawbreaking could be translated into reality. But the meaning of these developments and events is not limited to Essex-county England during the reign of Elizabeth alone. And though we warned against drawing conclusions about a whole country from one community we should not fall into the equally dangerous error of viewing Essex in a vacuum.

The shifts in crime and the administration of justice in Essex illustrate only a portion of a larger story about early modern society. Movements beyond the county's borders were going on, movements that must be considered in order to avoid too narrow a view of crime and justice in Essex county. Thus do we turn from Essex county to the national and even international arena of which it was a part.

Royal will and national trade, deeper if subtler demographic and economic shifts in the whole country, and even the great transformations occurring in Western Europe during the sixteenth century ultimately shaped the configuration of crime and the concept of law and order in Elizabethan Essex. The effects of these developments have not been, and only with great difficulty might they ever be, reduced to statistical correlation coefficients. Connections between events in the larger world and the degree of their impact on the number of crimes in the county can, at this point, only be determined by inferences based on proximity in time and space: associations and relationships, for example, between bureaucratic innovations at Westminster and concurrent law enforcement (administrative) improvements in Chelmsford, or between the trend in food prices in England and the contemporaneous number of crimes in Essex. What happened in the county, then, was intimately related to national and European events and developments, but it cannot be measured with statistical precision.

Royal government was one example of this connection. Elizabethan England was a much governed country. The Queen, her temperament ranging from that of a doting mother to that of a carping, childless, husbandless old maid, made close royal supervision of local affairs inevitable. Efficient execution of her surveillance was assured by bureaucratizing the Crown's agencies. A clerk and his staff was created, and a minute book and regularly scheduled meetings were introduced into the Privy Council. Careers of such lackluster men as Sir Walter Mildmay (his equally dull cousins were managing Essex county) whose administrative abilities were recognized by every monarch from Henry VIII to Elizabeth, proved both the permanence of the Tudor bureaucracy and its acknowledged value in running sixteenth-century government. A government resting upon so firm an administrative foundation was able not only to withstand the strong ideological shocks of the period, but also to intensify its active participation in ruling the countryside. And rule it did. The Queen and her counsellors egregiously exploited the power they had at their command. Lord Treasurer Burghley of England and Secretary Sir Francis Walsingham, for example, were frequently involved in Essex affairs. As Lord Lieutenant, Burghley of Essex can be seen ordering parish constables' behavior checked, scrutinizing the list of names on the Queen's loan of 1589, and giving testimony about highway obstruction in the county. Sir Francis as Recorder of Colchester, picked candidates for MP, chastised the borough for unruliness, and true to his reputation as secret service director, actively participated in ferreting out libelers in the town. No more eloquent example exists of how extensive Elizabethan government was, however, than the power the Queen held in theory and exercised in person over the appointment of JPs. No local gentleman, no matter how much he may have wanted to be in it, was entitled as a matter of right to be in the Commission of Peace. He was there solely by royal sufferance. More than one country gentleman found this out to his sorrow, as for example when the Queen threw several Essex men off the bench for their Roman Catholic leanings in 1569. The intrusive policies and direct intervention of central government in local affairs, especially since Essex was so close to Westminster, were bound to have an effect on the country's life. To link the improvement of government at court to the extension of law enforcement in Essex, therefore, is eminently plausible, if not subject to conclusive proof. Other parallels are striking and support this contention. Thicker parliament and plea rolls in London matched fatter Quarter Sessions Rolls and Assize files for Essex. Regularly scheduled Privy Council meetings at Westminster equalled routinized local court sessions in Chelmsford, and central government bureaucracy was mirrored in the Clerk of Assize, the Clerk of the Peace, and their staffs.

The spread of active government and the proliferation of a burgeoning bureaucracy created additional places for men in public life. Fortunately, the ranks from whence they sprang grew apace with the need for their services. The universities and the Inns of Court were invaded by waxing numbers of students who were learning skills that suit them for careers in government. A new philosophy of education stressed the *usefulness* of schools that were called upon to train civil servants as well as (perhaps even instead of) priests and scholars. The secularization of education and the practical bent that learning took did not change, however, the essentially traditional world view that society rested upon order and degree, not liberty and equality. The latter two were largely unknown, or, if known, they were thought to be highly dangerous ideas in the sixteenth century. Such were the aspirations, if not the reality, of society summed up by Shakespeare's lines: "Take but degree away, untune that string/And hark! what discord follows."

Preaching the ideas of obedience to superiors and the duty to preserve degree was bound to have its influence on the new governors of Essex society, and their especial zeal in rooting out lawlessness is understandable in the context of the dominating philosophy of the age. This is especially likely, since most Essex JPs and preachers went off to Cambridge for a spell, and the JPs added to their college education a stint at the Inns of Court where they were sure to imbibe a strong dose of the prevailing pedagogy and social philosophy. But philosophers rarely become kings, and though ideas may be the standard of the community's stability, they reflect rather than determine social reality. Deeper social forces were playing upon the delicate crime indices—and many of these forces were in flux throughout the Tudor period, particularly during the reign of Elizabeth.

Even as early as the sixteenth century, comtemporaries claimed that the roots of crime lay in the soil of an unstable society. Vagabonds and criminals, they believed, were stamped from the same mold. Idleness bred poverty, and poverty spawned crime according to contemporary commentators—English and continental alike. Criminals, they claimed, stemmed from the poverty-stricken ranks of decayed gentlemen, uprooted peasants, ruined craftsmen, unpaid soldiers, and unemployed or under-paid laborers. Of course, particular crises played their part in creating peaks in the graph of crime. Famine caused the figures to skyrocket, dramatically indicating that basic survival was the most that many ordinary people could hope for. This was especially true during the series of bad harvests in the 1590s. But the peaks in crime only punctuate a rising record of deviance, which leads one to the conclusion that there was more to the problem than periodic famine. In England during the late sixteenth century, the pressures of a rising population forced a readjustment in the exploitation of resources, mainly in the direction of increasing the country's food supply. The readjustment was not completely successful, even though it spurred on the commercialization of agriculture and increased the country's wealth generally. In part this was because the distribution of wealth was so uneven. Only those who could sell on the expanding and ever higher priced food market made large profits. These were the more enterprising landholders drawn from the ranks of gentry, yeomen, and some peasants. The material improvement of their lives is clearly related to the steadily declining numbers of them found among felons' ranks. But at the bottom of the scale the situation differed markedly. Wage earners suffered terribly due to two factors—and here is the heart of the crime problem in Essex. The rising population contributed to a labor surplus, driving wages down while the crisis in the food supply, especially with the heavy added drain caused by the proximity of London and Colchester, sent food prices skyrocketing.

Rising crime figures, seen from this perspective, reflect more rather than better law enforcement, and a philosophy and world view based on hierarchy, order, and degree. Hardening community attitudes toward lawlessness, swelling ranks of law-enforcement personnel, and revamped machinery of justice have at least two meanings. They not only mean more and better records of crime, but they also represent a change in society's response to a real increase in deviance. The development of Elizabethan machinery of justice and the crimes it recorded, therefore, measure the achievement and the cost of one preindustrial community's effort to cope with the problem of feeding and disciplining a growing population, an accomplishment that should not be measured by the extensive commercialization of agriculture and general increase in wealth alone. The tremendous success represented by the development of sophisticated instruments of law enforcement, the recruitment of competent judicial personnel, and in general the wide community participation in keeping the peace divulge another dimension of the achievement that the subsistence crisis fostered. But that such a highly developed criminal justice administration came into being in Elizabethan Essex is ample proof that a great price was paid for producing more food. The discontinuity that these efforts generated can be measured in part by the number of crimes committed by those who did not share in the general growth in prosperity and who had no stake in the land or the new uses to which it was put. Just as the courts and the law, the policemen and jurors, the clerks and the justices reflect the crowning achievement of society in coping with social discontinuity, the high prices and low wages, the crimes committed and the punishments suffered by ordinary men and women in Essex mirror the pain that was attendant on the beginning of the great transformation of England from a preindustrial to a modern society.

APPENDIX I

CRIME DISTRIBUTION IN ELIZABETHAN ESSEX

The two tables in this appendix elaborate the information included in Chapter I. They are more detailed in one respect: They break down violent felony as a group into its component offenses. In Chapter I, most conclusions are based on combining all violent felonies and treating them as a whole. These tables sort out and correct any distortions which such grouping created. They render the movement in crime trends smoother, both among individual violent felonies and the three categories of felony used in the text. This is achieved by 5-year moving averages. Such computation smooths out any distortion which an individual year might create in a simple 5-year total (compare Tables 1 and 2 in Chapter I). Five-year averages are based on figures which take the first five years in the period (1559–1563) and average them, then take the group of 5 years beginning with 1560 (1560–1564) and so on through the whole 45-year period. The tables included here should help the reader both to categorize more specifically trends in violent felonies and to see a rather more blended view of the trends in all types of felony for the period. At the same time, however, caution is required so that one is not misled by this bunching, a distortion which Table 1 in Chapter I corrects.

TABLE A-1 *Violent Crimes—Five-Year Moving Averages (1558–1603)*

Murder	Homi-cide	Suicide	Infan-ticide	Rape	Group total
.6	1.4	1.2	.6	.6	4.4
.8	1.0	1.6	.8	.6	4.8
.8	.2	1.8	1.0	—	3.8
.4	.2	1.8	1.2	.2	3.8
1.0	.4	2.6	1.2	.4	5.6
1.0	.8	1.4	.8	.6	4.6
.8	.8	1.4	.6	.6	4.2
.8	1.2	3.0	.4	.6	6.0
1.2	1.2	3.8	.2	.4	6.8
.6	1.0	3.0	.2	.2	5.0
.6	.8	3.0	.2	.2	4.8
.8	1.2	4.6	.8	.2	7.6
.8	1.2	4.6	.6	.4	7.6
.2	1.0	3.8	.6	1.0	6.6
.2	2.4	3.6	.6	1.0	7.8
.2	2.6	3.6	.6	.8	7.8
.2	.3	1.6	.4	1.2	3.7
.6	3.4	1.2	1.0	1.8	8.0
.6	5.4	1.6	1.0	2.6	11.2
.8	4.4	1.4	1.2	3.2	11.0
1.0	5.0	1.6	1.4	4.0	13.0
.8	5.0	2.4	1.6	3.4	13.2
.4	5.0	2.4	1.0	3.0	11.8
.8	3.6	2.8	1.6	2.8	11.6
.8	3.2	3.4	1.4	1.2	10.0
1.2	3.2	3.4	1.2	.8	9.8
1.2	3.2	2.6	1.2	.6	8.8
1.4	3.4	2.0	1.2	.8	8.8
1.0	4.2	1.4	.6	1.2	8.4
1.2	4.6	1.0	.8	1.2	8.8
.6	5.4	.8	.8	1.0	8.6
.6	5.8	1.6	.8	1.2	10.0
.4	5.4	1.4	1.2	1.2	9.6
.4	4.0	1.2	1.0	.6	7.2
—	4.4	1.8	1.0	.6	7.8
—	3.4	2.4	1.0	.4	7.2
.6	2.4	2.8	.8	.2	6.8
1.2	2.2	3.4	.4	.4	7.6
2.0	2.2	3.8	1.0	.4	9.4
2.4	4.8	3.2	1.2	.4	12.0
2.4	4.6	2.2	1.2	.4	10.8

TABLE A-2 *Common-Law Felonies Five-Year Moving Averages (1558–1603)*

Violent crimes	Body and goods	Theft
4.4	10.8	15.2
4.8	6.8	12.2
3.8	7.4	10.2
3.8	8.4	11.6
5.6	12.2	15.4
4.6	12.6	15.0
4.2	11.8	20.4
6.0	12.2	27.6
6.8	11.4	28.4
5.0	8.6	30.4
4.8	7.6	35.2
7.6	9.2	43.6
7.6	8.8	44.4
6.6	9.4	46.0
7.8	11.2	46.8
7.8	10.6	47.6
3.1	13.4	40.8
8.0	15.6	45.6
10.2	16.0	49.2
11.0	15.4	59.4
13.0	15.2	57.8
13.2	11.8	61.4
11.8	12.4	62.2
11.6	13.4	61.2
10.0	17.0	56.8
9.8	20.8	66.2
8.8	23.2	72.0
8.8	22.4	78.6
8.4	20.2	97.6
8.8	16.0	91.0
8.6	12.4	89.2
9.2	10.8	87.0
9.6	10.6	84.6
7.2	9.6	74.8
7.8	15.0	120.6
7.2	25.4	138.8
6.8	24.2	130.0
7.6	25.2	136.2
9.4	31.4	134.8
12.0	25.4	101.4
10.8	20.4	73.8

APPENDIX II

DISPOSITION OF CASES

Gaol delivery calendars were schedules made up by the Clerk of Assize and his staff which summarized the dispositions of cases at Assizes. They add an important dimension to our knowledge of court decisions because they often explain why no sentence was given in an indictment—usually because the prisoner did not appear. Even more important, they give the total numbers of persons hanged rather than the number of hanging sentences. Most important of all, however, they tell us how many prisoners were freed because no one came to prosecute them. The conclusions drawn from these data are included in Chapter II.

TABLE A-3 *Summary of Extant Gaol Delivery Calendars in P.R.O. Asz. 35/3–45*

Year	Hanged	Freed on procla-mation	Total in calendar
1582H[a]	11	37	72
1582T[b]	—	34	74
1584H	7	6	53
1584T	7	15	31
1585H	11	19	67
1585T	—	24	68
1587H	—	39	47
1587T	17	19	59
1588H	11	15	66
1588T	—	10	48
1590H	—	24	74
1590T	11	27	67
1592T	10	17	47
1593H	—	13	65
1593T	12	13	47
Total	97	312	885

[a] Hilary Term (Winter Assizes).
[b] Trinity Term (Summer Assizes).

APPENDIX III

CRIME AND PUNISHMENT IN ELIZABETHAN ESSEX

The 40 tables that follow are divided into four categories. Tables A-4 to A-14 show the numbers of accused offenders and the punishments, if any, they received. Tables A-15 to A-23 set out the number of *offenses* as opposed to *offenders* and disposition of the cases. Tables A-24 to A-34 break down the offenders by social status and show the distribution of types of felony that the various groups in society committed or were charged with committing. Tables A-35 to A-42 again plot social status of offenders, but instead of crossing status with crime, the suspected offender's status is crossed with the punishment, if any, received.

TABLE A-4 *Crime and Punishment (1559–1562)*

	Guilty	Benefit of clergy or pregnancy	Unknown	Acquitted	Row total
Violent crimes	1[a]	2	2	9	14
	7.1[b]	14.3	14.3	64.3	12.8
	3.7[c]	11.1	9.5	20.9	
	.9[d]	1.8	1.8	8.3	
Robbery and burglary	17	5	11	11	44
	38.6	11.4	25.0	25.0	40.4
	63.0	27.8	52.4	25.6	
	15.6	4.6	10.1	10.1	
Theft	9	11	8	23	51
	17.6	21.6	15.7	45.1	46.8
	33.3	61.1	38.1	53.5	
	8.3	10.1	7.3	21.1	
Column total	27	18	21	43	109
	24.8	16.5	19.3	39.4	100.0

Key for Tables 1–13 and 23–38:
[a] Total number of persons.
[b] Row percentage.
[c] Column percentage.
[d] Percentage of total matrix.

TABLE A-5 *Crime and Punishment (1563–1567)*

	Guilty	Benefit of clergy or pregnancy	Unknown	Acquitted	Row total
Violent crimes	5	3	1	9	18
	27.8	16.7	5.6	50.0	11.9
	10.2	7.9	12.5	16.1	
	3.3	2.0	.7	6.0	
Robbery and Burglary	10	7	3	11	31
	32.3	22.6	9.7	35.5	20.5
	20.4	18.4	37.5	19.6	
	6.6	4.6	2.0	7.3	
Theft	34	28	4	36	102
	33.3	27.5	3.9	35.3	67.5
	69.4	73.7	50.0	64.3	
	22.5	18.5	2.6	23.8	
Column total	49	38	8	56	151
	32.5	25.2	5.3	37.1	100.0

TABLE A-6 *Crime and Punishment (1568–1572)*

	Guilty	Benefit of clergy or pregnancy	Unknown	Acquitted	Row total
Violent crimes	6 27.3 12.0 4.1	4 18.2 8.2 2.8	6 27.3 75.0 4.1	6 27.3 15.8 4.1	22 15.2
Robbery and burglary	7 46.7 14.0 4.8	2 13.3 4.1 1.4	0 0.0 0.0 0.0	6 40.0 15.8 4.1	15 10.3
Theft	37 34.3 74.0 25.5	43 39.8 87.8 29.7	2 1.9 25.0 1.4	26 24.1 68.4 17.9	108 74.5
Column total	50 34.5	49 33.8	8 5.5	38 26.2	145 100.0

TABLE A-7 *Crime and Punishment (1573–1577)*

	Guilty	Benefit of clergy or pregnancy	Unknown	Acquitted	Row total
Violent crimes	4 44.4 9.3 2.6	0 0.0 0.0 0.0	3 33.3 11.1 2.0	2 22.2 4.4 1.3	9 6.0
Robbery and burglary	13 36.1 30.2 8.6	6 16.7 16.7 4.0	11 30.6 40.7 7.3	6 16.7 13.3 4.0	36 23.8
Theft	26 24.5 60.5 17.2	30 28.3 83.3 19.9	13 12.3 48.1 8.6	37 34.9 82.2 24.5	106 70.2
Column total	43 28.5	36 23.8	27 17.9	45 29.8	151 100.0

TABLE A-8 *Crime and Punishment (1578–1582)*

	Guilty	Benefit of clergy or pregnancy	Unknown	Acquitted	Row total
Violent crimes	11 37.9 14.3 4.3	4 13.8 4.7 1.6	6 17.2 10.9 2.0	9 31.0 18.4 3.5	29 11.3
Robbery and burglary	22 43.1 28.6 8.6	10 19.6 11.8 3.9	13 25.5 28.9 5.1	6 11.8 12.2 2.3	51 19.8
Theft	44 24.9 57.1 17.1	71 40.1 83.5 27.6	28 15.8 62.2 10.9	34 19.2 69.4 13.2	177 68.9
Column total	77 30.0	85 33.1	46 17.9	49 19.1	257 100.0

TABLE A-9 *Crime and Punishment (1583–1587)*

	Guilty	Benefit of clergy or pregnancy	Unknown	Acquitted	Row total
Violent crimes	11 30.6 14.7 2.7	5 13.9 3.4 1.2	7 19.4 9.2 1.7	13 36.1 11.3 3.1	36 8.7
Robbery and burglary	13 32.5 17.3 3.1	9 22.5 6.1 2.2	9 10.0 5.3 1.0	14 35.0 12.2 3.4	40 9.7
Theft	51 15.1 68.0 12.3	134 39.6 90.5 32.4	65 19.2 85.5 15.7	88 26.0 76.5 21.3	338 81.6
Column total	75 18.1	148 35.7	76 18.4	115 27.8	414 100.0

TABLE A-10 *Crime and Punishment (1588–1592)*

	Guilty	Benefit of clergy or pregnancy	Unknown	Acquitted	Row total
Violent crimes	6	5	5	6	22
	27.3	22.7	22.7	27.3	6.0
	9.1	3.7	7.2	6.1	
	1.6	1.4	1.4	1.6	
Robbery and burglary	25	9	15	13	62
	40.3	14.5	24.2	21.0	16.8
	37.9	6.7	21.7	13.3	
	6.8	2.4	4.1	3.5	
Theft	35	121	49	79	284
	12.3	42.6	17.3	27.8	77.2
	53.0	89.6	71.0	80.6	
	9.5	32.9	13.3	21.5	
Column total	66	135	69	98	368
	17.9	36.7	18.7	26.6	100.0

TABLE A-11 *Crime and Punishment (1593–1597)*

	Guilty	Benefit of clergy or pregnancy	Unknown	Acquitted	Row total
Violent crimes	9	4	13	5	31
	29.0	12.9	41.9	16.1	6.1
	5.3	3.8	16.3	3.3	
	1.8	.8	2.6	1.0	
Robbery and burglary	16	6	2	8	32
	50.0	18.7	6.3	25.0	6.3
	9.4	5.7	2.5	5.3	
	3.2	1.2	.4	1.6	
Theft	145	95	65	137	442
	32.8	21.5	14.7	31.0	87.5
	85.3	90.5	81.3	91.3	
	28.7	18.8	12.9	27.1	
Column total	170	105	80	150	505
	33.7	20.8	15.8	29.7	100.0

TABLE A-12 *Crime and Punishment (1598–1602)*

	Guilty	Benefit of clergy or pregnancy	Unknown	Acquitted	Row total
	7	2	9	7	25
Violent	28.0	8.0	36.0	28.0	7.4
crimes	7.6	2.1	13.2	8.4	
	2.1	.6	2.7	2.1	
Robbery	33	6	10	20	69
and	47.8	8.7	14.5	29.0	20.5
burglary	35.9	6.4	14.7	24.1	
	9.8	1.8	3.	5.9	
	52	86	49	56	243
Theft	21.4	35.4	20.2	23.0	72.1
	56.5	91.5	72.1	67.5	
	15.4	25.5	14.5	16.6	
Column	92	94	68	83	337
total	27.3	27.9	20.2	24.6	100.0

TABLE A-13[a] *Crime and Punishment (1668–1713)*

	Guilty	Benefit of clergy or pregnancy	Unknown	Acquitted	Row total
	6	4	3	8	21
Violent	28.6	19.0	14.3	38.1	18.4
crimes	16.2	12.5	15.8	30.8	
	5.3	3.5	2.6	7.0	
Robbery	13	4	6	4	27
and	48.1	14.8	22.2	14.8	23.7
burglary	35.1	12.5	31.6	15.4	
	11.4	3.5	5.3	3.5	
	18	24	10	14	66
Theft	27.3	36.4	15.2	21.2	57.9
	48.6	75.0	52.6	53.8	
	15.8	21.1	8.8	12.3	
Column	37	32	19	26	114
total	32.5	28.1	16.7	22.8	100.0

[a] This table is based on a sample drawn from every fourth year from 1668 to 1713 and is included only for purposes of comparison.

TABLE A-14 *Murder*

Year	Hanged	Guilty	Reprieve	Clergy	Unknown	Pardon	Acquitted
1559	—	—	—	—	—	—	—
1560	—	—	—	—	2	—	1
1561	—	—	—	—	2	—	1
1562	—	—	—	—	—	—	—
1563	—	—	—	—	—	—	—
1564	—	—	—	—	1	—	—
1565	—	—	—	—	—	—	—
1566	—	1	—	—	—	—	—
1567	—	—	—	1	2	—	—
1568	—	—	—	—	—	—	—
1569	—	—	—	—	—	—	—
1570	—	—	—	—	—	—	—
1571	—	1	—	—	—	—	2
1572	—	—	—	—	—	—	—
1573	—	—	—	—	—	—	—
1574	—	—	—	—	1	—	—
1575	—	—	—	—	—	—	—
1576	—	—	—	—	—	—	—
1577	—	—	—	—	—	—	—
1578	—	—	—	—	—	—	—
1579	—	—	—	1	—	—	—
1580	—	—	—	—	2	—	—
1581	—	—	—	—	—	—	—
1582	—	—	—	—	1	—	—
1583	—	—	—	—	—	—	1
1584	—	—	—	—	—	—	—
1585	—	—	—	—	—	—	—
1586	—	1	—	—	1	—	—
1587	—	—	—	—	1	—	—
1588	—	3	—	—	—	—	—
1589	—	—	—	—	—	—	—
1590	1	—	—	—	—	—	—
1591	—	—	—	—	—	—	—
1592	—	—	1	—	—	—	1
1593	—	—	—	—	—	—	—
1594	—	—	—	—	—	—	—
1595	—	—	—	—	—	—	—
1596	—	—	—	—	—	—	—
1597	—	—	—	—	—	—	—
1598	—	—	—	—	—	—	—
1599	—	—	—	—	3	—	—
1600	—	—	—	2	—	—	1
1601	1	—	—	—	1	—	1
1602	—	—	1	—	1	—	—
1603	—	—	—	—	—	—	—

TABLE A-15 *Manslaughter*

Year	Hanged	Guilty	Reprieve	Clergy	Unknown	Pardon	Acquitted
1559	—	—	—	—	—	—	2
1560	—	—	1	—	—	—	—
1561	—	—	—	1	—	—	—
1562	—	—	—	—	—	—	—
1563	—	—	—	—	—	—	—
1564	—	—	—	—	—	—	—
1565	—	—	—	—	—	—	—
1566	—	—	—	—	—	1	—
1567	—	—	—	—	1	—	—
1568	—	—	—	—	1	—	1
1569	—	—	—	—	—	—	—
1570	—	1	—	—	—	—	1
1571	—	—	—	—	—	—	1
1572	—	—	—	—	—	—	—
1573	—	—	—	—	1	—	—
1574	—	1	—	—	1	—	—
1575	—	—	—	1	1	—	—
1576	—	—	—	—	—	—	—
1577	—	—	—	—	4	—	3
1578	—	—	—	1	1	—	—
1579	—	—	—	—	2	—	2
1580	—	—	—	4	—	—	—
1581	—	2	—	—	4	1	3
1582	—	—	—	1	—	—	—
1583	—	—	—	—	1	—	4
1584	1	2	—	1	—	—	—
1585	—	—	—	—	—	1	2
1586	—	1	—	1	—	—	1
1587	—	—	—	—	—	—	—
1588	—	—	—	—	1	—	5
1589	—	—	—	1	2	—	—
1590	1	—	—	—	3	—	—
1591	—	1	—	1	3	—	2
1592	1	—	—	1	—	—	—
1593	1	—	1	2	3	3	—
1594	—	1	1	—	1	—	2
1595	—	—	—	1	1	—	1
1596	—	—	—	—	—	—	—
1597	1	—	—	—	3	—	—
1598	2	—	—	1	2	—	—
1599	—	—	—	—	—	—	—
1600	—	—	—	1	—	—	—
1601	—	—	—	—	—	—	—
1602	1	—	1	8	5	—	2
1603	—	—	—	1	2	—	1

TABLE A-16 *Infanticide*

Year	Hanged	Guilty	Reprieve	Clergy	Unknown	Pardon	Acquitted
1559	—	—	—	—	—	—	—
1560	—	—	—	—	—	—	—
1561	—	—	—	—	—	—	1
1562	—	—	—	—	—	—	—
1563	2	—	—	—	—	—	—
1564	—	—	—	—	—	—	—
1565	—	—	—	—	1	—	—
1566	—	—	—	—	—	—	2
1567	—	—	—	—	—	—	—
1568	—	—	—	—	—	—	—
1569	—	—	—	—	—	—	—
1570	—	—	—	—	—	—	—
1571	—	—	—	—	1	—	—
1572	—	—	—	—	—	—	—
1573	—	—	—	—	—	—	—
1574	—	—	2	—	—	—	—
1575	—	—	—	—	—	—	—
1576	—	2	—	—	—	—	—
1577	—	—	—	—	—	—	—
1578	—	—	—	—	—	—	—
1579	—	—	—	—	1	—	—
1580	—	2	—	—	—	—	1
1581	—	—	—	—	—	—	1
1582	—	—	—	—	—	1	1
1583	1	—	—	—	—	—	1
1584	1	—	—	—	4	—	—
1585	—	—	—	—	—	—	—
1586	—	1	—	—	2	—	1
1587	—	—	—	—	—	—	—
1588	—	—	—	—	1	—	—
1589	—	—	1	—	—	—	—
1590	—	—	—	—	—	—	—
1591	—	1	—	—	—	—	—
1592	—	—	—	—	1	—	—
1593	1	—	—	—	—	—	—
1594	—	—	1	—	—	—	—
1595	—	—	—	1	—	—	1
1596	—	—	—	—	—	—	—
1597	1	—	—	—	—	—	—
1598	—	—	—	—	1	—	—
1599	—	—	—	—	—	—	—
1600	—	—	—	—	—	—	—
1601	1	—	—	—	—	—	2
1602	—	—	—	—	2	—	—
1603	—	—	—	—	—	—	1

TABLE A-17 *Suicide*

Year	Hanged	Guilty	Reprieve	Clergy	Unknown	Pardon	Acquitted
1559	—	—	—	—	—	—	—
1560	—	—	—	—	1	—	—
1561	—	—	—	—	—	—	—
1562	—	—	—	—	3	—	—
1563	—	—	—	—	2	—	—
1564	—	—	—	—	2	—	—
1565	—	—	—	—	2	—	—
1566	—	—	—	—	—	—	—
1567	—	—	—	—	7	—	—
1568	—	—	—	—	1	—	—
1569	—	—	—	—	2	—	—
1570	—	—	—	—	5	—	—
1571	—	—	—	—	4	—	—
1572	—	—	—	—	—	—	—
1573	—	—	—	—	1	—	—
1574	—	—	—	—	10	—	—
1575	—	—	—	—	5	—	—
1576	—	—	—	—	—	—	—
1577	—	—	—	—	2	—	—
1578	—	—	—	—	1	—	—
1579	—	—	—	—	—	—	—
1580	—	—	—	—	3	—	—
1581	—	—	—	—	2	—	—
1582	—	—	—	—	—	—	—
1583	—	—	—	—	3	—	—
1584	—	—	—	—	—	—	—
1585	—	—	—	—	3	—	—
1586	—	—	—	—	4	—	—
1587	—	—	—	—	3	—	—
1588	—	—	—	—	3	—	—
1589	—	—	—	—	—	—	—
1590	—	—	—	—	—	—	—
1591	—	—	—	—	1	—	—
1592	—	—	—	—	—	—	—
1593	—	—	—	—	2	—	—
1594	—	—	—	—	3	—	—
1595	—	—	—	—	—	—	—
1596	—	—	—	—	—	—	—
1597	—	—	—	—	4	—	—
1598	—	—	—	—	5	—	—
1599	—	—	—	—	5	—	—
1600	—	—	—	—	3	—	—
1601	—	—	—	—	2	—	—
1602	—	—	—	—	1	—	—
1603	—	—	—	—	—	—	—

TABLE A-18 *Sedition*

Year	Hanged	Guilty	Reprieve	Clergy	Unknown	Pardon	Acquitted
1559	—	—	—	—	—	—	—
1560	—	—	—	—	—	—	—
1561	—	—	—	—	—	—	—
1562	—	—	—	—	—	—	—
1563	—	—	—	—	—	—	—
1564	—	—	—	—	—	—	—
1565	—	—	—	—	—	—	—
1566	—	—	—	—	—	—	—
1567	—	—	—	—	—	—	—
1568	—	—	—	—	—	—	—
1569	—	—	—	—	—	—	—
1570	—	—	—	—	—	—	—
1571	—	—	—	—	—	—	—
1572	—	—	—	—	—	—	—
1573	—	—	—	—	—	—	—
1574	—	—	—	—	—	—	—
1575	—	—	—	—	—	—	—
1576	—	—	—	—	—	—	—
1577	—	—	—	—	—	—	—
1578	—	—	—	—	—	—	—
1579	—	—	—	—	—	—	—
1580	—	—	—	—	—	—	—
1581	1	—	—	—	—	—	—
1582	1	—	—	—	—	—	—
1583	—	—	—	—	—	—	—
1584	—	—	—	—	—	—	—
1585	—	—	—	—	—	—	—
1586	—	—	—	—	1	—	—
1587	—	—	—	—	—	—	—
1588	—	—	—	—	—	—	—
1589	—	—	—	—	—	—	—
1590	—	—	—	—	—	—	—
1591	—	—	—	—	—	—	—
1592	—	—	—	—	—	—	—
1593	—	—	—	—	—	—	—
1594	—	2	—	—	—	—	—
1595	—	—	—	—	—	—	—
1596	—	—	—	—	—	—	—
1597	—	—	—	—	1	—	—
1598	—	—	—	—	—	—	—
1599	—	—	—	—	—	—	—
1600	—	—	—	—	—	—	—
1601	—	—	—	—	—	—	—
1602	—	—	—	—	—	—	—
1603	—	—	—	—	—	—	—

TABLE A-19 *Sex Crimes*

Year	Hanged	Guilty	Reprieve	Clergy	Unknown	Pardon	Acquitted
1559	—	—	—	—	—	—	—
1560	—	—	—	—	—	—	3
1561	—	—	—	—	—	—	—
1562	—	—	—	—	—	—	—
1563	—	—	—	—	—	—	—
1564	—	—	—	—	—	—	—
1565	—	—	—	—	—	—	—
1566	—	1	—	—	—	—	—
1567	—	—	—	—	1	—	—
1568	—	—	—	—	1	—	—
1569	—	—	—	—	—	—	—
1570	—	—	—	—	—	—	—
1571	—	—	—	—	—	—	—
1572	—	—	—	—	3	—	—
1573	—	1	—	—	—	—	—
1574	—	—	—	—	—	—	—
1575	—	—	—	—	1	—	—
1576	—	2	—	—	1	—	—
1577	—	—	—	—	—	—	—
1578	—	—	—	—	—	—	—
1579	—	1	—	—	—	—	1
1580	—	3	—	—	1	—	—
1581	—	—	—	—	7	—	—
1582	—	—	—	—	1	—	2
1583	1	—	—	—	—	—	3
1584	—	—	—	—	—	—	1
1585	—	—	—	—	—	—	—
1586	—	—	—	—	—	—	1
1587	—	—	—	—	—	—	—
1588	—	—	—	—	—	—	—
1589	—	—	—	—	—	—	—
1590	—	—	—	—	—	—	1
1591	—	—	—	—	—	—	3
1592	—	—	—	—	—	—	—
1593	—	—	—	—	1	—	—
1594	—	—	—	—	1	—	—
1595	1	—	—	—	1	—	—
1596	—	—	—	—	—	—	—
1597	—	—	—	—	—	—	—
1598	—	—	—	—	—	—	—
1599	—	—	—	—	—	—	—
1600	1	—	—	—	—	—	1
1601	—	—	—	—	—	—	1
1602	—	—	—	—	—	—	—
1603	—	—	—	—	—	—	—

TABLE A-20 *Robbery*

Year	Hanged	Guilty	Reprieve	Clergy	Unknown	Pardon	Acquitted
1559	4	—	—	—	—	—	2
1560	—	—	—	—	—	—	3
1561	—	—	—	—	—	—	—
1562	—	—	—	—	—	—	—
1563	—	—	—	—	3	—	—
1564	—	3	—	1	1	—	3
1565	—	—	—	1	—	—	1
1566	—	—	—	1	—	—	1
1567	—	—	—	—	—	—	—
1568	2	2	—	—	1	—	3
1569	—	2	—	—	—	—	—
1570	—	—	—	—	1	2	—
1571	—	1	—	—	—	1	1
1572	—	—	—	—	—	—	—
1573	—	—	—	—	—	2	1
1574	—	2	1	1	—	1	7
1575	3	—	1	1	—	—	—
1576	2	—	2	—	—	—	—
1577	—	2	—	—	6	—	—
1578	—	—	—	2	—	—	1
1579	—	—	1	5	4	2	2
1580	—	—	—	—	—	—	—
1581	1	3	—	4	4	—	2
1582	1	—	—	—	3	—	1
1583	—	—	—	—	2	—	—
1584	—	1	—	1	—	—	2
1585	2	3	—	2	3	—	2
1586	—	3	1	2	—	1	7
1587	—	4	—	8	2	—	1
1588	—	4	1	—	2	—	1
1589	—	3	—	—	—	—	3
1590	3	—	—	—	6	—	—
1591	—	1	—	—	3	—	1
1592	—	—	—	—	—	—	—
1593	—	—	—	—	—	—	—
1594	—	—	—	—	4	—	—
1595	—	—	—	—	—	—	—
1596	—	—	—	3	—	—	—
1597	7	—	—	—	3	—	2
1598	8	—	—	2	8	—	—
1599	1	—	—	—	—	—	—
1600	1	3	—	—	2	—	6
1601	3	1	—	2	7	—	1
1602	1	—	—	—	2	—	2
1603	8	—	2	2	3	—	7

TABLE A-21 *Burglary*

Year	Hanged	Guilty	Reprieve	Clergy	Unknown	Pardon	Acquitted
1559	9	—	—	3	7	—	4
1560	—	—	—	1	—	—	—
1561	—	3	—	2	—	—	5
1562	—	—	—	—	—	—	—
1563	—	—	—	2	1	—	5
1564	—	—	—	—	—	—	1
1565	—	—	—	4	—	—	1
1566	—	3	—	1	5	—	4
1567	6	5	—	3	4	—	1
1568	—	—	—	—	3	—	2
1569	—	—	—	—	1	—	2
1570	—	1	—	3	1	—	1
1571	—	5	—	3	—	—	—
1572	—	—	—	—	5	—	—
1573	—	2	—	—	2	—	1
1574	—	—	—	—	—	—	—
1575	2	—	—	—	—	—	—
1576	—	4	—	—	2	—	4
1577	—	5	—	1	—	—	—
1578	—	2	—	—	—	—	—
1579	—	7	—	1	4	—	1
1580	—	3	—	4	6	—	5
1581	—	—	—	1	1	—	—
1582	1	1	—	3	—	—	—
1583	1	—	—	—	1	—	—
1584	—	3	—	1	1	—	1
1585	1	1	—	—	4	—	3
1586	—	3	—	—	2	—	2
1587	—	1	—	8	3	—	2
1588	7	—	4	1	—	—	3
1589	—	6	2	—	8	—	—
1590	2	—	—	—	4	—	2
1591	—	1	—	1	2	—	2
1592	4	—	1	2	1	—	—
1593	1	—	—	2	—	—	2
1594	—	6	—	1	1	—	4
1595	3	2	1	1	7	—	2
1596	—	—	—	1	—	—	1
1597	10	—	—	5	2	—	6
1598	18	3	—	1	9	—	9
1599	3	—	—	2	—	—	3
1600	3	2	—	—	—	—	4
1601	6	—	—	—	7	—	7
1602	6	—	—	1	—	—	3
1603	—	—	—	—	—	—	—

TABLE A-22 *Theft*

Year	Hanged	Guilty	Reprieve	Clergy	Unknown	Pardon	Acquitted
1559	2	—	—	6	6	1	2
1560	—	2	2	4	3	—	11
1561	—	3	—	2	5	—	11
1562	—	—	—	—	—	—	—
1563	7	—	1	2	1	2	3
1564	—	1	—	—	—	—	1
1565	—	3	—	—	6	—	1
1566	—	6	—	8	8	—	8
1567	—	—	1	3	6	4	5
1568	—	10	—	4	—	—	2
1569	Pressed	8	2	5	3	7	—
1570	—	10	3	21	—	—	12
1571	—	8	—	13	1	1	11
1572	—	—	—	5	18	—	6
1573	—	4	—	9	19	—	8
1574	21	—	—	8	14	—	25
1575	19	—	—	10	5	—	10
1576	19	—	—	11	9	1	12
1577	—	3	—	18	4	—	8
1578	—	19	—	8	15	—	2
1579	—	7	—	10	9	2	7
1580	—	14	1	29	14	—	6
1581	—	5	—	21	29	8	7
1582	5	11	3	37	5	—	23
1583	1	1	—	15	11	—	8
1584	1	5	—	16	6	—	25
1585	7	2	1	36	6	1	20
1586	—	6	—	13	27	—	19
1587	—	8	—	30	11	—	14
1588	11	2	1	36	10	1	22
1589	—	14	4	33	11	—	18
1590	7	1	1	25	40	—	27
1591	6	18	—	58	36	—	35
1592	1	—	—	16	5	—	6
1593	6	—	3	25	15	2	22
1594	—	19	—	16	16	—	20
1595	8	12	1	19	34	—	19
1596	12	8	1	46	26	—	19
1597	31	22	2	97	49	—	57
1598	20	10	—	83	33	3	16
1599	2	—	—	10	11	—	5
1600	16	32	—	25	32	—	15
1601	14	9	—	36	15	1	29
1602	12	1	8	14	33	3	16
1603	5	—	—	9	6	4	3

TABLE A-23 *Social Status and Crime (1558–1562)*

	Violent crimes	Robbery and burglary	Theft	Row total
Yeomen	5 19.2 41.7 4.8	19 73.1 43.2 18.1	2 7.7 4.1 1.9	26 24.8
Peasants	1 11.1 8.3 1.0	4 44.4 9.1 3.8	4 44.4 8.2 3.8	9 8.6
Artisans	2 6.9 16.7 1.9	11 37.9 25.0 10.5	16 55.2 32.7 15.2	29 27.6
Laborers	2 6.1 16.7 1.9	9 27.3 20.5 8.6	22 66.7 44.9 21.0	33 31.4
Women	2 25.0 16.7 1.9	1 12.5 2.3 1.0	5 62.5 10.2 4.8	8 7.6
Column total	12 11.4	44 41.9	49 46.7	105 100.0

TABLE A-24 *Social Status and Crime (1563–1567)*

	Violent crimes	Robbery and burglary	Theft	Row total
Yeomen	3 13.0 15.8 2.0	3 13.0 9.7 2.0	17 73.9 16.8 11.3	23 15.2
Peasants	1 11.1 5.3 .7	1 11.1 3.2 .7	7 77.8 6.9 4.6	9 6.0
Artisans	1 2.1 5.3 .7	14 29.2 45.2 9.3	33 68.8 32.7 21.9	48 31.8

TABLE A-24 *Continued*

	Violent crimes	Robbery and burglary	Theft	Row total
Laborers	4 8.2 21.1 2.6	11 22.4 35.5 7.3	34 69.4 33.7 22.5	49 32.5
Women	10 45.5 52.6 6.6	2 9.1 6.5 1.3	10 45.5 9.9 6.6	22 14.6
Column total	19 12.6	31 20.5	101 66.9	151 100.0

TABLE A-25 *Social Status and Crime (1568–1572)*

	Violent crimes	Robbery and burglary	Theft	Row total
Yeomen	9 23.1 45.0 6.3	4 10.3 26.7 2.8	26 66.7 24.3 18.3	39 27.5
Peasants	0 0.0 0.0 0.0	1 25.0 6.7 .7	3 75.0 2.8 2.1	4 2.8
Artisans	3 9.7 15.0 2.1	6 19.4 40.0 4.2	22 71.0 20.6 15.5	31 21.8
Laborers	4 7.1 20.0 2.8	4 7.1 26.7 2.8	48 85.7 44.9 33.8	56 39.4
Women	4 33.3 20.0 2.8	0 0.0 0.0 0.0	8 66.7 7.5 5.6	12 8.5
Column total	20 14.1	15 10.6	107 75.4	142 100.0

TABLE A-26 *Social Status and Crime (1573–1577)*

	Violent crimes	Robbery and burglary	Theft	Row total
Yeomen	1	5	21	27
	3.7	18.5	77.8	18.6
	14.3	15.6	19.8	
	.7	3.4	14.5	
Peasants	2	3	10	15
	13.3	20.0	66.7	10.3
	28.6	9.4	9.4	
	1.4	2.1	6.9	
Artisans	2	7	23	32
	6.3	21.9	71.9	22.1
	28.6	21.9	21.7	
	1.4	4.8	15.9	
Laborers	2	16	45	63
	3.2	25.4	71.4	43.4
	28.6	50.0	42.5	
	1.4	11.0	31.0	
Women	0	1	7	8
	0.0	12.5	87.5	5.5
	0.0	3.1	6.6	
	0.0	.7	4.8	
Column total	7	32	106	145
	4.8	22.1	73.1	100.0

TABLE A-27 *Social Status and Crime (1578–1582)*

	Violent crimes	Robbery and burglary	Theft	Row total
Yeomen	3	7	29	39
	7.7	17.9	74.4	16.0
	11.1	14.0	17.5	
	1.2	2.9	11.9	
Peasants	6	8	16	30
	20.0	26.7	53.3	12.3
	22.2	16.0	9.6	
	2.5	3.3	6.6	
Artisans	5	6	37	48
	10.4	12.5	77.1	19.8
	18.5	12.0	22.3	
	2.1	2.5	15.2	

TABLE A-27 *Continued*

	Violent crimes	Robbery and burglary	Theft	Row total
Laborers	9	25	65	99
	9.1	25.3	65.7	40.7
	33.3	50.0	39.2	
	3.7	10.3	26.7	
Women	4	4	19	27
	14.8	14.8	70.4	11.1
	14.8	8.0	11.4	
	1.6	1.6	7.8	
Column total	27	50	166	243
	11.1	20.6	68.3	100.0

TABLE A-28 *Social Status and Crime (1583–1587)*

	Violent crimes	Robbery and burglary	Theft	Row total
Yeomen	4	7	21	32
	12.5	21.9	65.6	7.8
	11.4	17.9	6.3	
	1.0	1.7	5.1	
Peasants	4	3	29	36
	11.1	8.3	80.6	8.8
	11.4	7.7	8.7	
	1.0	,7	7.1	
Artisans	12	12	98	122
	9.8	9.8	80.3	29.9
	34.3	30.8	29.3	
	2.9	2.9	24.0	
Laborers	7	16	160	183
	3.8	8.7	87.4	44.9
	20.0	41.0	47.9	
	1.7	3.9	39.2	
Women	8	1	26	35
	22.9	2.9	74.3	8.6
	22.9	2.6	7.8	
	2.0	.2	6.4	
Column total	35	39	334	408
	8.6	9.6	81.9	100.0

TABLE A-29 *Social Status and Crime (1588–1592)*

	Violent crimes	Robbery and burglary	Theft	Row total
Yeomen	8 26.7 38.1 2.2	7 23.3 11.7 1.9	15 50.0 5.3 4.1	30 8.3
Peasants	0 0.0 0.0 0.0	5 22.7 8.3 1.4	17 77.3 6.0 4.7	22 6.1
Artisans	5 5.0 23.8 1.4	20 19.8 33.3 5.5	76 75.2 27.0 20.9	101 27.8
Laborers	3 1.7 14.3 .8	24 13.3 40.0 6.6	153 85.0 54.3 42.1	180 49.6
Women	5 16.7 23.8 1.4	4 13.3 6.7 1.1	21 70.0 7.4 5.8	30 8.3
Column total	21 5.8	60 16.5	282 77.7	363 100.0

TABLE A-30 *Social Status and Crime (1593–1597)*

	Violent crimes	Robbery and burglary	Theft	Row total
Yeomen	6 20.7 21.4 1.2	2 6.9 6.3 .4	21 72.4 4.8 4.2	29 5.8
Peasants	0 0.0 0.0 0.0	3 12.0 9.4 .6	22 88.0 5.0 4.4	25 5.0
Artisans	9 7.8 32.1 1.8	4 3.4 12.5 .8	103 88.8 23.5 20.6	116 23.2

TABLE A-30 *Continued*

	Violent crimes	Robbery and burglary	Theft	Row total
Laborers	8 3.0 28.6 1.6	19 7.1 59.4 3.8	239 89.8 54.4 47.9	266 53.3
Women	5 7.9 17.9 1.0	4 6.3 12.5 .8	54 85.7 12.3 10.8	63 12.6
Column total	28 5.6	32 6.4	439 88.0	499 100.0

TABLE A-31 *Social Status and Crime (1598–1602)*

	Violent crimes	Robbery and burglary	Theft	Row total
Yeomen	4 36.4 16.7 1.2	0 0.0 0.0 0.0	7 63.6 2.9 2.1	11 3.3
Peasants	7 20.0 29.2 2.1	10 28.6 14.9 3.0	18 51.4 7.4 5.4	35 10.5
Artisans	5 6.2 20.8 1.5	8 9.9 11.9 2.4	68 84.0 28.1 20.4	81 24.3
Laborers	3 1.9 12.5 .9	42 25.9 62.7 12.6	117 72.2 48.3 35.1	162 48.6
Women	5 11.4 20.8 1.5	7 15.9 10.4 2.1	32 72.7 13.2 9.6	44 13.2
Column total	24 7.2	67 20.1	242 72.7	333 100.0

TABLE A-32 *Social Status and Crime (1668–1713)*[a]

	Violent crimes	Robbery and burglary	Theft	Row total
Yeomen	0	5	0	5
	0.0	100.0	0.0	4.5
	0.0	20.0	0.0	
	0.0	4.5	0.0	
Peasants	0	1	0	1
	0.0	100.0	0.0	.9
	0.0	4.0	0.0	
	0.0	.9	0.0	
Artisans	0	1	0	1
	0.0	100.0	0.0	.9
	0.0	4.0	0.0	
	0.0	.9	0.0	
Laborers	16	15	58	89
	18.0	16.9	65.2	80.2
	80.0	60.0	87.9	
	14.4	13.5	52.3	
Women	4	3	8	15
	26.7	20.0	53.3	13.5
	20.0	12.0	12.1	
	3.6	2.7	7.2	
Column total	20	12.0	12.1	111
	18.0	22.5	59.5	100.0

[a] This table was based on a sample drawn from every fourth year from 1668 to 1713 and is included only for purposes of comparison.

TABLE A-33 *Social Status and Court Decisions (1558–1562)*

	Guilty	Benefit of clergy or pregnancy	Unknown	Acquitted	Row total
Yeomen	10	1	9	6	25
	38.5	3.8	34.6	23.1	24.8
	37.0	5.9	47.4	14.3	
	9.5	1.0	8.6	5.7	
Peasants	2	1	2	4	9
	22.2	11.1	22.2	44.4	8.6
	7.4	5.9	10.5	9.5	
	1.9	1.0	1.9	3.8	

TABLE A-33 *Continued*

	Guilty	Benefit of clergy or pregnancy	Unknown	Acquitted	Row total
Artisans	9 31.0 33.3 8.6	9 31.0 52.9 8.6	2 6.9 10.5 1.9	9 31.0 21.4 8.6	29 27.6
Laborers	6 18.2 22.2 5.7	4 12.1 23.5 3.8	6 18.2 31.6 5.7	17 51.5 40.5 16.2	33 31.4
Women	0 0.0 0.0 0.0	2 25.0 11.8 1.9	0 0.0 0.0 0.0	6 75.0 14.3 5.7	8 7.6
Column total	27 25.7	17 16.2	19 18.1	42 40.0	105 100.0

TABLE A-34 *Social Status and Court Decisions (1563–1567)*

	Guilty	Benefit of clergy or pregnancy	Unknown	Acquitted	Row total
Yeomen	9 33.3 18.0 5.8	4 14.8 10.8 2.6	1 3.7 12.5 .6	13 48.1 21.3 8.3	27 17.3
Peasants	3 33.3 6.0 1.9	2 22.2 5.4 1.3	1 11.1 12.5 .6	3 33.3 4.9 1.9	9 5.8
Artisans	15 31.3 30.0 9.6	10 20.8 27.0 6.4	5 10.4 62.5 3.2	18 37.5 29.5 11.5	48 30.8
Laborers	14 28.6 28.0 9.0	19 38.8 51.4 12.2	1 2.0 12.5 .6	15 30.6 24.6 9.6	49 31.4
Women	9 39.1 18.0 5.8	2 8.7 5.4 1.3	0 0.0 0.0 0.0	12 52.2 19.7 7.7	23 14.7
Column total	50 32.1	37 23.7	8 5.1	61 39.1	156 100.0

TABLE A-35 *Social Status and Court Decisions (1568–1572)*

	Guilty	Benefit of clergy or pregnancy	Unknown	Acquitted	Row total
Yeomen	15 38.5 29.4 10.5	6 15.4 12.8 4.2	6 15.4 75.0 4.2	12 30.8 32.4 8.4	39 27.3
Peasants	1 25.0 2.0 .7	2 50.0 4.3 1.4	0 0.0 0.0 0.0	1 25.0 2.7 .7	4 2.8
Artisans	13 40.6 25.5 .1	11 34.4 23.4 7.7	1 3.1 12.5 .7	7 21.9 18.9 4.9	32 22.4
Laborers	19 33.9 37.3 13.3	23 41.1 48.9 16.1	0 0.0 0.0 0.0	14 25.0 37.8 9.8	56 39.2
Women	3 25.0 5.9 2.1	5 41.7 10.6 3.5	1 8.3 12.5 .7	3 25.0 8.1 2.1	12 8.4
Column total	51 35.7	47 32.9	8 5.6	37 25.9	143 100.0

TABLE A-36 *Social Status and Court Decision (1573–1577)*

	Guilty	Benefit of clergy or pregnancy	Unknown	Acquitted	Row total
Yeomen	9 33.3 21.4 6.2	13 48.1 36.1 9.0	2 7.4 9.1 1.4	3 11.1 6.7 2.1	27 18.6
Peasants	5 33.3 11.9 3.4	2 13.3 5.6 1.4	2 13.3 9.1 1.4	6 40.0 13.3 4.1	15 10.3
Artisans	7 21.9 16.7 4.8	10 31.3 27.8 6.9	2 6.3 9.1 1.4	13 40.6 28.9 9.0	32 22.1

TABLE A-36 *Continued*

	Guilty	Benefit of clergy or pregnancy	Unknown	Acquitted	Row total
Laborers	20	9	16	18	63
	31.7	14.3	25.4	28.6	43.4
	47.6	25.0	72.7	40.0	
	13.8	6.2	11.0	12.4	
Women	1	2	0	5	8
	12.5	25.0	0.0	62.5	5.5
	2.4	5.6	0.0	11.1	
	.7	1.4	0.0	3.4	
Column total	42	36	22	45	145
	29.0	24.8	15.2	31.0	100.0

TABLE A-37 *Social Status and Court Decisions (1578–1582)*

	Guilty	Benefit of clergy or pregnancy	Unknown	Acquitted	Row total
Yeomen	10	5	12	5	32
	31.3	15.6	37.5	15.6	15.0
	15.6	6.9	32.4	12.8	
	4.7	2.3	5.6	2.3	
Peasants	4	8	8	6	26
	15.4	30.8	30.8	23.1	12.2
	6.3	11.1	21.6	15.4	
	1.9	3.8	3.8	2.8	
Artisans	13	13	5	9	40
	32.5	32.5	12.5	22.5	18.8
	20.3	18.1	13.5	23.1	
	6.1	6.1	2.3	4.2	
Laborers	31	40	9	12	92
	33.7	43.5	9.8	13.0	43.2
	48.4	55.6	24.3	30.8	
	14.6	18.8	4.2	5.6	
Women	6	6	4	7	23
	26.1	26.1	17.4	30.4	10.8
	9.4	8.3	10.8	17.9	
	2.8	2.8	1.9	3.3	
Column total	64	72	38	39	213
	30.0	33.8	17.9	18.3	100.0

TABLE A-38 *Social Status and Court Decisions (1583–1587)*

	Guilty	Benefit of clergy or pregnancy	Unknown	Acquitted	Row total
Yeomen	2 6.5 2.8 .5	7 22.6 4.9 1.7	12 38.7 16.2 3.0	10 32.3 8.8 2.5	31 7.7
Peasants	4 11.4 5.6 1.0	13 37.1 9.1 3.2	10 28.6 13.5 2.5	8 22.9 7.0 2.0	35 8.7
Artisans	18 15.1 25.0 4.5	45 37.8 31.5 11.2	20 16.8 27.0 5.0	36 30.3 31.6 8.9	119 29.5
Laborers	38 20.8 52.8 9.4	74 40.4 51.7 18.4	25 13.7 33.8 6.2	46 25.1 40.4 11.4	183 45.4
Women	10 28.6 13.9 2.5	4 11.4 2.8 1.0	7 20.0 9.5 1.7	14 40.0 12.3 3.5	35 8.7
Column total	72 17.9	143 35.5	74 18.4	114 28.3	403 100.0

TABLE A-39 *Social Status and Court Decisions (1588–1592)*

	Guilty	Benefit of clergy or pregnancy	Unknown	Acquitted	Row total
Yeomen	11 36.7 16.7 3.0	4 13.3 3.0 1.1	4 13.3 6.2 1.1	11 36.7 11.3 3.0	30 8.3
Peasants	4 18.2 6.1 1.1	10 45.5 7.5 2.8	2 9.1 3.1 .6	6 27.3 6.2 1.7	22 6.1
Artisans	12 11.9 18.2 3.3	40 39.6 29.9 11.0	18 17.8 27.7 5.0	31 30.7 32.0 8.6	101 27.9

TABLE A-40 *Continued*

	Guilty	Benefit of clergy or pregnancy	Unknown	Acquitted	Row total
Laborers	38 21.2 57.6 10.5	73 40.8 54.5 20.2	35 19.6 53.8 9.7	33 18.4 34.0 9.1	179 49.4
Women	1 3.3 1.5 .3	7 23.3 5.2 1.9	6 20.0 9.2 1.7	16 53.3 16.5 4.4	30 8.3
Column total	66 18.2	134 37.0	65 18.0	97 26.8	362 100.0

TABLE A-40 *Social Status and Court Decisions (1593–1597)*

	Guilty	Benefit of clergy or pregnancy	Unknown	Acquitted	Row total
Yeomen	10 37.0 6.0 2.0	3 11.1 2.9 .6	11 40.7 14.3 2.2	3 11.1 2.0 .6	27 5.4
Peasants	12 48.0 7.2 2.4	3 12.0 2.9 .6	7 28.0 9.1 1.4	3 12.0 2.0 .6	25 5.0
Artisans	42 36.2 25.1 8.5	22 19.0 21.2 4.4	18 15.5 23.4 3.6	34 29.3 22.8 6.8	116 23.3
Laborers	84 31.6 50.3 16.9	69 25.9 66.3 13.9	33 12.4 42.9 6.6	80 30.1 53.7 16.1	266 53.5
Women	19 30.2 11.4 3.8	7 11.1 6.7 1.4	8 12.7 10.4 1.6	29 46.0 19.5 5.8	63 12.7
Column total	167 33.6	104 20.9	77 15.5	149 30.0	497 100.0

TABLE A-41 *Social Status and Court Decisions (1598–1602)*

	Guilty	Benefit of clergy or pregnancy	Unknown	Acquitted	Row total
Yeomen	0 0.0 0.0 0.0	3 27.3 3.2 .9	5 45.5 7.8 1.5	3 27.3 3.7 .9	11 3.3
Peasants	6 17.1 6.6 1.8	16 45.7 17.2 4.8	9 25.7 14.1 2.7	4 11.4 4.9 1.2	35 10.6
Artisans	21 25.9 23.1 6.4	26 32.1 28.0 7.9	16 19.8 25.0 4.8	18 22.2 22.0 5.5	81 24.5
Laborers	52 32.7 57.1 15.8	44 27.7 47.3 13.3	28 17.6 43.8 8.5	35 22.0 42.7 10.6	159 48.2
Women	12 27.3 13.2 3.6	4 9.1 4.3 1.2	6 13.6 9.4 1.8	22 50.0 26.8 6.7	44 13.3
Column total	91 27.6	93 28.2	64 19.4	82 24.8	330 100.0

TABLE A-42 *Social Status and Court Decisions (1668–1713)*[a]

	Guilty	Benefit of clergy or pregnancy	Unknown	Acquitted	Row total
Yeomen	0 0.0 0.0 0.0	0 0.0 0.0 0.0	5 100.0 25.0 4.2	0 0.0 0.0 0.0	5 4.2
Peasants	1 100.0 2.4 .8	0 0.0 0.0 0.0	0 0.0 0.0 0.0	0 0.0 0.0 0.0	1 .8
Artisans	1 100.0 2.4 .8	0 0.0 0.0 0.0	0 0.0 0.0 0.0	0 0.0 0.0 0.0	1 .8
Laborers	32 33.7 78.0 26.9	28 29.5 93.3 23.5	14 14.7 70.0 11.8	21 22.1 75.0 17.6	95 79.8
Women	7 41.2 17.1 5.9	2 11.8 6.7 1.7	1 5.9 5.0 .8	7 41.2 25.0 5.9	17 14.3
Column total	41 34.5	30 25.2	20 16.8	28 23.5	119 100.0

[a] This table was based on a sample drawn from every fourth year from 1668 to 1713 and is included only for purposes of comparison.

APPENDIX IV

THE JUSTICES OF THE PEACE

For most counties it is extremely difficult, if not impossible, to compile adequate lists of active justices of the peace for the Elizabethan period. Only a small number of Commissions of the Peace survive, a few of which were copied on to the *dorse* of the Patent Rolls. The list of names from one of these copies is reproduced in Table A-44. Lists like this one have serious limitations. Since so few are extant it is impossible to uncover trends in the membership of the commission during the period. Furthermore, since only names appear, they tell nothing of the extent of activity of the justices. Indeed, any attempt to use these lists for that purpose would definitely be misleading. A glance at Table A-44 shows why. Only a small number of those named in the commission took an active part in the county's judicial administration.

Another source, the calendars of the justices of the peace in the Assize files for Essex, are preserved. Few counties are this fortunate. These calendars are contemporary documents that the Clerk of the Peace drew up for the Clerk of Assize, handing them over shortly before the Assize opened. The Clerk of Assize used them as an attendance roster and put some revealing notes on them. The names of the justices who were ill, excused for other reasons, or dead were also noted; and, from 1575, those who were present at the Assizes. Fines for those absent and unexcused were also noted. These calendars form an almost unbroken series, and since the Assize Clerk annotated them they are especially important. From them it is possible to compile complete and current lists of the names of justices. They are thus more valuable than the few commissions on the Patent Rolls. It is also possible to determine attendance at Assizes from the

Assize Clerk's notes on the calendars. They do not, however, state whether and to what extent the justices were active at their own Quarter Sessions. Justices who often attended Assizes may have attended Quarter Sessions rarely. For example, Christopher Chibborne, one of the hardest-working justices in Elizabethan Essex, rarely attended Assizes. For Essex there is, however, another source by which to measure the extent of the justices' activity. The Sessions Rolls include an almost complete set of rosters of justices who attended Sessions. Such lists for other counties during this period are almost nonexistant. Unlike the later lists for Somerset which Professor Barnes found inaccurate[1] and a few other incomplete lists which give a few names followed by a tantalising "and others," the Essex rosters are both accurate and complete.

The names in Table A-44 and the attendance figures in Tables A-43 and A-44 are derived from these rosters. Though no better source for measuring a justice's activity exists, it has some limitations. The rosters include only justices who attended Quarter Sessions. Since the tables derive from them and since all justices in the commissions did not attend Quarter Sessions, it follows that some justices in the commission will not appear in Table A-43, which, in fact, should be termed more accurately a table of *active* justices. Furthermore, attendance at sessions did not always indicate which justices were most active. Sometimes between sessions an individual justice took many recognizances either for good behavior or to keep the peace, committed many suspected felons to the Colchester Castle gaol to await trial, quelled affrays, and together with a fellow justice tried cases of forcible entry, and yet did not attend the session following. This is not common, but it happened occasionally.

All information on the justices' university background is based on Venn's *Alumni Cantabrigienses* and Foster's *Alumni Oxonienses.* Similarly, the information concerning their professional background included in Table A-43 and summarized in Table 7, p. 75 is based on the registers of admissions to the various Inns of Court. Again, information was included only when it seemed certain that justices with the same names were identical. Because of this restriction on entries it is fair to assume that these lists and the summaries based on them represent an absolute minimum.

Despite the limitations, the tables provide some interesting biographical information about a socially significant segment of Essex society. And they do more: Taken together with the tables in Appendices I and III, they demonstrate some important developments. The growth in numbers of justices of the peace, in the number of sessions they attended, and in the average attendance at Quarter Sessions parallels the increase in the Court's business. The increasing percentage of those who attended an university

[1] T. Barnes, *Somerset 1629–1640*, Ch. 3 (Cambridge, U.S.A., 1961).

(usually Cambridge) points to a better-educated group of individuals. At the same time that their education improved, their professional training, however, declined. This decline should be compared with Professor Gleason's findings in the counties he studied.[2]

Together these tables tell an interesting and important story. In Elizabethan Essex a growing number of more active, better educated and truly amateur men in the county were devoting their own time to what they considered a crisis in law and order. For the most part, they were purely local men who did not cast their ambition beyond the boundaries of Essex. These unpaid and to a large extent unnoticed men, who spent so much time in the dull and often unprofitable business of administering their county, deserve their place in English history.

[2] J. Gleason, *The Justices of the Peace in England, 1558–1640* (Oxford, 1969).

TABLE A-43 *Names, Status, Education and Professional Training; Years Attended Quarter Sessions and Number of Sessions Attended*

Name	Status	University	Legal background	Quarter sessions	Sessions attended
Abell, John	gentleman			1573–1575	3
Altham, James	gentleman		Gray's Inn	1564–1581	11
Amys, Israel	gentleman	Cambridge (St. John's) B.A., M.A.	Middle Temple	1586–1589	4
Amys, Roger	gentleman			1564–1569	4
Appleton, Hen.	gentleman			1574–1588	14
Archer, Hen.	gentleman			1575–1585	11
Ayloff, Wm.	gentleman		Lincoln's Inn (Justice, Queen's Bench)	1562–1590	7
Ayloff, Wm. of St. Osyth	gentleman			1590–1603	20
Barlie, Rich.	gentleman			1586–1590	9
Barrett, Edw.	gentleman	Oxford	Lincoln's Inn	1566–1580	5
Barrington, Frs.	knight	Cambridge, M.A., 1580		1586–1603	25
Barrington, Tho.	gentleman		Gray's Inn	1564–1580	17
Beckingham, Tho.	gentleman			1603	1
Bendishe, Tho.	gentleman	Cambridge (Peterhouse)	Middle Temple	1589–1599	6
Bendlowes, Wm.	gentleman	Cambridge (St. John's)	Lincoln's Inn (barrister sergeant)	1562–1564	4
Bocking, Edmund	gentleman			1563–1576	16
Bradbury, Matthew	knight			1563–1582	16
Browne, Anthony			Justice (Queen's Bench)	1563–1564	2
Browne, Wistan	gentleman			1578–1580	3
Bury, Edward	gentleman			1563–1569	5
Butler, Edward	gentleman			1602	1
Butler, John	gentleman			1582–1601	21
Capell, Gamaliel	gentleman			1599–1603	10
Capell, Hen.	gentleman			1576–1581	6
Cardynall, Wm.	gentleman	Cambridge (St. John's)	Gray's Inn (bench reader)	1562–1584	9
Cheshall, Wm.	gentleman			1563–1564	2

TABLE A-43 *Continued*

Name	Status	University	Legal background	Quarter sessions	Sessions attended
Chibborne, Christr.	gentleman			1575–1602	36
Clarke, Rob.	knight		Baron of Exchequer	1582–1595	20
Clovile, Eustace	gentleman			1582–1589	22
Cole, Nich.	gentleman			1602	1
Colshill, Tho.	gentleman			1583	1
Cooke, Anthony	gentleman	Cambridge	Gray's Inn	1563–1564	2
Darcy, Brian	gentleman		Lincoln's Inn	1582	2
Darcy, John	baron		Middle Temple	1564–1588	15
Darcy, Rich.	gentleman			1562	1
Darcy, Tho.	knight		Lincoln's Inn	1583–1593	2
Darrell, Geo.	gentleman			1577–1581	3
Deane, Wm.	gentleman			1582	2
Eliott, Edward	gentleman	Cambridge (Christ's) B.A., M.A.	Priest	1586–1595	18
Fortescue, Hen.	gentleman			1568–1575	8
Franke, Rich.	gentleman			1591–1602	9
Franke, Rob.	gentleman			1598	1
Franke, Tho.	knight			1566–1574	10
Gaines, John				1595	1
Gardner, Tho.	gentleman	Cambridge (Peterhouse) B.A.	Priest	1600–1603	3
Gente, Tho.	knight	Cambridge	Middle Temple (barrister, Baron of Exchequer)	1572–1591	27
Golding, Hen.	gentleman		Gray's Inn	1566–1576	10
Golding, Tho.	gentleman	Cambridge (Gonville)	Middle Temple	1566–1569	2
Graye, Hen.	knight		Gray's Inn	1573–1589	12
Grimston, Edward	gentleman	Cambridge (Christ's) age 13	Gray's Inn (Master of Chancery)	1591–1602	6
Hadley, Geo.	gentleman			1564	1
Hall, Rob.	gentleman			1579	1

Harlackendon, Rog.	gentleman	Cambridge (Magdalene)		1593–1601	7
Harleston, John	gentleman			1600	1
Harrys, Arthur	gentleman		Lincoln's Inn	1572–1595	19
Harrys, Tho.	gentleman		Lincoln's Inn	1593–1603	5
Harrys, Vincent	gentleman			1571–1572	4
Harrys, Wm.	gentleman			1600	1
Harvey, Frs.	gentleman		Gray's Inn	1569–1598	16
Harvey, Geo.	gentleman			1590–1593	3
Heygate, Reg.	gentleman	Cambridge	Gray's Inn	1571–1576	8
Higham, Wm.	gentleman		Inner Temple	1585–1598	7
Hubbard, Edward	gentleman			1582–1598	15
Huddleston, Edmund	knight			1581–1588	5
Isaake, Edward	gentleman		Gray's Inn	1566–1568	2
Ive, John	gentleman			1594–1597	2
Josselyn, John	gentleman			1599–1600	3
Kempe, Rob.	gentleman		Lincoln's Inn	1564–1569	9
Kighley, Tho.	gentleman	Cambridge (Trinity)		1600–1603	10
Killingworth, John	gentleman			1603	1
Leigh, Rob.	gentleman		Gray's Inn	1588–1603	12
Lucas, Tho.	knight	Cambridge (Trinity)	Gray's Inn	1564–1599	13
Mackwilliam, Hen.	gentleman			1569–1577	3
Mackwilliam, Wm.	gentleman			1574	1
Maxye, Anthony	gentleman	Cambridge (Corpus)		1580–1591	25
Maxye, Hen.	gentleman	Cambridge (Queen's)		1598–1603	8
Maynard, Hen.	gentleman			1599–1603	7
Meade, Tho.	gentleman	Cambridge (Christ's)	Middle Temple (sergeant)	1568–1595	14
Medley, Hen.	gentleman	Cambridge (Magdalene)	Middle Temple	1573–1577	5
Mildmay, Hen.	gentleman	Cambridge (Christ's)	Gray's Inn	1581–1600	43
Mildmay, Hum.	gentleman	Cambridge (Peterhouse)	Gray's Inn	1591–1599	5
Mildmay, Tho.	knight	Cambridge (Christ's)	Lincoln's Inn (*Custos rotulorum*)	1569–1603	92
Mildmay, Tho. of Barnes	knight			1586–1603	50
Mildmay, Walter	knight	Cambridge (Christ's)	Gray's Inn	1575–1589	16

TABLE A-43 *Continued*

Name	Status	University	Legal background	Quarter sessions	Sessions attended
Mordaunt, John	knight		Middle Temple	1564–1568	4
Morley, Edward	baron			1585	1
Morrice, James	gentleman		Middle Temple (reader, barrister, Attorney for the Court of Wards)	1573–1593	22
Nicolls, Geo.	gentleman			1562–1583	20
Nicolls, Tho.	knight			1566	1
Nightingale, Geof.	gentleman	Cambridge (Christ's)	Gray's Inn	1595–1602	11
Paschall, Andrew	gentleman	Oxford (Exeter)		1587–1602	50
Petre, John	knight		Middle Temple	1573–1603	67
Petre, Wm.	knight	Oxford (Exeter)	Oxford, D.C.L. (*Custos rotulorum*)	1564	1
Pinchon, John	gentleman	Oxford	Inner Temple	1568–1573	11
Powell, Steven	gentleman	Oxford, B.A., M.A.	Middle Temple	1597–1598	2
Pyrton, Edmund	gentleman			1574–1588	6
Rawlens, Tho.	gentleman		Inner Temple	1600–1601	4
Raynsford, Rich.	gentleman			1594–1601	3
Riche, Edward	gentleman			1562–1598	35
Riche, Rich.	baron			1564	1
Riche, Rob. I	baron			1567–1581	24
Riche, Rob. II	baron		Gray's Inn	1582–1603	21
Riche, Rob.	gentleman		Inner Temple	1601–1603	4
Saltonstall, Rich.	gentleman			1602	1
Sammes, John	gentleman	Cambridge (Emmanuel)	Lincoln's Inn	1595–1601	16
Sandell, Leon.	gentleman			1569–1570	3
Smythe, John	knight			1584–1596	11
Smythe, Wm.	gentleman	Cambridge (St. John's)	Lincoln's Inn	1591–1603	23
Sisley, Clement	gentleman			1566	1

Smythe, Tho.	knight	Cambridge (Queen's), B.A., M.A.	Padua, LL.D.	1562–1570	6
Southerton, Geo.	gentleman			1591–1593	4
Stannap, Edward	gentleman			1589	1
Stern, John	bishop	Cambridge (Trinity) Colchester M.A., D.D., D.D.		1594–1603	13
Sulyard, Edward	gentleman		Lincoln's Inn	1579–1601	14
Sussex, Rob.	earl			1595–1601	3
Tabor, Wm.	gentleman		Doctor of Divinity	1599–1601	4
Taye, Tho.	gentleman			1574–1582	4
Throgmorton, Kenelm	gentleman			1562–1579	8
Towse, Wm.	gentleman		merchant	1592–1603	25
Tuke, Geo.	gentleman			1562–1572	2
Tuke, Peter	gentleman			1591–1603	16
Turner, Edward	gentleman	Cambridge (Emmanuel)	priest	1598–1603	11
Turner, John	gentleman			1574	2
Twedye, Rich.	gentleman			1572–1590	4
Tyndall, John	gentleman	Cambridge (Gonville)	Lincoln's Inn (barrister)	1593–1598	6
Waldegrave, Edward	gentleman	Cambridge (Peterhouse)	Gray's Inn	1600–1601	6
Waldegrave, Tho.	gentleman			1577–1602	8
Waldegrave, Wm.	gentleman		Lincoln's Inn	1568–1571	3
Warryn, Rich.	gentleman			1593–1596	7
Wentworth, John	gentleman		Lincoln's Inn	1584–1585	2
Wentworth, Reg.	gentleman			1580	1
West, Richard	gentleman		Justice of Queen's Bench	1564	1
Weston, Jerome	gentleman			1586–1603	29
Whestone, Bernard	gentleman			1589–1598	8
Wilson, Jerome	gentleman			1586	1
Wiseman, John	gentleman	Oxford (Queen's)	Inner Temple	1582–1590	9
Wiseman, Ralph	gentleman			1598–1603	13
Wiseman, Wm.	gentleman	Cambridge (Peterhouse)	Lincoln's Inn	1592–1602	14
Wrothe, Rob.	gentleman	Cambridge (St. John's)		1580–1595	7

TABLE A-44 *Essex Commission of the Peace (11 February 1562)*
(P.R.O. Calendar of Patent Rolls, 4 Eliz., Part X, No. 935)

*Nicholas Bacon
*William, Marquis of Winchester
*Henry, Earl of Arundel
*John, Earl of Oxford
*Thomas, Earl of Sussex
*Edward, Bishop of London
*Henry, Lord Morley
*Richard, Lord Rich
*John, Lord Darcy
*Henry, Lord Hundson
John, Lord Graye
*William Petre, knight
*Ranold Chomley, sergeant
*Gilbert Gerrarde, Attorney General
*†Anthony Browne, Judge of Common Pleas
*Richard Weston, Judge of Common Pleas
*Robert Riche
*†Anthony Cooke
*John Wentworth
*Thomas Worthe
Francis Jobson
*†Thomas Smythe, knight
Peter Mewtas
Thomas Josselyn
*†William Bendlowes, sergeant
*†Thomas Mildmay
*Thomas Powle
*George Medley
*Richard Cooke
†Kenelm Throgmorton
†William Ayloff
†William Cardynell
Edward Barrett
†Edward Bury
*John Tonworth
*George Hadley
*†George Nicolls
*†Edmund Bocking
Clement Sisley
George Christmas
Henry Golding
Edmund Daniel
†Matthew Bradburie
†Edward Riche
Roger Amys

* J.Ps who were made of the *quorum*.
† J.Ps who appeared at Quarter Sessions at least once within 2 years of appointment.

APPENDIX **V**

MODERNIZATION OF ELIZABETHAN CRIMINAL COURTS

The overall purpose of this appendix is once again to spell out in detail what is treated summarily in the chapter on courts (Chapter IV) in the text. Table A-45 is a tabulation of the sessions of Assize in Essex during Elizabeth's reign, including the date and place of meeting. From a study of this tabulation it is possible to follow the slow and sometimes halting movement toward more regular meetings and more certain times and places of holding the Assizes. Basically, the tabulations in Table A-46 do for Quarter Sessions what those in Table A-45 did for the Assizes, and again the movement toward more frequent and regular meetings can be traces in detail where in the text it is generally summarized. Table A-47 indicates the gaol deliveries held in conjunction with Quarter Sessions.

Tables A-48 and A-49 depict the growth and then the decay of the manor court in Essex during the reign of Elizabeth. They are intended to show the movement of cases both as to number and type during the 45-year period under review. They should be helpful in understanding both the discussion of centralization of courts and in the argument about manorial decay discussed in Chapters I and IV.

Table A-50 is a general summary based on a few sample years of the relative number of documents found in the main sources used in the text. It should help to put into perspective the place and the weight of various court records in compiling data about felony statistics. To be sure, they are not complete, but totals of all documents, not separated into various courts, and repositories of records are available in Table 2 and Figure 2 in Chapter I.

Table A-51 shows the total number of coroners' inquisitions by decades.

Table A-52 indicates the total number of coroners and the names of those who served during the period. It is important because it might have been that shifts in officials affected the numbers of murders or other violent deaths which were recorded during the period. But a study of the graph in Chapter I shows that the number of violent deaths remained fairly constant and that when it did not, the shift was not directly related to changes in officials who served as coroners.

TABLE A-45 *Meetings of the Assize in Essex (1559–1602)*[a]

Year	Date	Day	Place
1559	22 February	Wednesday	Brentwood
1559	13 July	Thursday	Chelmsford
1560	29 March	Friday	Chelmsford
1560	4 July	Thursday	Chelmsford
1561	20 March	Thursday	Chelmsford
1563	1 April	Tuesday	Brentwood
1564	21 July	Friday	Colchester
1565	30 March	Friday	Chelmsford
1566	14 March	Thursday	Brentwood
1566	26 July	Wednesday	Chelmsford
1567	13 March	Thursday	Brentwood
1567	7 July	Monday	Chelmsford
1568	11 March	Thursday	Chelmsford
1569	7 March	Monday	Chelmsford
1570	2 March	Thursday	Chelmsford
1570	17 July	Monday	Chelmsford
1571	8 March	Thursday	Chelmsford
1572	12 July	Thursday	Chelmsford
1572	28 August	Thursday	Chelmsford
1573	2 March	Monday	Chelmsford
1573	29 June	Monday	Chelmsford
1574	24 March	Wednesday	Chelmsford
1575	9 July	Friday	Brentwood
1575	3 March	Thursday	Chelmsford
1576	19 March	Monday	Brentwood
1576	30 July	Monday	Chelmsford
1577	6 March	Wednesday	Chelmsford
1578	10 March	Monday	Chelmsford

[a] The information in this table is taken from the writs of *venire facias* in the Assize files for the whole period. Fortunately, most of them are extant. They are taken from AF 35/1/3 to AF 35/44/T.

TABLE A-45 *Continued*

Year	Date	Day	Place
1578	14 July	Monday	Chelmsford
1579	2 April	Thursday	Chelmsford
1580	17 March	Thursday	Brentwood
1580	25 July	Monday	Chelmsford
1581	13 March	Monday	Brentwood
1581	17 July	Monday	Braintree
1582	29 March	Thursday	Chelmsford
1582	2 August	Thursday	Chelmsford
1583	29 July	Monday	Witham
1584	2 March	Monday	Chelmsford
1584	27 July	Monday	Witham
1585	8 March	Monday	Chelmsford
1585	19 July	Monday	Brentwood
1586	3 March	Tuesday	Chelmsford
1586	11 July	Monday	Witham
1587	13 March	Monday	Chelmsford
1587	24 July	Monday	Chelmsford
1588	4 March	Monday	Chelmsford
1588	15 July	Monday	Braintree
1589	Hilary	unknown	Chelmsford
1589	3 July	Tuesday	Chelmsford
1590	19 February	Thursday	Chelmsford
1590	27 July	Monday	Chelmsford
1591	4 March	Thursday	Chelmsford
1591	Trinity	unknown	Chelmsford
1592	10 July	Monday	Chelmsford
1593	28 March	Wednesday	Chelmsford
1593	26 July	Thursday	Chelmsford
1594	18 March	Monday	Chelmsford
1594	8 August	Thursday	Brentwood
1595	3 March	Monday	Chelmsford
1596	15 July	Thursday	Brentwood
1597	28 February	unknown	Chelmsford
1597	30 June	Thursday	Brentwood
1598	27 February	Monday	Chelmsford
1600	6 March	Thursday	Chelmsford
1601	12 March	Thursday	Brentwood
1601	23 July	Thursday	Chelmsford
1602	4 March	Thursday	Brentwood
1602	18 July	Thursday	Chelmsford

TABLE A-46 *Meetings of Quarter Sessions in Essex (1558–1603)*

Year	Number of Sessions	Time of Session[a]	Number of days
1558–1561	Session Rolls missing		
1562	4	Epiphany	1
		Easter	1
		St. Peter & Paul	1
		St. Michael	1
1563	2	Epiphany	1
		St. Peter & Paul	1
1564	3	Easter	1
		St. Peter & Paul	1
		St. Michael	1
1565	2	St. Peter & Paul	2
		St. Michael	1
1566	3	Epiphany	1
		Easter	1
		St. Peter & Paul	1
1567	4	Epiphany	1
		Easter	1
		St. Peter & Paul	1
		St. Michael	1
1568	4	Epiphany	1
		Easter	1
		St. Peter & Paul	1
		St. Michael	1
1569	3	Easter	1
		St. Peter & Paul	1
		St. Michael	1
1570	3	Epiphany	1
		St. Peter & Paul	1
		St. Michael	1
1571	4	Epiphany	1
		Easter	1
		St. Peter & Paul	1
		St. Michael	1

[a] All sessions were held on the Thursday following the named feasts or holy days. Epiphany came in early January; Easter, of course, in late March or early April; St. Peter and Paul in early July; and the Feast of St. Michael in early October.

TABLE A-46 *Continued*

Year	Number of Sessions	Time of Session	Number of days
1572	4	Epiphany	1
		Easter	1
		St. Peter & Paul	1
		St. Michael	1
1573	4	Epiphany	1
		Easter	1
		St. Peter & Paul	1
		St. Michael	1
1574	5	Epiphany	1
		Easter	1
		St. Peter & Paul	1
		12 August	1
		St. Michael	1
1575	4	Epiphany	1
		Easter	1
		St. Peter & Paul	1
		St. Michael	1
1576	4	Epiphany	1
		Easter	1
		St. Peter & Paul	1
		St. Michael	1
1577	5	Epiphany (1)	1
		Epiphany (2)[b]	1
		Easter	1
		St. Peter & Paul	1
		St. Michael	1
1578	4	Epiphany	1
		Easter	1
		St. Peter & Paul	1
		St. Michael	1
1579	4	Epiphany	1
		Easter	1
		St. Peter & Paul	1
		St. Michael	1
1580	4	Epiphany	1
		Easter	1
		St. Peter & Paul	1
		St: Michael	1

[b] A special Epiphany session was held during this year.

TABLE A-46 *Continued*

Year	Number of Sessions	Time of Session	Number of days
1581	2	Epiphany	1
		St. Peter & Paul	1
1582	3	Easter	1
		St. Peter & Paul	1
		St. Michael	1
1583	4	Epiphany	1
		Easter	1
		St. Peter & Paul	1
		St. Michael	1
1584	3	Easter	1
		St. Peter & Paul	1
		St. Michael	1
1585	4	Epiphany	1
		Easter	1
		St. Peter & Paul	1
		St. Michael	1
1586	4	Epiphany	2
		Easter	2
		St. Peter & Paul	2
		St. Michael	2
1587	4	Epiphany	1
		Easter	2
		St. Peter & Paul	1
		St. Michael	1
1588	4	Epiphany	1
		Easter	1
		St. Peter & Paul	1
		St. Michael	1
1589	4	Epiphany	1
		Easter	1
		St. Peter & Paul	1
		St. Michael	1
1590	4	Epiphany	2
		Easter	2
		St. Peter & Paul	2
		St. Michael	1

TABLE A-46 *Continued*

Year	Number of Sessions	Time of Session	Number of days
1591	4	Epiphany	1
		Easter	1
		St. Peter & Paul	1
		St. Michael	1
1592	4	Epiphany	1
		Easter	1
		St. Peter & Paul	1
		St. Michael	1
1593	4	Epiphany	1
		Easter	1
		St. Peter & Paul	1
		St. Michael	1
1594	2	Easter	2
		St. Peter & Paul	1
1595	3	Epiphany	2
		St. Peter & Paul	1
		St. Michael	1
1596	4	Epiphany	2
		Easter	3
		St. Peter & Paul	2
		St. Michael	1
1597	4	Epiphany	3
		Easter	2
		St. Peter & Paul	1
		St. Michael	1
1598	4	Epiphany	3
		Easter	2
		St. Peter & Paul	1
		St. Michael	1
1599	4	Epiphany	3
		Easter	1
		St. Peter & Paul	1
		St. Michael	1
1600	4	Epiphany	3
		Easter	1
		St. Peter & Paul	1
		St. Michael	2

TABLE A-46 *Continued*

Year	Number of Sessions	Time of Session	Number of days
1601	4	Epiphany	3
		Easter	1
		St. Peter & Paul	1
		St. Michael	1
1602	4	Epiphany	3
		Easter	1
		St. Peter & Paul	1
		St. Michael	1
1603	4	Epiphany	3
		Easter	1
		St. Peter & Paul	1
		St. Michael	1

TABLE A-47 *Goal Deliveries Held in Conjunction with Quarter Sessions*[a]

Year	Session	Quarter Sessions Roll	King's Bench Indictment
1584	Epiphany	Q/SR 87	KB9/659/86
1587	Epiphany	no roster	KB9/667/66
1595	Epiphany	Q/SR 129	KB9/687/113
1596	Epiphany	Q/SR 132	KB9/689/150
1597	Epiphany	Q/SR 136	KB9/692/11
1598	Epiphany	Q/SR 140	KB9/695/59
1599	Epiphany	Q/SR 144	KB9/699/25
1600	Epiphany	Q/SR 148	KB9/703/95
1600	Lent	no roster	KB9/704 Part II
1601	Epiphany	Q/SR 152	KB9/707/50
1602	Epiphany	Q/SR 156	no document found
1603	Epiphany	Q/SR 160	no document found

[a] This table is based on the Quarter Sessions Rolls and King's Bench Indictments Ancient (P.O.R. K.B.9) noted in the last column.

TABLE 48 *Offenses in the Manor Court of Weathersfield*[a]

Offenses	1558–1569	1570–1579	1580–1589	1590–1599	1600–1603
Felony	0	0	0	0	0
Assault	1	0	2	2	0
Wounding	3	3	0	0	0
Ill behavior[b]	0	3	1	0	0
Abusing officials[c]	0	0	0	0	0
Public welfare[d]	18	151	52	124	7
Trade[e]	84	67	49	73	25
Woodcutting	10	3	0	9	1
Vagrancy	0	2	0	13	0
Official misconduct[c]	0	0	0	0	0
Total	116	229	104	221	33

[a] D/DFy M18–21. I am indebted to Mr. K. C. Newton, Essex County Archivist, who generously shared his typescript calendar of this court.

[b] Includes gaming, causing disturbances in public places, nightwalking, scolding, and other minor disturbances.

[c] Officials here is used to describe anyone acting for public purposes, including jurors, constables, watchmen, etc.

[d] Includes offences like scouring ditches, clearing roadways, obstructing ways, public health measures like throwing dung into streets, throwing entrails into streets, selling rotten meat, etc.

[e] Includes mainly licensing or selling without licenses, but also overcharging and violations of weights and measures.

TABLE A-49 *Offenses in the Manor Court of Ingatestone*[a]

Offenses	1558–1569	1570–1579	1580–1589	1590–1599	1600–1603
Felony	1	1	0	0	0
Assault	0	1	0	0	0
Wounding	0	0	3	0	1
Ill behavior[b]	47	4	3	0	3
Abusing officials[b]	1	1	0	0	1
Public welfare[b]	125	105	65	86	19
Trade[b]	65	35	109	104	41
Woodcutting	9	17	7	2	0
Vagrancy	15	5	0	1	2
Official misconduct[b]	1	1	89[c]	7	0
Total	253	160	276	200	66

[a] D/DP M99–101. I am indebted to Mr. K. C. Newton's generous offer to share his typescript calendar of this court with me.
[b] See notes in Table A-48 on Weathersfield Manor.
[c] This figure is inflated by the large number of jurors who did not appear.

TABLE A-50 *Number of Documents Related to Criminal Cases in Various Courts*[a]

Years	King's Bench (P.R.O. K.B.9)	Assize Files (P.R.O. Asz. 35)	Quarter Sessions (E.R.O. Q/SR)	Manor Courts[b] (E.R.O. D/DP M)
1559–1560	22	71	no rolls	16
1570–1571	29	107	262	37
1580–1581	18	152	383	68
1588–1589	14	258	479	93
1601–1602	26	339	564	40

[a] This table is based on the sample years.
[b] The figures for manor courts are based on Ingatestone Manor which has a full setof manor court rolls for the Elizabethan period. This manor was owned by Sir William Petre and afterward by his son, Sir John Petre. They are all found under the heading D/DP M99–101. For a detailed summary of the number of cases each year, see Table A-49 on Ingatestone Manor.

TABLE A-51 *Coroners' Inquisitions in Essex (1564–1603)*

Years	Number of inquisitions
1564–1574	97
1575–1584	123
1585–1594	119
1595–1603	122

TABLE A-52 *Coroners of Essex*[a]

Name	Years	Inquisitions	
		Total	Annual average
Clement Tusser	1559–	3	3
Thomas Knott	1559–1578	118	6
William Vernon	1567–1581	46	3
John Latham	1578–1580	15	5
John Luckyn	1580–1582	9	4
Henry Longe	1581–1583	13	2
	1585, 1593–1595		
Thomas More	1582–1596	72	5
Thomas Meade	1582–1584	0	
John Gosse	1585–1587	12	6
Thomas Drywood	1587–1596	13	1
Charles Chute	1595	0	
John Nashe	1596–1603	47	6
Thomas Shaa	1596–1600	4	1
Richard Freeman	1600–1603	10	3

[a] These names and figures are drawn from PRO/KB9 in which coroners' inquisitions were filed. They do not include the coroners from special jurisdictions like the boroughs, the duchy of Lancaster, the Liberty of Havering-atte-Bower, the Manor of Writtle, and other specially exempt areas which had their own coroners. The coroners played a critical role in determining recorded violent crimes, since their primary duties included taking inquisitions of all suspicious deaths in the county. All statistics which involved murder, manslaughter, infanticide were made up from the documents these members of the lesser gentry of Essex produced.

APPENDIX VI

RELATIONSHIP OF HARVEST ABUNDANCE AND CRIMES

This graph plots the quality of harvest alongside the number of felonies recorded for the years of Elizabeth's reign. Harvest quality was divided into five categories, following the figures in Hoskins, W. G., "Harvest Fluctuations and English Economic History," *Agricultural History Review*, Volume XII (1964). The felony figures are based on the tallies in Appendix I. Notice that until 1588 the correlation between poor harvests and high felony figures is not perfectly clear. But from that year on to the end of the reign, the two are quite closely connected; only in 1591 does crime move in the opposite direction from harvest and this is explained by possible inadequacy in the criminal court records of that particular year. The years 1592 through 1599, on the other hand, represent a distinct and sustained harvest trend for the worse and correspondingly higher felony figures. This period is perhaps, therefore, the only one for which an unquestionable case for the correlation between poor harvests and high crime figures can be made. This limitation in the data should be taken into account when interpreting the significance of relating quality of harvest to the numbers of felonies recorded during the reign of Elizabeth.

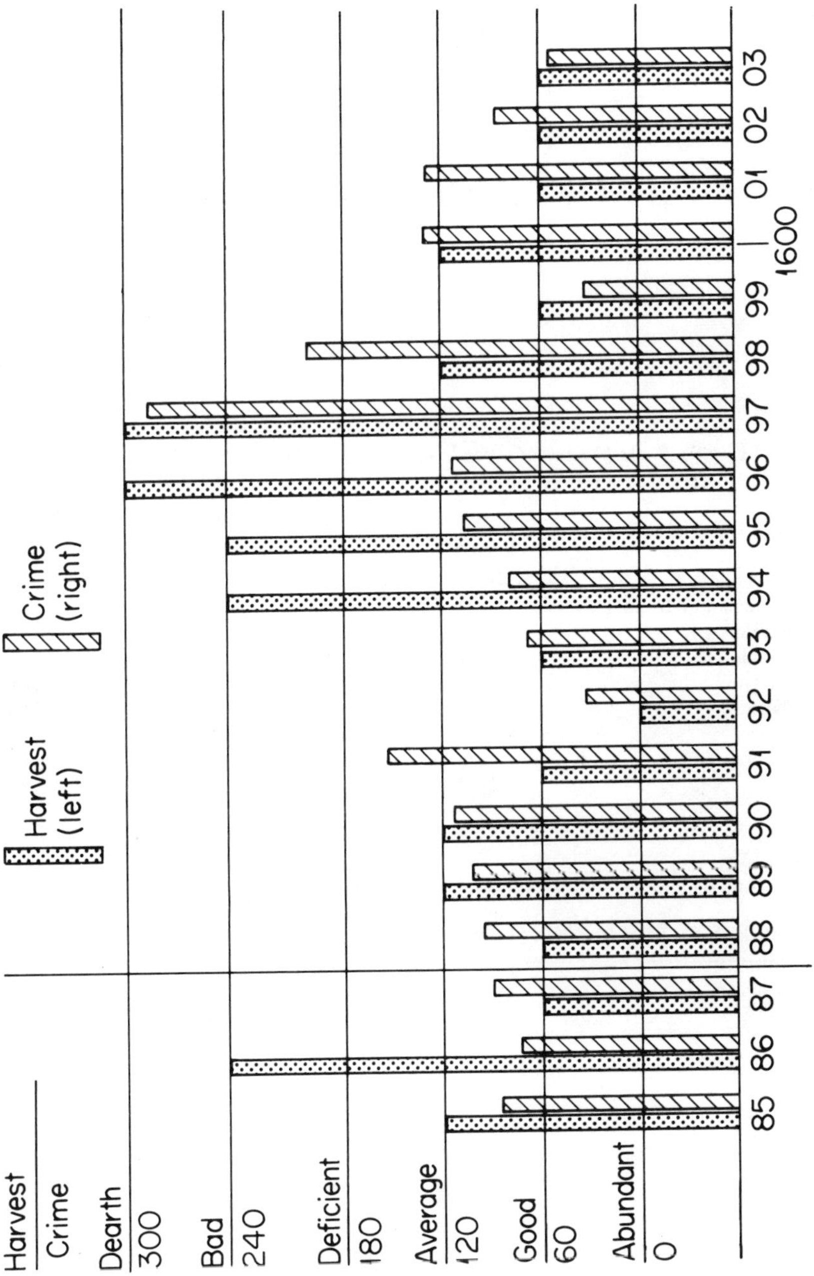
Harvest
Crime
Dearth
300
Bad
240
Deficient
180
Average
120
Good
60
Abundant
0
Harvest (left)
Crime (right)
85
86
87
88
89
90
91
92
93
94
95
96
97
98
99
1600
01
02
03

APPENDIX **VII**

RAW DATA FOR CHAPTERS I AND II

TABLE A-53 *Total Number of Offenders by Social Status*

Social status	Absolute frequency	Relative frequency (%)	Adjusted frequency (%)	Cumulative adjusted frequency (%)
Gentleman or Esquire	27	1.1	1.1	1.1
Yeoman	254	10.4	10.6	11.7
Husbandman	181	7.4	7.6	19.3
Artisan	542	22.3	22.6	41.9
Weaver	60	2.5	2.5	44.4
Laborer	1085	44.6	45.3	89.7
Woman	246	10.1	10.3	100.0
Blank	37	1.5	missing	100.0
Total	2432[a]	100.0	100.0	100.0

[a] Total includes valid observations (2395) and missing observations (37).

TABLE A-54 *Total Number of Crimes by Month*

Month	Absolute frequency	Relative frequency (%)	Adjusted frequency (%)	Cumulative adjusted frequency (%)
January	297	12.2	12.4	12.4
February	298	12.3	12.4	24.8
March	193	7.9	8.0	32.8
April	178	7.3	7.4	40.2
May	278	11.4	11.6	51.8

TABLE A-54 *Continued*

Month	Absolute frequency	Relative frequency (%)	Adjusted frequency (%)	Cumulative adjusted frequency (%)
June	191	7.9	8.0	59.8
July	123	5.1	5.1	64.9
August	112	4.6	4.7	69.6
September	150	6.2	6.2	75.8
October	173	7.1	7.2	83.0
November	180	7.4	7.5	90.5
December	228	9.4	9.5	100.0
Blank	31	1.4	missing	100.0
Total	2432[a]	100.0	100.0	100.0

[a] Total includes valid observations (2395) and missing observations (37).

TABLE A-55 *Total Number of Offenders by Type of Crime*

Type of crime	Absolute frequency	Relative frequency (%)	Adjusted frequency (%)	Cumulative adjusted frequency (%)
Violent crimes	206	8.5	8.5	8.5
Robbery and burglary	376	15.5	15.5	24.0
Theft	1839	75.6	76.0	100.0
Blank	11	.5	missing	100.0
Total	2432[a]	100.0	100.0	100.0

[a] Total includes valid observations (2395) and missing observations (37).

TABLE A-56 *Total Number of Offenders by Disposition of Case*

Disposition of case	Absolute frequency	Relative frequency (%)	Adjusted frequency (%)	Cumulative adjusted frequency (%)
Guilty	642	26.4	26.6	26.6
Clergy	622	25.6	25.8	52.3
Pregnancy	34	1.4	1.4	53.7
Pardon	41	1.7	1.7	55.4
Unknown	401	16.5	16.6	72.0
Acquited	674	27.7	27.9	100.0
Blank	17	.7	missing	100.0
Total	2432[a]	100.0	100.0	100.0

[a] Total includes valid observations (2395) and missing observations (37).

BIBLIOGRAPHY

Manuscript Sources

British Museum, *Egerton Manuscripts,* 2644.
British Museum, *Landsdowne Manuscripts,* 49.
Cambridge University, *Baker Manuscripts,* 40.
Essex Record Office, *Manor of Hatfield Broadoak.* Steward's Papers (D/DHtM49).
Essex Record Office, *Manor of Ingatestone.* Court Rolls D/DP M99–10/.
Essex Record Office, *Manor of Weathersfield.* Court Rolls D/DFy M18–21.
Essex Record Office, *Morant Manuscripts.*
Essex Record Office, *Petre Manuscripts* (D/DP).
Essex Record Office, *Plea Roll of the Quarter Sessions,* 1.
Essex Record Office, *Survey of the Manor of Chelmsford, 1591* (D/DGe M50).
Essex Record Office, *The Quarter Sessions Rolls,* 1–160.
Essex Record Office, *Wills, Bishop's Commisary* N. Essex and Hertfordshire Jurisdiction (D/ABW) .
Public Record Office, *Assizes* 35/1–45.
Public Record Office, *King's Bench Indictments Ancient.*
Public Record Office, *Star Chamber*, 5.
Public Record Office, *State Papers Domestic*, 12.

Printed Sources

Acts of the Privy Council

Statutes of the Realm: 36 Edward III, cap. 12
27 Elizabeth, cap. 6
18 Elizabeth, cap. 7
18 Henry VI,
4 Henry VII, cap. 14
12 Henry VII, cap. 7
4 and 5 Philip and Mary, cap. 4
8 Elizabeth, cap. 4
39 Elizabeth, cap. 15

Articles and Books

Anglian, J. Pascal. *The Archdeaconry Courts in Essex*. U.C.L.A. Ph.D. dissertation, 1965.

Barnes, Thomas G. *The Clerk of the Peace in Caroline Somerset*. Leicester University Press, 1961.

Barnes, Thomas G. *Somerset Assize Orders 1629–1640*. Frame England, 1959.

Bonger, William. *Criminality and Economic Conditions*, Translated by Henry P. Horton. New York: Agathon Press, Inc., 1967.

Cheyney, Edward P. *A History of England from the Defeat of the Armada to the Death of Elizabeth*, Vol. II. New York, 1948.

Cockburn, J. S. "Seventeenth century clerks of Assize: Some anonymous members of the legal profession." *The American Journal of Legal History*, 13(1969):315–332.

Cockburn, J. S. *A History of the English Assizes: from 1558 to 1714*. London: Cambridge Univ. Press, 1972.

Coke, Sir Edward. *Third Institute*. London, 1837.

Cressey, Donald R. and Ward, David A. *Delinquency, Crime and Social Process*. New York: Harper, 1969.

Elton, Geoffffrey R. *England Under the Tudors*. New York: Barnes & Noble, 1955.

Emmison, Fredrick G. *Elizabethan Life: Disorder*. Chelmsford, England: Essex County Council, 1970.

Erikson, Kai T. *Wayward Puritans: A Study in the Sociology of Deviance*. New York: Wiley, 1966.

Essex Record Office. *Essex Towns*. Chelmsford, England: County Council of Essex.

Essex Record Office Publication. *Law and Order in Essex*. Chelmsford, England: County Council of Essex, 1970.

Essex Record Office Publication Number 51. *Guide to the Essex Record Office*. Chelmsford, England: County Council of Essex, 1969.

Finberg, H.P. and Thirsk, Joan, eds. *The Agrarian History of England and Wales, 1500–1640*. Vol. IV. London: Cambridge Univ. Press, 1971.

Firth, C. B. "Benefit of clergy in the time of Edward IV." *English Historical Review*, 32(1917): 175–191.

Fisher, F. J. "The development of the London road market, 1540–1640." *Economic History Review*, 5(1935).

Fisher, F. J. "Commercial trends and policies in sixteenth century England." *Economic History Review*, 10:95–117.

Gleason, John *The Justices of the Peace in England 1558–1649: A Later Eirenarcha*.

Harrison, William, *The Description of England*, Georges Edelen, ed. Ithaca: Cornell Univ. Press, 1968.

Holdsworth, Sir William. *Some Makers of English Law*. Vol. I. London: Cambridge Univ. Press, 1969.

Hughes, Paul and Larkin, James *Tudor Royal Proclamations: The Later Tudors*. Vols. II and III. New Haven, Connecticut: Yale Univ. Press, 1969.

Hull, Felix *Agriculture and Rural Society in Essex, 1540–1640*. University of London Ph.D. dissertation, 1950.

Italian Relation of England. Camden Society, 1847.

Jacob, Giles. *Law Dictionary*. London, 1809.

Jayewardene, C. H. S. "Criminal culture and subcultures." *Probation and Child Care Journal*. 2(1963):1–5.

Judges, Arthur V., ed. *The Elizabethan Underworld*. London, 1930.

Lambarde, William. *Eirenarcha*. London, 1589.

Lambarde, William. *Of the Duties of Constables*. London, 1602.

Laslett, Peter. *The World We Have Lost*. New York: Scribner, 1966.

Lehmberg, Stanford E. *Sir Walter Mildmay and Tudor Government.* Austin: Univ. Texas Press, 1964.

Lopez-Rey, Manuel. "Economic conditions and crime with special reference to less-developed countries." *International Annuals of Criminology.* Pt. I(1964):33–40.

Macfarlane, Alan. *Witchcraft in Tudor-Stuart England 1560–1680.* New York: Harper, 1970.

McClintock, F. H. and Avison, N. Howard. *Crime in England and Wales.* London: Heineman Educational Books, Ltd., 1968.

Metcalf, Walter, ed., *Visitations of Essex.* Vols. XIII–XIV. London, 1904.

Nef, John V. "A comparison of industrial growth in France and England, 1540–1640." *Journal of Political Economy* 44:289–317, 503–533, 643–666.

Norden, John. *Speculi Britanniae Pars.* Camden Society Publication, London. 1840.

Phillips, Sir Richard. *On the Powers and Duties of Juries.* London, 1811.

Pound, Roscoe. "The causes of the popular dissatisfaction with the administration of justice." *American Bar Association.* 29(1906):395–417.

Pulton, Fernando. *An Abstract of All Penal Statutes.* London, 1577.

Read, Conyers. *William Lambarde and Local Government.* Ithaca: Cornell Univ. Press, 1962.

Rich, E.E. "The population of Elizabethan England." *Economic History Review.* 2nd ser. Vol. 2, 1950.

Rowse, Alfred L. *The England of Elizabeth.* New York: Macmillan, 1967. (New York: Crowell-Collier, paperback edition, 1966).

Secretariat Paper, Third United Nations Congress on the Prevention of Crime and the Treatment of Offenders, "Social Change and Criminality." United Nations, Stockholm, 1965.

Shoham, Shlomo. "The Approach of the 'Culture-Conflict' Hypothesis to the Criminality of Immigrants to Israel." *Journal of Criminal Law, Criminology, and Police Science.* 53 (1962): 207–214.

Smith, Sir Thomas. *De Republica Anglorum.* L. Alston, ed. Cambridge, 1906.

Stephens, Sir James Fitzjames. *A History of Criminal Law of England.* Vols. I–III. London, 1882.

Stone, Lawrence. *The Crisis of the Aristocracy, 1558–1641.* Abridged edition. New York: Oxford Univ. Press, 1967.

Stone, Lawrence. "The educational revolution in England, 1540–1640." *Past and Present.* 28(July, 1964):41–80.

Venn, John and Venn, S. A. *Alumni Cantabrigiensis.* Cambridge University, 1922–1927.

Venter, Herman J. "Urbanization as crimenogenic factors in the Republic of South Africa." *International Review of Criminal Policy.* 20(1962):59–71.

Victoria County History of Essex. Vol. II. London, 1907.

Williams, G. Ogden. *Caernarvonshire Quarter Sessions Records.* Vol. I. Caernarvon, 1956.

Wilson, Thomas. *The State of England 1600.* Camden Miscellany. Fisher, F. J., ed. Vol. XVI, 1936.

The Office of the Clerk of Assize Together with the Office of the Clerk of the Peace. London, 1676.

INDEX